Not Your Mother's Life

Also by Joan K. Peters:

When Mothers Work

Not Your Mother's Life

Changing the Rules of Work, Love, and Family

Joan K. Peters

DA CAPO PRESS
Cambridge, Massachusetts

 Printed in the United States of America.

Cataloging-in-Publication Data is available from the Library of Congress
ISBN 0–7382-0346-7

Perseus Publishing is a member of the Perseus Books Group.
Find us on the World Wide Web at http://www.perseuspublishing.com
Perseus Publishing books are available at special discounts for bulk purchases in the United States by corporations, institutions, and other organizations. For more information, please contact the Special Markets Department at HarperCollins Publishers, 10 East 53rd Street, New York, NY 10022, or call 1–212–207–7528.

Text design by Rachel Hegarty
Set in 10-point Stone Informal by Perseus Publishing Services

First printing, March 2001

1 2 3 4 5 6 7 8 9 10—03 02 01

For my 81-year-old mother, Bette,
my 10-year-old daughter, Lily,
and my ageless husband, Peter
. . . feminists all

Contents

Acknowledgments ix
First Thoughts xi

"In Dreams Begin Responsibilities" **1**

Generation XX:
No More Business as Usual **21**

Reality Bites **39**

Rethinking Modern Romance **59**

Designing a Life:
Finding a Direction/Choosing Work **83**

Understanding the Workplace 2000 **107**

If You're Considering
Medicine, Business, or Law **129**

Striking Out on Your Own:
The Entrepreneur **161**

Work And Family:
If You're Thinking of Kids
(And Most of You Are) **183**

New Rules, New Parents, New Choices **217**

No Woman Is An Island **245**

Notes 267
Bibliography 289
Index 301

Acknowledgments

Writing my last two books, both based heavily on interviews, I've often felt more like a conductor than a composer, one who coordinates voices and talents, interprets, and, if successful, renders the whole greater than its parts. With this book, as with my last, I've been blessed in finding eloquent people whose stories and insights shaped my ideas, enriching my writing and myself.

To those subjects who became mentors, many many thanks, especially: Carol Ann and Greg Kalish, Kemba Extavour, Niven Youssef, Hillary Billings, Trini and Willie Quinn, Sarah Luck Pearson, Dr. Tamara Sachs, Dr. Beth Davis Phillpotts and Garfield Phillpotts, Dr. Elizabeth Kavaler, Dr. Shlomo Raz, Carol Malnick, Col. Kimber McKenzie, Sarah Vickers Willis, Bob and Bonnie Gemmell, Risa Gerson, Galia Swetschinsk, Joline Godfrey, Jordan and Sherry Levy, Barbara Marcus, and Jean Feiwel.

To those experts in their fields who clarified and stimulated my thinking, much gratitude, especially psychologists Carol Zulman, Drs. Joyce Abrams and Diane Gottlieb (a dear friend and colleague of so many years), psychiatrists Drs. Arthur Kornhaber and Ethel Person, Professor Kathleen Allen, and Gen X commentators Heather Neely and Jennifer Kushell.

But, of course, none of their ideas or mine would ever have seen the light of day without the guidance and wisdom of my agent, Susan Ginsburg; my wonderful editor, Elizabeth Carduff, who doubles my luck bringing her expertise as director of marketing and associate publisher of Perseus Books; the smart, enthusiastic staff there, especially marketing associate Margaret Lamont; publicity director Lissa Warren, who talked through many central ideas with me; and Donna MacLetchie, who worked on the publicity.

A whole other kind of gratitude to my friends of decades as well as my family—Peter, Lily, Bette, and my father Dan, recently deceased—who cheered me on and cheered me up, provided respite from work, and raised my spiritual currency to untold value.

First Thoughts

Three generations of women—the silent generation, the baby boomers, and what has become known as Gen XY—coexist peacefully as the twenty-first century begins. But in some deep philosophic ways, they politely ignore one another, strangers at the core. Subtle resentments abound, though rarely are they expressed as more than an over-the-shoulder, "like, who *are* you?" Given the chill, it may be a foolhardy act of political passion for me, a baby boomer, to offer this generation her vision for changing the rules so that everyone can have "balance," as we now call life. But I've been staring at some of the same problems for a long time now. And, anyway, foolhardy acts of political passion characterize my generation.

For us, politics dominated everything. It created friendships and destroyed them. It gave people's lives direction, it informed every decision—the way we worked, married, had families (or didn't). It fused with music and movies, with the drug culture, the hippies, the yippies, the rock-and-rollers. We were one great tie-dye of a group, hallucinating ourselves into the future. The cacophony of theories, critiques, and hollering was often so deafening that people dropped out, some into isolation in Vermont or Colorado. Many did an about-face, embracing capitalism with a capital C, creating the workaholism Gen XY inherited and the workplaces that demand body and soul.

It's easy to dismiss us, the way we dismissed the women of our mothers' generation. But what a waste. Without the ballast of our stolid elders, our political ideals tipped toward the unattainably purist, leaving many of our imperfect selves by the wayside. Yet without political ideals as a beacon, this very practical new generation of women suffers, mostly silently—from overwork, financial pressures, fiercely materialist values, and, despite society's slick lip service, from discrimination in salary, promotions, bank loans, and law. They, too, risk falling by the wayside when these realities stifle dreams.

But that needn't happen. If this generation were to use its unprecedented economic power—power we boomers never attained—it could remake the workplace and home life in its own image, one woman at a time. Think of it as a merger of the best of the boomers' analytical sensibilities with the best of Gen XY's professional savvy.

Of course, this may be a challenge given the barriers of age and experience. Women, it is almost too obvious to mention, have changed dramatically since the Depression and World War II. The very earth they grew up on seems different, not to mention the air, water, weather, food, drugs (think antibiotics, birth control pills), ideas, family constellations, economics, communications, and global perspective. It's as if we come from different countries, and in some ways we do.

Interviewing women in their twenties, thirties, and early forties to learn about their goals and life strategies, I've been told many times that they're tired of hearing how hard it was for their parents. They don't want to be guilted into the boomers' political agenda. They don't feel they have to prove that women can make it in a man's world. Growing up knowing that women can do whatever they want, and often as not feeling pushed to achieve, they prefer to figure out for themselves how they'll live. Not surprisingly, a lot of them reject what their female boomer bosses have: no life, no kids—or kids they never see because they're working so hard. Those women, so I have heard, can be tougher bosses than men, more exacting, never giving the younger women a break, as in: "I worked my tail off to get here, you better do the same." Or, "I took off ten years to raise my children, so don't expect any special considerations." Nor do most wish to emulate the moms who took them to India on their quests for enlightenment or who dragged them to every march on Washington to support the revolution.

The revolution. Now, there's a bone of contention. While the silent generation sat on the sidelines, disapproving, boomer women rallied, rebelled, and even ran for president (remember Shirley Chisholm?). Whole lives were dedicated to gaining equality for women, blacks, and other minorities. Gen XY women are bored of hearing about it, just like we boomers got bored of hearing about breadlines and fighting Nazis, even though they permanently affected our parents and our culture. So I'm not going to dwell on it and I certainly understand why a lot of young women want Family, with a capital F.

Much of the boomer wisdom just doesn't seem relevant, especially when this new generation is doing so well on its own, thank you very much. Young women are dot-comming, networking, decoding the genome, and making more money than boomer girls ever dreamed of. But doing all this and still having a life, no less a family, has gotten harder. And boomer wisdom, like hiring a nanny or creating universal quality childcare (a rather tall order), doesn't address the problem as they see it.

There is, however, one thing boomers had that might further empower this remarkably accomplished generation to achieve its stated goals: a sense of ourselves as a group. Whatever the challenges of our lives, we had each other in support groups of every flavor and action committees for every cause. We were aware of our differences, our strengths, and our vulnerabilities—as a group.

By contrast, Gen XY is almost defined by its individuality. Although there are young women creating new kinds of pro-woman activism, from Riot Grrrls to Third Wave feminism, the majority seems to be setting out, each in her own life, with few references to a broader culture. The popularity of Susan Faludi's *Backlash*, Naomi Wolf's *The Beauty Myth* and *Fire with Fire*, Eve Ensler's *Vagina Monologues*, Elizabeth Wurtzel's *Prozac Nation* and *Bitch* testify to a craving for the powerful commentary they offer. But, on the whole, young women have few books to read about their lives as a generation, few organizations to help guide their life strategies, few action groups to implement their beliefs.

In *ManifestA: Young Women, Feminism and the Future*, an impressive attempt to remedy this problem, authors Jennifer Baumgardner and Amy Richards write that "lack of consciousness is one reason that the movement is stalled." Whatever collective wisdom is out there isn't informing the greater generation's thinking. Even words like "movement" or "collective wisdom" sound scary when "groupthink" is out, as I'm told it is.

Collective wisdom, however, isn't the same as groupthink. Knowing how your contemporaries deal with challenges doesn't mean you adopt their ideas. It just means you understand yourself as one among many, an advantage that expands individual choices and perspectives. Knowing who you are as a generation can clarify your efforts to become a whole person. That is one great gift we boomers can give. It is what I presume to offer in *Not Your Mother's Life: Changing the Rules of Work, Love, and Family:* more than a mirror reflecting today's women, it is an interpretation of their strengths and weaknesses based on interviews, studies, and their own writings. More than a lament about the way things are, it is an analysis, based on the research, of their options, schools, workplaces, culture, and, finally, of society's response to them.

As each individual identifies herself in this cultural portrait, she can use it to plan her life effectively, building on the strengths and insight of her peers, avoiding the pitfalls that felled others. She can exploit what is valuable in the boomer legacy instead of rejecting it whole cloth, the way we did the silent generation's.

My mother and her peers seemed too different from me and mine to make the connections. She grew up (literally) speaking a different language, quitting school at 14 to help support her family, marrying at 16, and then, as a 26-year-old widow, barely supporting me and my brother by modeling fur coats in New York City's Garment District. Like everyone in our neighborhood, I was a latchkey kid. My mother hoped that I'd be a model or an executive secretary, then marry one of the rich bosses, have kids, and live the protected suburban life she never had.

By the time I was 16, I decided she had nothing to tell me about life. To her chagrin, I passed by rich husbands and went to the University of Chicago, where I got a doctorate in comparative literature and married an unemployed poet. With birth control pills in hand, I vowed never to have children and thereby never to run the risk of getting stuck in the suburban Valhalla she so coveted.

My biases, which obscured our similarities, were as much formed by my culture as my mother's were by hers. Lacking penicillin and adequate nutrition, six of her ten siblings never made it out of childhood. Because they grew up in the shadow of the Depression, economic insecurity was a major life force, just as extended family was a major life support. Staying close to home and getting on with the basics of life while the getting was good, they clung together, married early, and had children immediately. Women she knew worked only out of necessity.

The Depression that scarred my mother's childhood made her feel like a vulnerable speck in the universe. The world war that loomed over her twenties left her in awe of incomprehensible political forces and charismatic male leaders. I grew up economically secure, enjoyed an elite education, and chose to make a revolution—if only a cultural one. One day, when a popular woman I knew on campus asked me to sign up for a march on Washington to stop the war in Vietnam, I explained I wasn't interested in politics. "That's what people said when soldiers rounded up the Jews and sent them to concentration camps," she sneered. At that moment, I joined the force of history, as I saw it.

Of course, my perspective was as limited as my mother's. Had I not completely rejected her wisdom, I would have suspected that sooner or later (it was later), I might want to be a mother. Or that family, friends, and community would turn out to be the most important thing in my life, too. I would have realized that my feminist politics was based on a wish that women wouldn't need the male protection my mother did, or wouldn't suffer as much as she (and we, her children) did without it.

Unfortunately, the politics that dominated my life made hers seem meaningless to me. They strangled individuality and created intergenerational estrangement. But they nourished us, too. Indifference to politics can leave you rudderless. It can mean history towers above you, perplexing, out of your control. You focus too narrowly, moving only within the confines of the status quo.

With some notable exceptions, like the ones mentioned above, the majority of women's books today reflect these limits. They either describe women's struggles trying to have it all, tell women how to play by men's rules to climb the corporate ladder, or counsel them to quit work to take care of their children.

The broader perspective—connecting the personal, the political, the psychological, the economic—seems to me just what this new generation is missing, at least outside of feminist political circles. It's what's missing in the self-image of a phenomenally successful young surgeon I spoke with who lacked both the self-confidence and the supportive friends to keep her family intact while pursuing a prestigious fellowship. Without a well-conceived life design, her marriage fell apart. But she might have prevented the storm if she had examined the powerful currents moving her husband, her child, and herself. Betsy will change medicine because she understands its myths and its weaknesses, and because she has power. But she could have changed her personal life as well if she'd been similarly perceptive and understood her power there.

Like everyone in the book, Betsy is quite real. I use her name and the actual circumstances of her life. There are only two exceptions. One, a woman I call Erin Martin, preferred that I not use her name, perhaps because she felt she would get so little of what she wanted. But her choices are telling, as is the narrowness of her perspective. The other, whom I call Amy Lowe, felt she could not use her name because professional protocol at her office requires that executives not discuss their personal lives.

Most portraits I draw are of college graduates. This is not because women with degrees are the only important story today, but because college attendance, which is the most certain catalyst for women, is rising remarkably for them. All the couples I interview are heterosexual, not because same-sex couples don't face daunting problems or have wisdom to share, but because the problems facing heterosexual women in love and parenting relationships go a long way in explaining women's stalled progress.

If the women portrayed in these pages seem too perfect, it's because they've succeeded on their own terms. But notice how they have all sacrificed valuable things, like the most prestigious job or big money or simply having playtime in their twenties. None of them has it all, but they (and their life-partners) have all gotten most of what they want by focusing on priorities.

What you see in each portrait is contentment, not perfection; an inner glow rather than cover-girl beauty. As varied as they are, to whatever degree they've achieved their goals, each of their stories is a variation on the theme of understanding private choices in a public context. It is in this way that the lessons of their lives apply to us all. Including me, who has learned so much from this next generation of women and taken so much inspiration from their accomplishments.

"In Dreams Begin Responsibilities"

I can start with a proposition or a story. But the story's more engaging, as stories tend to be. Besides, it foretells what's illustrated, tabulated, verified, and at times, expounded in the rest of the book.

So let's cut to a real-life protagonist, one of several you'll meet along the way. She's a lawyer and the mother of a three-year-old. A heroine, but not the destined-for-success kind. More your average female college grad who muddles through her twenties, dating the wrong guys, unsure about what she's doing with her life (aside from paying back student loans). But one who gets a grip. She figured out who she was, what she wanted, and how best to get it in the light of workplace realities. Not so much acted upon as acting, changing the rules as much as playing by them—and thus, changing them for everyone. In other words, she planned her life well and is making a personal workplace revolution.

Carol Ann and Greg Kalish

That said, meet Carol Ann Kalish, a 36-year-old litigator at the most prestigious law firm in Sarasota, Florida, where she lives with her husband of ten years, Greg, a 45-year-old cardio-rehabilitation therapist. A year after she became a mother (at age 33), she described her life to me in an e-mail:

> When my baby Benjamin was born, I took about 10 days off, then came back to the office part-time, working 5 a.m. to noon each day. Ben would come to the office with me, usually sleeping of course, until about 8 or 9 a.m. when Greg or my mom would pick him up. This went on for about two months, then I came back to work full time. Now, Ben is with Greg two days a week, my mom three days, and Greg and me together two days. His care is a family effort and he is the happiest little guy I've ever seen. This works for us and for Ben.

Although she didn't mention it, her mother-in-law later told me that her 36 colleagues volunteered to make one dinner each, which they delivered to the new parents' home during Ben's first month. Checking back with Carol Ann a year later, this time meeting her and Greg at a family gathering, I find the same profoundly satisfied mother, effective attorney, and happy family. On a later visit when Benjamin is three, there they were again, balanced as gymnasts on the beam, though far less strained.

We meet at the house they bought four years back, a "Florida-cracker style house," they explain on my tour. It's old fashioned, in "a real neighborhood," like they wanted, small (two-bedroom) but with ample porches and a cypress-paneled dining room all decked out in Christmas greenery, tree and trim.

Out back, maternal grandma Margaret (whom they pay $1000 a month for childcare) plays with Ben on his swing-set. He hurries over for parental kisses when we poke our heads out, then hurries back.

Do you enjoy your work? I ask grandma casually, expecting a weary sigh. "I love it," she says flatly, "no more stress." Lucky for everyone, Carol Ann's mother retired the year Ben was born.

Under the lazy noonday sun, Greg and Carol Ann look out of place in work clothes, but there they are: Carol Ann in her lawyer duds: a black pinstriped suit with an ankle-length skirt; Greg in aqua hospital scrubs. The two are a study in opposites: Carol Ann, a diminutive blonde all-American type with peachy skin and cropped hair and Greg, an immigrant hodgepodge (in looks, that is) of tawny Mediterranean tones, angular Greek cheekbones, and a prominent Native American nose.

We head for the sunporch while Ben plays with Margaret and my own eight-year-old, whose school holiday meant an extra take-your-daughter-to-work day. We all put our feet up on the coffee table and meander through their lives.

Their schedule's changed. Both work full time now, but they usually get home for lunch with Ben and Margaret. Greg works 35 hours a week so he's home more—though, as a serious athlete (he's done three triathlons), he's often out running, biking, or thrashing through ocean currents. Actually, I find out from neighbors that he's famous for running in his skimpy Speedo swimsuit so he can dive directly into the surf after covering five miles. Admiring ladies call him "the streaker."

Although they both have that glowing, well-toned look of Sun Belt athletes, Carol Ann assures me she's not athletic at all. Outside of work, which keeps her at the office from 9 to 5-ish, she does community work with "Lawyers for Literacy" or the local chapter of the American Cancer Society. Later in the week, in fact, Greg's going to play Santa at Carol Ann's "Young Lawyers Xmas in July" program.

"You have time for this?" I inquire. She tells me her firm gives the attorneys credits for 15 hours of charity work a week so it's not so hard to fit in.

Sure, I'm thinking: ideal people, ideal community, ideal law firm. And they all found each other. What about ordinary mortals slaving away 24/7, arguing with our spouses about who's making dinner, and never having time to go to the gym or play Santa. Well, it turns out, the rest of us may not have planned as carefully.

Part of the charm of Carol Ann and Greg's life is the ease with which they live it. But daily *ease* doesn't mean their life was *easy* to create. Living Carol Ann's version of work/life balance takes a great deal. Most notably,

- a willing grandmother living close by,
- a willing husband with a flexible schedule,

- a willing employer who offers flexibility and part-time options;
- an energy level to perform demanding office work on a few hours sleep despite nursing Ben at night;
- a mellow, healthy baby;
- and a second set of adoring grandparents living close by.

Carol Ann is lucky. But she also lined her ducks in a row before plunging into her future. She made some clear decisions, such as living near her mother, whom she knew would help. She married a man who never put his work above hers. She chose an employer whose stated priority, after excellence, is "family comes first." All three are choices that require the courage to buck substantial social pressure.

A lot of high achievers Carol Ann's age live far from their families, leaving home in order to strike out on their own and go to "the best" school they can get into or take "the best" job offer, wherever it may be. Carol Ann was very tempted to do the same. After graduating from the University of South Florida at Tampa, she came close to choosing one of the great law schools. As she tells it, "My L.S.A.T.'s were so high that I got courted by everyone. I felt a sort of intestinal pressure to go somewhere *important*. But I just didn't. I stayed local instead. With hindsight, it was the best decision I could have made."

It may have helped that Carol Ann took plenty of time to make the decision. After college, she worked for three years as an assistant buyer for a local department store before settling on law school. Her conscious motive was to save money, an excellent strategy in itself. But as you'll see from a lot of the real-life stories that follow, people who take a break to think about what they're doing with their lives often get a better perspective on crucial decisions. In Carol Ann's case, she realized how much she liked her hometown, and what an advantage it was to have deep roots in a place. Alone in her early twenties, she also understood the value of a supportive family nearby and friends from as far back as fourth grade. Having grown up relatively poor, she wanted the opportunity to enjoy Sarasota's middle-class pleasures and to participate in the community at a leadership level. She chose law because of the community's ready acceptance of lawyers as leaders.

In the planning department, Carol Ann had learned the hard way. Her father, who died when she was ten, was a successful lawyer. But because he had made no provision for his family, his early death plunged them from the middle class to a much humbler existence. With barely restrained emotion, Carol Ann said, "I learned that you don't do that to yourself or others."

When she finally graduated from Stetson Law School in St. Petersburg, chosen because she knew she wanted to practice locally and because she could commute to live with Greg in Sarasota, she faced another great temptation: a job in a big Atlanta firm where she could easily have gotten a starting salary of $70,000 instead of $50,000 in Sarasota. The bigger offer was particularly appealing because she had $82,000 in school debt. Also, as she explains, "law school is so competitive, kids take the 'plum' job because it's the prize, not because it's what they want to do or at a law firm they like." But when she interviewed for those plum jobs, she found herself uncomfortable with the high pressure and the competitive atmosphere. She knew that the young associates worked night and day, which she didn't want, particularly because she'd just married Greg.

Then she interviewed at Williams, Parker, Harrison, Dietz and Getzen in Sarasota and loved it. "They were collegial, not competitive. They were interested in me as a person, not just as a lawyer. They told me that a lot of firms will give you a Disneyland clerkship, taking you drinking and dining every night, but you have to wonder, where are their spouses while they're out till all hours? They said, we don't do that. Family comes first here. Everyone goes home at night. Once a year, the whole firm goes on a family weekend."

Being a smart cookie, Carol Ann didn't believe them so she drove by the parking lot on Saturday morning: an excellent strategy, and a good outcome. The lot was empty. It would be well worth the forfeit of $20,000, in her estimation.

Seven years later, Carol Ann can say the firm is what it seemed. They really do grow young attorneys. They don't want anyone to burn out. They want all of the associates to make partner, which is rare elsewhere. Usually two-thirds drop out or don't make it, she tells me. That's why other law firms are so much more competitive.

She was the first woman in the litigation department, but her mentor helped and listened: "I was comfortable revealing my insecurities and asking for direction. He was generous and reasonable. Later, when I was pregnant and told the senior partners I was going to work from 5:00 A.M. to noon *and* bring the baby to the office, they said, 'fine.' They trusted me as an attorney and simply went with my plan."

And why shouldn't they? "It's not like there's a law that workplaces have to be a certain way," asserts Carol Ann. "Some are, the largest, maybe, but in many others you can go in, find a like-minded mentor who believes in a decent work ethic, and help to make the office reflect your beliefs. Most lawyers leave the field instead of trying to change it."

Carol Ann is now the lead outside counsel for the firm's premier client, an important Sarasota hospital. It's a very demanding job, but she's got it under control: "I think about my job all the time. Inspiration for strategies can come in the shower or at lunch. It's a career, not a job. But I'm honest about what I can deliver. I do excellent work, but I won't be on call after hours or on weekends." She has also never worked on a case in which she felt the hospital wasn't right, nor would she be pressured to; they all respect her judgment. As for the money, Carol Ann now earns $100,000 instead of the $150,000–$175,000 she'd be pulling down in Atlanta—with no regrets on her part. And she was just made a shareholder.

She told me about a new recruit from the University of Virginia Law School who accepted a job at her firm (over the more "plum" possibilities), explaining her choice to Carol Ann by saying, "I don't want to always be trying to get somewhere. I want to love where I am."

When I visit the law offices, I can see why a new recruit would love WPHD&G (as they call it). Despite it's staid colonial exterior, thickly carpeted hush corridors, and formal Ethan Allen furniture, the firm is filled with friendly people, all of whom come to meet me, to be interviewed, or just to tell me something I might not know about Carol Ann.

Carol Ann introduces me to the senior partner, the man responsible for setting the tone, explaining that he had custody of small children while he went to law school, so he really understood the importance of family. I meet another partner who took a month off when he and his wife adopted a child. "Now, he does mornings with his son Henry," Carol Ann whispers. I meet Susan, a very pregnant tax attorney (wearing one of Carol Ann's hand-me-down velvet-trimmed silk maternity suits), who is planning to take six weeks off, then work from home for a while. Susan says that the senior partners told her to wait and see how much she can do so she won't feel pressure. "If I'm less productive, they'll adjust my salary. They won't penalize me professionally."

The firm is "reasonable," Carol Ann says, but Carol Ann also scouted for work within it that helps her to maintain a work/life balance. Though it can be different in big cities, in Sarasota litigation gives her more control over her time than standard transactional work would. Here the courts have established rules for how long lawyers can take to do things; they create clear deadlines. However, she still has a big say over trial dates. In her view, attorneys who work with big business clients seem to have hysterical deadlines when they're closing a deal. It's very hectic because the clients choose the dates and drive the work. Again, Carol Ann designed her life thoughtfully.

Her most thoughtful decision, though, may have been her choice of a husband. An awful lot of women find security in marrying someone *more* ambitious or higher salaried than themselves. It's what feels "normal" and is all too often encouraged by parents who often still ask their daughters, "how will he support you?"

Before she met Greg, Carol Ann lived with a successful broker. "He was everything I wanted—on paper. It was the go-go '80s. He was doing great. But in reality, he was a mean-spirited person with very little self-confidence, a disappointment to his dad, who expected him to be a billionaire. He was all work, with no real life. I think I realized all this when he never even visited my dying grandfather, whom I was very, very close to."

On her first date with Greg, she saw what she really valued:

> We were caught in a rainstorm so we went to his house and I was charmed. It was a real home, with Mexican tiles and plants and pictures of people in his life: family, friends, himself with three basset hound puppies, him on a dive. I saw he had passions, he wasn't waiting for someone to give them to him. When I got to know him, I saw that he wasn't running around with his hair on fire trying to accomplish. He was living his life. That, to me, was so appealing. I liked that he talked about people lovingly and with respect. I felt I could learn from him to put life first. He was living in a way I really admired.

As Greg is quick to point out, he "makes as much in a day as Carol Ann spends on panty hose." But work was never the center of Greg's life. He thought a lot about finding work he genuinely loved, but he earned money just to "go on his next dive." Graduating from Michigan State in fine arts, he took a graduate degree in therapeutic recreation. "I loved art, but working so introspectively, in isolation, was not for me. I was also very athletic and enjoyed helping people, so I decided on physical therapy."

Eventually, he found cardio-rehabilitation, which was very satisfying to him. In six weeks, he'd see post-op bypass patients transformed. "I could really help them to live healthier lives."

Greg liked how intimate the job was, how well he got to know his clients. Now he monitors patients on pacemakers, a job with less of the patient contact that he likes so much. But he works closer to home and has less rigid hours so that he can be more available in Ben's early years.

There's not a lot of money in the helping professions. And though he wishes it were otherwise, it's something he can live with in order to do what he likes. "It doesn't bother me that Carol Ann makes more money than I do. It bothers me that I don't make more money doing the work I do. I make less than anyone I know, anyone I went to school with."

Does he regret his choice? Was this a bad life design?

"I have my moments," Greg says, "but I'm comfortable with my choice. I enjoy the hell out of my life."

I was thinking that Greg must take it on the chin from men who make so much more than he does. But when I ask them how men react to Greg, Carol Ann blurts out, "They're fascinated by him. Everyone talks about 'the Greg and Ben' show. It's Greg with Ben at the store, at the park, at a playdate. The other cookie-cutter men envy Greg's relationship with Ben. They tell him, 'I wish I could do that,' meaning take off early and go to the beach with their children, have lunch, stroll around town as a dad."

I wonder if Carol Ann isn't playing the cheerleader here. Especially when Greg adds that it's hard to find friends who are like him. "Other guys here like to play golf or watch football. They sometimes treat me like I'm gay because I cook and take care of my son. But I have my family. I swim. I run. That's enough." In fact, Greg has more friends than he acknowledges, as I learn when one of the attorneys in Carol Ann's office introduces himself to me as Greg's "best friend." And some genuine admiration. The husband of Susan (the very pregnant tax attorney), a builder, is so taken with Greg's lifestyle he's modeling his parenthood on him.

People tell Carol Ann how lucky she is that Greg's such a great father, but both of them know it wasn't luck. Some men—some *people*—are naturally great with small children. But great parents are mostly made, not born. Greg was quite fearful of fatherhood and unusually honest about it. "I never liked babies or kids. I had no experience. The only reason I agreed to have one was that I thought I should have this experience before I died. But we were very close to never having children."

Nor did he take to fatherhood immediately. "Infancy *horrified* me. I remember thinking, this is as close as I'll get to being air-dropped into Vietnam. There I was with this screaming, pooping larvae. I couldn't relate."

But unlike many men (who may suddenly have an awful lot of office work to do), he persevered because he'd agreed to, and he "tag teamed" with Carol Ann, taking care of Ben when she wasn't. "I got to be alone with Ben. Carol Ann totally ceded him to me on my days. She never criticized me. We each took turns, doing what had to be done."

Then Ben smiled. "I remember the day. That's when I knew he was actually a little person and that's when I bonded. I never thought I'd have those feelings. Now it's as if I'm seeing life through a child's eyes and getting so much insight into my own childhood. I never felt so loved by anyone, or have loved so much."

If any two people have been true to their dreams, it's Greg and Carol Ann, and it shows in their happiness. Neither regrets their major choices. Neither feels stuck, or as if life's been unfair or they've had to give up too much. They have lives, not just livelihoods. But we can't forget how much they each sacrificed for their dreams. Greg relinquished standard male salary and status, for which he's paid a price. Though not *the* price men fear they'll pay: rejection by women (he's always had great girlfriends) and derision from other men. She's given up the big-city fast track and the role of big-status breadwinner.

However, that's them. As much as we may admire how Carol Ann and Greg designed their lives, as much as we all know we should be true to our dreams, it's hard to do. And yet this is the first generation in which both women and men really can design their lives—and should if they want to work and also have a life.

Renaming Gen XY, Claiming Its Powers

In combining the polar opposites of dreams and responsibilities, poet Delmore Schwartz' mysterious phrase, "in dreams begin responsibilities," conveys what we all, deep down, suspect: If we don't take responsibility for our dreams, we betray them, and ourselves. We know we're our own worst enemies in the dream department. Especially women.

Most Y Gen women coming of age in this new millennium, as well as the so-called Gen X'ers between the ages of 25 and 45, do dream what women have rarely dared to before: of having rich work and personal lives. Just as unprecedented, they have a good shot at getting both if they design their lives thoughtfully. But there's much more to life-design than individual happiness, not that I'm knocking individual happiness. There's potential for a cultural revolution here. Think of it this way: the cumulative effect of each woman creating a balanced life (by demanding decent work hours and flexibility and insisting spouses do the same) will restore a sane work ethic to America's current obsession with ever-greater productivity.

What makes this sound more pipe dream than possibility is that no one's yet stated the obvious loudly enough: Women who are now of childbearing age are the first generation with the training needed to compete at every level in the market place. They are the first to create predominantly dual-income marriages—more than 30 million, compared to 11 million with a male earner only. They are also the first to live rich (no pun intended) lives as singles, more than half of whom own their own homes. Single women not only dominate the formerly male home renovation market, they dominate other formerly male upscale markets, such as adventure travel.

The economic position of women today is strong enough that simply by planning to work in a way that ensures personal time they will save us from marching lockstep into what *San Francisco Chronicle* columnist, Jon Carroll, has called "the Stepford economy," where people unquestioningly work every waking hour. Which is why X and Y are such misleading names.

Calling the 51 million people born between 1960 and 1980 by the dismissive moniker, Gen X, was clearly a misnomer that stuck. But, then, who's had the last laugh? Where would the new economy be without Gen X? And where would Gen X be without the women of Gen X?

The women of Gen X have had so much impact on our culture and our economy that if we're as committed to throwing around alphabet letters as we seem to be, the generation should rightfully be called Gen XX after the double XX chromosome that creates the female. This *could* be the women's generation, the first time in history when women live up to their full economic potential and implement policies based on conventionally female values such as caring, connecting, and celebrating life.

If any group is to reform our workaholic materialist culture, it will probably be women because most aren't prepared to forego a personal life or children for remunerative work or positions of power. Most men would rather not have to but give in more easily to work pressure. Although in the case of Greg and Carol Ann, it was he who encouraged her to put life before work, they are unusual that way. In most couples, it's the women who must encourage men to make time for their personal lives, especially if they've had a child. This is what's happening according to the cutting-edge people who describe their lives throughout this book. More than anything else, it's what solves the "life factor" problem that most twenty-somethings ruminate about.

THE LIFE FACTOR

The electronic revolution sent the American economy into orbit, but it's also produced a backlash. As much as we love our Palm Pilots and Nokias, we all see our private life slipping away with each technological advance. Clearly, the now quite common cry for "balance" is part of the attempt to preserve our personal lives before we find ourselves permanently plugged into work. But balance requires a cultural revolution to accompany the economic one, and that means a whole new way of thinking about work. Which, as I said, depends on women and their dreams.

It's scary to explore personal dreams for fear that if we look too closely we will glimpse their painful impossibility. The dream of combining work with family—or any kind of satisfying personal life—may seem impossible. Especially with a chorus of skeptics chanting in the background, "Women can't have it all. Who wants to be an executive anyway? Your husband's going to leave you for someone who cooks." Yet it's a reasonable dream for women today, who have been schooled to live full economic lives as well as raised to be mommies.

Pick a twenty-something woman at random and you'll find a helter-skelter version of the dream. It's floating through high schools, colleges, professional schools, and workplaces all over America. You'll also find the one in twenty-five who, without any extraordinary advantage, lives her own version of the dream. It doesn't mean everyone should race headlong down her particular path. But like Carol Ann, her strategy can serve as a blueprint for achieving balance in today's driven workplace, or an inspiration, or even a glimmer of hope. And remember, Carol Ann and her ilk are the law partners of tomorrow, as well as the CEO's and the entrepreneurs and the scientists and the heads of the Senate Finance Committee. They will be among the people who run things.

Unfortunately, there aren't yet enough of them. Carol Ann and Greg are exceptions, even in their own world. Most of the young attorneys at Carol Ann's firm and the doctors at Greg's cardiology clinic have wives who stay home with the children, though they all worked before the children were born. Carol Ann and her colleague, Susan, tell me that most of those women didn't like their jobs all that much and quit when they became mothers.

That's an all-too-typical path. It's as if there's a fork in the road for women, though not for men. One sign says: "Job," often "Boring Job" or "Exhausting Job"; the other, "Motherhood." This is how it looks through the eyes of 24-year-old Margaret Lamont, marketing associate at Perseus, the publisher of this book: "Nobody knows what they're going to do about the life factor. It's hard to meet people after college. If there's kids later on, no one seems to want to stay home with them." Her colleague, Lissa Warren, 28-year-old Publicity Director, says, "The more I work, the more a family becomes either/or. I can have this career and work really hard. Or I can quit and raise kids. For a decade, I'll have given work my all. I can't imagine how I could do as good a job if I didn't give my all." Their conflicts echo throughout their peer group.

Peggy Orenstein's book, *Flux*, has shown this so vividly with its medley of young women's voices. In a section she calls "The Crunch," Orenstein reports that "nearly all of the women I spoke with liked children; that wasn't the issue. Their ambivalence pivoted on a lack of conviction that even under the best of circumstances they could navigate motherhood with their essential selves intact." As she shows, the conflict isn't limited to job versus family, but encompasses identity versus family as well.

Their apprehension is based on the very real evidence they see around them of mothers struggling, and often failing, to work as hard as they do. And it might be justified if neither they nor the workplace were to change in any way. However, single women in their twenties rarely consider how much children can empower you to be more yourself. Or how a desire to be with them can motivate you to do your job more efficiently. And you have so much more time when you're not putting prodigious energy into finding yourself, let alone a companion in life. Children enrich you in ways you can't anticipate. Ann S. Moore, President of *People* magazine, succinctly explained one:

> I probably use less of what I learned at the Harvard Business School and more of what I learned as a parent. The single best thing to equip you for management in the Fortune 500 is good parenting skills. Everything from "Nobody loves a whiner" to "Look both ways" or "Do your homework" or "Say thank you."

That is, in some ways children can help make a worklife easier.

Another short view: Margaret, Lissa, and other twenty-somethings don't factor in their own power to change the way work gets done. They don't realize that men can be their allies in parenting, exerting their influence as well to change our work ethic. Often, I find, they don't believe in their power to shape a relationship.

Margaret's boyfriend wants to make a lot of money. She knows that will affect their lives, should they stay together, but isn't sure where to go with that one. He probably assumes he can just go for it without ever having to fret about the life factor. Men, well, they're just different, a lot of women seem to think. If they have jobs they don't like, they either make their peace with them or find others. They don't opt out when they become parents. They're not tortured about how they're going to "have it all." But, then, they're also not pulled by tradition, by family, by those inner voices to quit and stay home with children. They don't have to relinquish work in order to prove that they're good fathers the way women think that good mothers have to do. For men, it's harder, not easier, to give up even a little work. In fact, as Greg points out, putting life before work can make you a bit of a freak.

Sadly, men and women don't seem to be talking a lot to one another about what this all means. Growing numbers are making the perfectly reasonable decision not to have children. But mostly, they're obsessing about the Life Factor in isolation. They tell themselves they'll think about it later, or they'll just drop out for a while when they do have kids (as if that course will be a breeze), or they'll just forget about kids, not because they wouldn't like them but because they're ambitious and that means working just as much as men do. Great.

However irrelevant children, or studying Buddhism, or exploring the world, or serving on the local zoning board may seem while you're in your twenties, by your thirties most women do want a life outside the office. So you can let life happen to you, or you can design your life so that you'll end up with what you really want. The trick is to be proactive, to understand the consequences of each choice.

This book isn't aimed at convincing you to have children or not or explaining the virtues (or vices) of staying home with them. It's about thinking strategically about your life choices. But the stark truth is that, for women, motherhood *is* "the crunch," the choice that has the greatest consequences and needs to be made wisely. As we'll see, the dirty little secret of today's version of equality is that men and women have very similar lives—and options—until women have children. It's mothers who are not equal to others, either to women without children or to men. Mothers are still way behind by every measure of professional success, and it's not because they don't care any more. They pay a big price for being mothers. Literally. While childless women earn wages close to men's, mothers earn up to 15 percent less and single mothers, up to 40 percent less. Mothers handle the lion's share of housework and childcare, letting their husbands off the hook. Often, these women end up without the work they trained for or the paychecks that are their due. They know it but they don't know what to do about it, so they keep on scaling back or opting out or accepting the mommy track.

No one's talking about what it means that most women, because most are mothers, can't remain major players in the world of work. Or that their reverting to the traditional division of family labor "frees" their husbands to continue working 60 hours a week. If you ask them, and a lot of researchers have, she'd actually like to work and he'd like to work less. Mostly, this arrangement is the result of letting life happen.

Carol Ann and Susan tell me that most of the women who left work to mother seem to have "lost part of themselves." Carol Ann wonders about the organizations cropping up, like the Young Mothers League. She tells me that they have a board of directors and daily activities, including play groups and sibling groups. "They attend to children with such exacting detail, it's as if children were a job." That's because they've been trained not to be housewives, but to work, so motherhood becomes their work instead of being a part of their lives.

Carol Ann and Susan sense something borne out by the research: Women who give up work for motherhood mostly chose what seemed the lesser of two evils instead of doing what they really want. "Women fear that combining work and family responsibilities is a big problem," confirms Cornell University medical sociologist Elaine Wethington, the coauthor of a recent study on the subject. But the study found that new mothers who left full-time jobs to care for their infants were more psychologically distressed than their counterparts who returned to work. These are the dilemmas considered in chapter nine. For now, suffice it to say, women are mostly reared to work these days. That's not the problem. The problem is how to work without "giving everything to work," as Lissa put it.

The men who give everything to work often don't like it either, but they can't risk change, especially if they're the sole support of their families. And here's the catch-22: The more they work, the less fulfilling family life (or any personal life) becomes. If you don't see kids much, it's much harder to know how to enjoy them, or they you. Said differently, if you don't practice the piano, that Scarlatti sonata will never get any easier.

The best defense against workaholism is a rich personal life. When people have a great personal life—with or without kids—they rarely allow work to push it aside. But of the various ingredients in anyone's personal life, kids are probably the most demanding. They can't be left in an empty apartment, like a cat. They make incredible messes. They need affection, attention, visits to Grandma, doctors, dentists, schools, playmates, soccer teams, all of which require quantity time. So I can see how tempting it would be to assume they just don't combine well with work as we know it. Yet work as we know it has pushed people to their limits, which has made an increasing majority pretty angry.

Women may have the most obvious motivation to humanize the workplace. But if women alone try to do it, the workplace will continue to marginalize them, creating separate work tracks, paying them less, maintaining the glass ceiling. That's in fact what's happening in medicine, where men are still working the 80-hour weeks demanded by the highest professional strata while women are choosing 40-hour-a-week work in clinics and hospitals they often wouldn't go to themselves. But, then, most of these women, just like the women who opt out of work to take up traditional motherhood, haven't figured out what else to do once they have kids.

Yes, women today are setting out with their great expectations but they don't always have the savvy to maximize their opportunities. Carol Ann designed a life with one kind of balance. There are infinite versions. The women whose portraits I've drawn in this book are wildly different in lifestyle, in values, in backgrounds, and in ages that range from 25 to 45. Some have children; others don't. But what they have in common with Carol Ann is strategic planning. They all planned their paths carefully, sticking to their real values, compromising lesser goals for more fulfilling ones, and turning mistakes into learning experiences. None had the advantage of special connections, deep pockets, genius, or glamour. All are activists in their own lives, making up the rules as they go along.

One "Gen X" expert, Heather Neely, a 32-year-old organizational psychologist who helps older managers to handle her generation of workers, characterizes her peers as largely "reactive." Their strong suit, she feels, is in adapting to the work situation, not in creating or changing it. "We came into this workplace thinking the boomers had it all figured out. Boomers created this workaholic life. We inherited it, and their dissatisfaction with it. We haven't really generated leaders the way they did; we accept their rules instead of creating our own. We see ourselves as rebuilding their world, but we do it without any dialogue. It's each person doing it quietly, on his or her own."

But Heather worries about rebuilding without any "big picture," any clear sense of what the generation as a whole faces today. She recalls how she graduated college in 1989, during the recession, and couldn't find any job except as a temp. "Everyone was so contemptuous of Gen X, muttering about what slackers we were, only taking temp jobs or working at coffee bars, how we had short attention spans, no company loyalty, no clear values. I felt awful, as if I'd personally failed, until my father made me realize it wasn't me, it was the changing economy and different generational outlooks." At that point, she began to use her temp experience to size up companies, to form ideas about who her contemporaries are and how people can adapt to different work situations, which eventually led to her present consulting career.

Heather's on to something. Only with this overview of work can individuals think aggressively, creatively, and fully in their self-interest. Only with an overview can women take the lead in creating a new work ethic and a more caring culture. As Heather says, "If we don't start talking about ourselves, we fall into the trap of just doing what we're told."

As Carol Ann pointed out, "It's not like there's a law that workplaces have to be a certain way. In many you can go in, find a mentor who believes in a decent work ethic, and help to make the office reflect your beliefs. Most lawyers leave the field instead of trying to change it."

That's true of every field. Women, especially, leave or adapt rather than try to change the way work gets done. They accept their spouses following the status quo instead of encouraging them to change the way work gets done. Yet, the more that this generation of women know about who they are, how much they've already accomplished, and what they are worth in today's marketplace, the easier it will be to create new options for themselves, along with everyone else.

Generation XX: No More Business as Usual

Next to the invention of the microprocessor, arguably the most significant change in the American workplace in the last half-century, has been the nearly doubling of women in the labor force. Yet apart from the still startling appearance of a few top dog women in boardrooms, legislatures, and operating rooms, society hasn't reacted. That's the good news and the bad.

Though close to 46 million women work full time and on average contribute a third of the family income, women are still mostly absent at the helm of government, business, and science. No surprise, they are also still at the helm of domestic life—tending children, the sick, and the elderly, shopping, cooking, and calling the plumber. But the stage is now set for a dramatic change: Finally we have a generation of women positioned to connect economic participation with power—most importantly, the power to make the workplace and public policy accommodate women and dual-income families.

The 51 million women and men born between 1960 and 1980 are the first in history to be equally educated and equally trained to earn a living. My generation longed for this kind of equality, but did not achieve it. Women flooded colleges back then, but the majority didn't train for lucrative careers. Mostly, they majored in education or English or other "women's" subjects that rarely led to power or money. Only a very few aimed to excel in a man's world and they had to put up with male professors who ignored them or barely concealed their contempt. A very short way into the twenty-first century, this generation has accomplished far more. Consider how much they have changed America's economic, political, and cultural landscape.

Who Is Gen XX?

Over 8 million women attend college and graduate schools today, earning more than half the B.A. and master's degrees. And while they still dabble in the gentler-sex professions of humanities and social sciences, the majority major in business. Forecasters predict that by the year 2007, they will also have achieved parity or majority in such traditionally "male" fields as business and biology.

A quarter-million women received master's degrees last year; while another 17,000 received doctorates. That's 40.6 percent of the total awarded (and almost four times the percentage since I got my degree back in the '70s). In the 1990s women earned twice as many veterinary degrees as men, fully half the dental degrees, almost half the law and medical degrees, and a third of the M.B.A's. They've even penetrated the male bastion of surgery, growing the numbers of female surgeons from 2,000 to 17,000 in just 20 years. Right now, more women than men are starting their own businesses and female entrepreneurs employ a quarter of America's workers.

As women aim higher, they're changing the culture. My late stepfather's oncological surgeon is a woman, as is my mother's ophthalmic surgeon, both chosen on the basis of their expertise. "Twenty years ago," my stepfather told me, "we wouldn't have felt comfortable with a woman doctor. Now, we don't even think about it."

Gen XX has made a norm of women in the professions. No one flinches any more at a female investment banker, attorney general, secretary of state, or Supreme Court justice, although all were inconceivable 30 years ago. Sixty years ago, when Al Gore's mother graduated from law school, she couldn't even get a job. Supreme Court Justices Sandra Day O'Connor and Ruth Bader Ginsburg couldn't get jobs as attorneys when they graduated, O'Connor became a state legislator instead, Ginsburg, a law professor. Women have changed those norms.

By the same token, let's not forget that millions more Gen XX women are beginning their rise in retail sales or office administration straight out of high school. Some of them, such as Patricia Dunn, the chairman of Barclay's Global Investors who began as an office temp 23 years earlier, are getting to the top in spite of the double handicap.

Every area of the workforce, with the exceptions of skilled manual labor and engineering, offers some evidence of women's expanding economic and professional presence. In 1999, for example, more than 40 percent of the legislators in Washington State were women, while women constituted more than 30 percent in Nevada, Arizona, Colorado, and Kansas. That same year three women held all the top posts in the launch of two spacecraft for Mars. Meanwhile, 42-year-old Col. Eileen M. Collins was the first women to command the space shuttle, leading a successful mission to carry the Chandra X-ray observatory into orbit. Even one-third of the scientists and staff working in Antarctica are now women, though barely a female face was seen there even two decades ago.

Women are showing up in the least likely places: A quarter of the Pittsburgh police force is female. Even the Avon ladies are now managed by a woman, Avon Products, Inc., having finally named its first woman CEO.

As a baby boomer, I take none of these accomplishments for granted and hope younger women fully appreciate their impact. Though boomers fought to make these gains possible, most of our energies went to establishing the *idea* of equality and creating exceptions to the gender rule, like Billy Jean King, the first woman who beat a man in professional tennis. Women today have definitely moved on from symbols to substance.

What They Want (At Least in Theory)

As they set out in life, women today seem certain about two things. First, they want good jobs—and by that they usually mean lucrative, creative, or meaningful ones. Work is so central to this generation's thinking that even the "Future Homemakers of America" recently voted to change their name to "Family, Career, and Community Leaders of America." True to their new name, the organization now offers programs in career development, leadership, and balancing career and family.

In fact, you rarely read about mothering nowadays without some mention of work. In a classic suburban parenting magazine, the kind they give away at the malls, the lead article is called "Motherhood: A Proud Profession." Yet buried amid the expected encomiums to nurturing the young is the fact that the author leaves her child at daycare while she and his father go to work every day. It's really an article about achieving balance, which brings us to the second clear goal of this new generation.

That goal—and it's one that holds true for young women and men alike—is having the kind of unhurried family life that few of them enjoyed growing up. Young men, lamenting their own fathers' absence from the dinner table and the soccer field, often express a desire for less taxing work so they can parent more. In the words of Kellyann Fitzpatrick, the founder of The Polling Company, a research firm that works with conservative political groups, "the biggest challenge for our generation is providing our own children with what we didn't have: fathers, time, attention, security." Insights like Fitzpatrick's may be why Meredith Bagby, former CNN reporter and author of *Rational Exuberance*, a book about her generation, explains that worklife balance is a priority for kids who grew up in the '60s and '70s because so many had parents, often divorced and supporting two households, who sacrificed time with their children in order to earn a better living. "Unlike the boomers," Bagby concludes, "few[er] of us measure our lives by our career status."

The younger the adults surveyed, the more steadfast the theme. A 1999 PricewaterhouseCoopers survey of 2,500 university students found that 57 percent name "attaining balance between personal life and career" as their primary goal—up from 45 percent in 1997. Teens report that they don't get enough time with their parents, and they don't want to be overloaded the way their parents are. In fact, they claim to value friends, family, home, and happiness ahead of wealth and professional success.

According to Ron Zemke, Claire Raines, and Bob Filipczak, the three authors of *Generations at Work*, a book about the generation clash, the younger generation wants balance. "In the eyes of Gen X, their parents devoted their lives to the religion of work, spending evenings and weekends at the office, bringing projects home, and expending all their energy and attention on work issues. . . . In the words of many an X'er their parents 'lived to work.' X'ers simply want to work to live."

Reeling from techno-paced workplaces, this generation is growing ever more insistent on a work-less-live-more ethic. *Fast Company* magazine's readership made that clear in their answers to a survey. Asked which of five job offers they would accept, readers overwhelmingly chose "Sanity. Balance. Butterfat." Yes, laid-back Ben and Jerry's in Burlington, Vermont, got one-third of the votes followed by Proctor and Gamble in "Cincinnati, where people are nice and the hours are reasonable." Both Wall Street and Silicon Valley, with far more money and round-the-clock hours, lost out. The editors' conclusion: "Sure, people want the big bucks, but most of them would rather have a life."

Like every generation, this one wants to achieve their parents' unfulfilled dreams. Yet they seem to have the wisdom to recognize the high-stress, fast-paced lives so many of their parents lead do not offer a successful model for the work/family blend they want. With long commutes and more than a 50-hour work week for managers and professionals, their parents rarely had the leisure to just be with their kids, particularly when the compressed housekeeping schedules of two-paycheck families can make family time feel like a forced march through a checklist of obligations.

Jamie Rubin, a 35-year-old senior stock analyst at Morgan Stanley whom we'll get to know better farther on, says, "We're a new generation. We're having kids and we have no models. The older women in the offices where I've worked work all the time and travel half of the year. Either they're single or, if they have children, they have two nannies to cover for them. I don't want that life." Like Jamie, most young women seem determined enough to blaze a new path—which is just what they have to do if they are to combine traditional male and female goals. Combining gender goals is essentially what they are doing although few among them would put it that way.

Expressions like "gender" and "sex roles" are not popular with this generation, probably because they sound retro like their parents, or because they seem too political for their apolitical sensibilities. Yet the 20- to 45-year-old set is, in fact, blending male and female goals more successfully than their parents were able to do. It seems normal to a majority of them for both men and women to care for children, normal for both of them to work. However, as most young women will tell you, the gap between what seems normal and what actually happens can be very wide.

Blending gender roles turns out to be much harder than people anticipate. Start with the fact that the average workplace still operates as if men were economic units instead of people. They're assumed to have women at home to run their personal lives so they need never be called away because of a sick child or dying parent, a flood in the basement, or a crisis at school. The workplace assumes that men will work 10- to 12-hour days and invites women to do the same. As late as 1994, even Catalyst, the leading research organization promoting women in business, counseled women who want to break through the glass ceiling to reassure male managers that, despite family responsibilities, they are no less committed than men: "Initiate discussions with managers about interest in assignments that may involve difficult hours, male-dominated work assignments . . . and relocation." In other words, even Catalyst bought into the boomer idea that equality in the workplace means anyone who wants can be a workaholic.

For most people, work-life balance, whether it's wanting to have time for a social life or a family life or just solitude, is hard to achieve in today's workplace. Once children are involved, punishingly long hours can stop dead any hope of blending of gender roles. To their credit, schools and colleges are beginning to address the problem. University courses and whole "Work and Family" departments have been created. Boston College's Carrol School of Management's database on the subject (available on the Internet) already contains thousands of scholarly articles. Even public high schools have begun to teach children about balancing work and family. More than 3,000 high schools now use *Career Choices*, a series of books that places heavy emphasis on work-life issues. But these courses and departments reach just a tiny portion of the legions of women and men dreaming of a blended, balanced life.

Women are a majority of the electorate today, but they haven't used this political leverage to change the work-life picture. The 1993 Family and Medical Leave Act, mandating three unpaid months' maternity leave in companies with more than 50 employees, is barely a beginning. According to surveys, women's priority issues are all about supporting families: improving health insurance, education, childcare, long-term care for the elderly, women's rights, spousal abuse. Improvements in any of them would lighten the burden for women, who shoulder most family responsibilities. Think what a 35-hour workweek could do for quality of life. Or paid parental leave and a month's vacation, which most of western Europe has. But we don't seem to think it's possible, even though we have the power to make all these changes. Work, work, and more work is our norm.

The Assault on Identity

Yes, women are "making it," but the greater society hasn't caught up with the resulting conflicts, as women soon realize when they confront 60-hour workweeks without understanding boyfriends or family who still expect them to carry out all the traditionally female caring tasks. For these women, a work identity can erode as it comes under slowly increasing cultural assault.

Our culture pays lip service to a woman's work identity, accepting her professional and economic intentions. However, she must usually fit herself into male work modes, which makes mothering, and sometimes even dating or just seeing friends, a very tight squeeze. This pressure to conform can be so dispiriting that many woman lose their direction and their sense of self, telling themselves they aren't as good at their work as they thought or that work just isn't as important as family. They assume it's their fault that they can't balance work and family. Without the big picture, you blame yourself. Also, the squeeze comes as a shock.

At college, a girl's work identity is usually solid. Her concerns are with grades and figuring out what she wants to do. She is preparing herself to work while still managing the traditional female role of creating intimate adult relationships. There is no conflict; she can do both. In fact, one activity enhances the other. The friends and lovers she's attached to are people with whom she shares the excitement of studying, finding herself, and reaching for the stars.

Trouble comes when moving into the second young-adult stage, in one's late twenties and early thirties, when the work-life conflict begins to pinch. Or even strangle women, as it did to Erin Martin, a very junior analyst at Morgan Stanley.

Erin, who is now 25, went straight from Yale to the investment banking firm where she quit in exasperation after two years. "I never saw my friends, I never went to the gym, I never had time to read a book. I couldn't even enjoy the perks, like traveling half the time. You'd take a thirteen-hour flight to Brazil, work the next day, then return to New York." Often, she worked 100-hour weeks, staying up two nights in a row to finish an assignment. But Erin doesn't know successful people who manage to work fewer hours and can't figure out how to plan a life of work and family down the road. "Most of the women I know don't think about the future.

They're pretending to themselves that everything will just work out. But it can't."

Not true; it can. At each stage, the questions and concerns may be different, but the underlying issues are the same. Whether you are choosing a college major or a first job, dating or getting married, maintaining a sense of self while giving 100 percent to advance in a career, you can create a successful balance by thinking strategically and hanging on to your values. But without a reference to a context—of your own life and the realities of today's workplace—you can inch toward a place you might not really want to be. As Erin is doing.

Erin's current plan is to find a work niche that is flexible enough so she can get a job wherever her medical-student boyfriend gets his. When she has children, she'll just quit and return to work later sometime. In her view, men want the most lucrative, prestigious jobs. She has lowered her sights so much that she considers herself lucky to be interviewing for a job now that demands only 12-hour days instead of the 16-hour marathons she put in at Morgan Stanley. She appreciates having a boyfriend who cares about personal life at all, unlike her former investment-banker beau who was "all work."

Erin hasn't ever considered what work might leave her time for a life; she just assumes there is none because her circle of friends is trying to make it big in New York City. By the same token, she doesn't consider the possibility that her boyfriend might find a specialty or a practice that would blend with her dreams. A great many women doctors do find less pressured niches, and male doctors could if they wanted to. Although she doesn't see herself as a materialist, she doesn't challenge the "prestige and income" values that lead to life-snatching job choices. As we'll see, she's hardly alone. Coming to terms with out-of-control materialism may actually be the most difficult challenge facing this generation.

Like many of her peers, Erin had a mother and stepmother who both put "work before family." She wants to quit work as a business manager to raise her children, although the field of software management she's now considering changes so rapidly that virtually any hiatus would leave her out of the loop. She believes that *either* family or work come first, not that the two can weigh equally in a woman's life. Given her limited experience and her unwillingness to research options or use the experience of others who have faced these choices before her, Erin lacks the perspective to analyze her life.

Even women who have a larger perspective, like Heather Neely, who makes her living from thinking big about the workplace, are still vulnerable. Well aware that Silicon Valley is "dangerously materialistic," she and her husband have steered clear of buying a home and the requisite BMW. Knowing that people who marry later have a better chance of making it work, she made a conscious choice not to marry till she was 30, and didn't. She also married a man who is very supportive of her work. "We negotiate everything," she tells me, and when I meet this soft-spoken, thoughtful, nice guy, it seems true.

Yet, as ambitious as she is, as determined to be a "part of the American dream," as she put it, by which she meant, "become a business woman," it is Heather, not her husband, who has begun to plan for cutting back when they have children. Her plan is a good one, mind you. She can cut her consulting hours and still keep a hand in while staying home with children. But husband Tim, a VP for Lucent Technologies, travels a lot and isn't designing his life with balance in mind. A trendsetter in most ways, Heather accepts the status quo in this regard. Her own wise words—"If we don't talk about it as a group, we fall into the trap of just doing what we're told without realizing it"—are as true for home life as they are for work.

For young women today, like the boomers before them who also wanted work and love, independence and intimacy, a paycheck and children, the seductive ease of the old route usually leads to a dead end. Many of their mothers started on a "career path," then either turned into workaholics, guiltily neglecting their children, or returned to the old route, cutting back on work or dropping out entirely to raise the kids. For everyone who trailblazed, many more gave up. Meg Whitman, CEO of eBay, who's been married 20 years and has two children, is quoted by *Fortune* as saying that half her female friends from Princeton and Harvard Business School quit work to raise children.

These were accomplished, ambitious women. How did it happen? Those women took small steps, often unconsciously, that led deeper and deeper into the traditional life because they couldn't think of other options. Some, like Heather, consciously plan for it. Many more than ever before achieve it, but most still do not. The Cornell University Careers Institute found that in 40 percent of dual-career professional couples they studied, one spouse had a career while the other had what they both perceived as a "job" instead, in order to take care of the family. Most of these were women. And although it is a significant sign of progress that in a third of the cases, women had the careers, a lot of women are still giving up the career part of their life plan; a lot still can't figure out another way.

On the new route, chaos and stress: arguments about who stays home with a sick child, anxieties over negotiating parental leave, missed meetings, dinnertime chaos, guilt over not having a traditional home life. On the old route, where *she* scales back to handle home life, the relief of manageability and familiarity. But the women now in school or starting careers do not see themselves on either road. Even those who are ready to have children typically believe they can carve out a third way. Those with savvy, luck, and steely determination, like Jamie Rubin, Carol Ann Kalish, and others we'll meet, do succeed. However, the statistics tell a more sobering tale: Unless they strategize, the majority of today's young women will end up failing to reach their work potential, and many of those who do succeed at work will sacrifice their dreams of a close-knit family.

Harvard economist Claudia Goldin took a cold look at women's earnings in relation to their work potential. What she found is that the earnings gap is now almost closed between men and *childless* women. But it has not narrowed for mothers these last two decades. That is, women can now compete with men—if they work the way men traditionally work—but not if they also want to have a family life. What's more, she found that the majority of women, who are, in fact, mothers, do not reach the potential of their training.

Mind you, it's not only mothers who risk losing their earning potential and fall short of their projected success. It's anyone who wants to have a rich personal life instead of defining themselves by work. I remember visiting the correspondent for the *New York Times* in Kenya some years ago. The assignment had seemed glamorous at first, particularly for an African-American woman eager to explore Africa. Two years in, however, she applied for a stateside assignment, although she knew it would mean a step down and exile from the fast track at the paper. Unlike the male correspondents, she didn't have a wife and kids to be with her. She was lonely.

If education is the great strength of this new generation, the greatest weakness is a naive belief that qualifications are enough. A public acceptance of equality of the sexes has fooled a lot of women into assuming we actually have achieved equality. "Your generation fought for equality, we have it," many women in their twenties have said to me. Dream on, ladies. As the next chapter will make clear, equality of the sexes is the lip service this culture pays to an idea it likes in theory but has not managed to produce in practice.

The difference between boomers and Gen XX'ers is that now women can have equality and balance. We may have raised consciousness, but this generation has actual clout, political and economic. That's only half the battle though: They'll have to know how to avoid female job ghettos or negotiate for what they want within them; they'll have to figure out how to avoid discrimination or to fight it; and they'll need partners and mentors and friends who support their goals. They'll have to use their economic power to change the rules about what constitutes a day's work, how work gets done and how it's rewarded. They'll have to level the playing field by creating a decent work ethic for everyone, not just for mothers.

Gen XX's Secret Weapons

Like other pioneering generations, the majority of women striving to blend work and family could end up as casualties so that a minority can settle a new world. In the past, however, there was very little communication between waves of trailblazers and very few guides to the challenges of the new territory. This generation has the advantage of both. Working women of the previous generation are ready to mentor them, as are a lot of men who now accept women in high places.

The basic tenet of this book is that this highly trained generation can succeed where others have failed, but only if they do things differently. First and foremost, life by conscious design has to replace the follow-your-nose trajectory so many women subscribe to. There is a seeming paradox in the idea that the more you consciously plan your work and private life in their early stages, the more freedom you'll have to create your own blend later on. If youth is synonymous with exploration and experimentation, who is going to sit down and strategize his or her life?

In *Passages*, Gail Sheehy argues that in your twenties, you should just try out different styles and identities. "Too much introspection would interfere with action," she writes. Well and good if twenty-somethings didn't have to make decisions about schools, jobs, lovers, children that set their lives on a particular course. Even so, what 20-year-old would subject his or her pleasures to such scrutiny? Who ever believes that personal merit won't triumph in the end? In my twenties, I certainly believed that.

I truly assumed that a Ph.D. from a well-respected university was enough in our perfect meritocracy to launch a college teaching career. So, wanting to live on a farm in the country, I casually accepted a job at Middlebury College in Vermont, even though I would be the only woman among 13 men in the department, as they cheerfully informed me, and, as I found out later, only one of three women teaching at the school. Even though, at the very job fair where I interviewed, a woman with a Middlebury professor's name tag responded to my passing question about the school by bursting into tears and telling me, "You're interviewing for *my* job. They've treated me terribly as a woman." This in a crowded elevator.

Still, no bells rang. I dismissed her as a sourpuss and an incompetent, unlike my suave self. Only later did I learn that she'd been "terminated" because she and her husband had a child which, in the eyes of the department, meant that she should be consigned to the mommy track at a community college.

OK, such attitudes seem too medieval to concern women today. Still, there are two lessons that apply:

- didn't know the playing field.
- arrogantly believed my own talents would overcome all barriers, as they had in graduate school.

Schoolroom and workplace, it turns out, play by different rules.

University professors, who generally know a lot more than their students, are parental with them, not competitive. Besides, students leave after a short time, and therefore, pose no direct threat. The transition from school to workplace can be a shock, even when the workplace is the university. Professors as colleagues behave quite differently from professors as educators, as most women faculty find out to their dismay.

I learned, of course, and by my next job placement (at the City College of New York), I'd chosen a department with lots of women and enlightened men. But personal experience isn't enough. There's just a lot more to know as you move around a field, more than any one place can teach you. By then I also had the advantage of understanding exactly what it meant to be a woman in the university system and in our broader culture. I'd started to read about the subject of women in the workplace and gender relations in general (sexual politics, we called it), which is what people have to do in times of social transition. Otherwise it's really hard to make sense of your life.

My goal was to be a college professor, and I would have become one by hook or by crook, I suspect, though in painful isolation. For me, the woman's movement was a second graduate school.

Theories about gender equality gave me greater confidence, as well as the means to deal with workplace discrimination. It helped me sustain an equal marriage (my first, I'm on my second now) and sanctioned my then-husband's desire to write poetry while I earned our living. It made me understand that, however talented I might be, to some extent, in the eyes of the culture and of a lot of men in positions of power, I had every assumed shortcoming of my sex. Unfortunately, a handful of notorious discrimination cases in the last five years (including a successfully prosecuted one at Morgan Stanley) confirm that discrimination is still a fact of life. No matter how perfect your present perch, or present dreams feel, it's worth arming yourself with information. I wish I had.

If I knew then what we, collectively, now know about women, life, and work, I would have made different choices. For example, having had only one female professor throughout college and graduate school—a childless one—I assumed I had to choose between career and motherhood. Everything I read suggested this was true, and so I simply convinced myself I couldn't have children. Nor did I until much later in life when I allowed myself to acknowledge how much I wanted to be a mother. Like many young women, I didn't know how the desire for children can grow in intensity instead of vanishing because you've bidden it.

In the same vein, I had no idea how much harder it is to have an equal relationship with children than without them; my first marriage was much easier because we didn't have children. Although my second husband is just as fair-minded as my first and we had the benefit of starting out in our thirties instead of our twenties, a child turned our marriage upside down. There again, I thought my strength of character plus my feminism would ensure equality in parenting. It doesn't.

Strategic Planning

This generation faces challenges no less dramatic than mine. But at least today, women are more aware that they are heading toward a work-life collision. In "Children of the Gender Revolution," a study in progress about young people now 18 to 28 years old, New York University sociologist Kathleen

Gerson learned that the young men don't believe they can support a family alone. Nor do they want to. She also found that young women assume they might have to support themselves and their children later in life. But the women are also acutely aware that they face a work-life conflict down the road and truly don't know how to resolve it.

Sarah Pearson, a 31-year-old freelance journalist married to Gabriel Roland, a musician, has postponed having children because she can't figure out how to maintain her independent work life: "I'm so frazzled with juggling an inconsistent lifestyle. Trying to factor in baby-sitters, car pools, and night feedings is beyond me." Without the money for nannies and hired help, she and her husband need realistic alternatives. "Workwise, I'm on call. When there's a story, I have to jump. Same with Gabriel. With a baby, he'd have to take over when I'm away and we haven't gotten there. I mean, when he washes the dishes, he's writing drum parts. How well do the dishes get done? Even if he's willing, he's so much less responsible than I am."

"Gabriel and I need a game plan," she tells me. "I want to read more on how it's done. This is the biggest research project of my life."

Dr. Beth Davis Phillpotts, a 34-year-old physician who had her first child at 32, spent a lot of her twenties trying to work out a life plan with her fiancé, Garfield, an account executive at Black Entertainment Television. She didn't know other women with the kind of marriage she wanted. "I was so worried we would just become these other people when we got married instead of being real friends, 50/50. I made Garfield read every book I could find and we even went to our minister for premarriage counseling."

It still wasn't enough. With a baby who unfortunately required a lot of emergency medical care, it was Beth who mostly took over and switched to part-time work. "It's so hard to change those patterns," she says, "especially right now in the middle-class African-American community, where everyone's riding around in Land Rovers and buying their first houses before they're thirty. The men are driven."

Sarah and Beth are the lucky ones. They're conscious of the problems they face and strive to solve them. They chose truly supportive men. And they're both politically aware enough to understand the larger context of their conflict instead of assuming it's a unique personal problem. The majority of their peers, though highly educated, aren't as aware of the forces acting on them or the information available that might help.

At whatever stage—college, first job, marriage, kids—analyzing relationships, work, and social pressures will ease conflicts and affirm identity. Whether you are choosing a college major or a first job, dating or getting married, moving up the corporate ladder or having a first child, knowing the challenges, vulnerabilities and strengths of your generation can help to design a well-balanced life.

Designing your life isn't some sort of radical social engineering. It's often just a matter of being aware of the probable results of choices. Had I known, for example, of the fatal oversupply of humanities professors during my twenties, a glut that meant many of us would never find entry-level positions or would ultimately lose the ones we had, I would have chosen a different field. In the same way, if women today understand the alarming implications of managed health care for the field of psychotherapy, an enormously popular profession for women, or the current glut of law school graduates, they, too, might adjust their plans. If they know which jobs lead to 16-hour workdays and which are flexible, they might be able to find satisfying work that allows for a personal life. Better to build your life now, to clear specifications, than to one day find yourself suffocating in a doll house or lost in a vast hall of corporate mirrors.

A lot of young people enjoy working long hours, in part because they like the social connections work can provide. But they will probably build personal lives that transform late nights at the office into drudgery. A lot of young women think they don't want children. That may be true at 24. In fact, it remains true more often than in the past and has quite rightly become a socially acceptable choice. But beware of how often those feelings do change. A lot of young people believe they'll never get divorced, but if the past is a reliable indicator, one out of two married couples will. Personal life of any stripe—abiding friendships, family crises, marriage, divorce, kids—does have a way of happening. The goal, then, is to avoid closing doors that may one day lead to where you may want or need to be. The next two chapters take a cold clear look at the territory, mapping the paths that avert some common dead ends.

Reality Bites

Overwork

Popular culture depicting daily life among the 20- and 30-year-olds divides along clear lines, depending whether it's about economic outsiders or insiders. The outsiders are either alternative, marginal or out-of-work types (i.e., aspiring actors, waiters, artists, messengers, dope-dealers); the insiders are the overworked lawyers, doctors, Wall Street guys. Movies like *Go* portray the harsh version of outsider life, where kids live from hand to mouth, from deal to deal, or their next supermarket check-out job. The fantasy version is the one on television shows like *Friends* whose twenty-somethings generally live in an eternal precareer paradise where they somehow make enough money to rent Manhattan apartments and keep themselves well stocked in great clothes. Even Ross, the anthropologist at the Museum of Natural History, seems to have plenty of time to keep the pot stirred with girlfriends past, current, and future.

At the other extreme are the insiders, professionals like that quintessential Gen XX'er—accomplished, superbly trained, competitive in the market place—*Ally McBeal* and her ilk in *ER*, *West Wing*, and *The Practice* who work all the time. Their closest relationships seem to be with colleagues, which is a good thing, because they don't have time for anyone else. Although they never seem to have to deal with family crises, aging parents, or needy children, they do pine for love, kids, and "a real life." Movies like *The 24-Hour Woman* document the explosions that ensue when one of the professionals, in this case a talk-show producer and her husband, the show's star, try to have a real personal life with—eek—a baby.

For most people in their twenties, prework paradise is rarely an option. More typical on the *Friends* side of the picture is my 26-year-old college graduate niece whose waitress jobs barely support her budding dance career. That means she lives in a cramped two-room San Francisco apartment with a roommate found through a newspaper ad—and, no, they're not friends. Even now that she's a licensed Pilates instructor, money is tight and she has little time to commiserate with friends.

The media's depiction of life among the professionals is far more realistic. A lot of the ones I've interviewed do pine for real life. Contrast Carol Ann's life with another, far more typical picture of the legal set (then, I promise, no more lawyers for a while). This time, meet Kemba Extavour, a 25-year-old Los Angeles attorney born in Trinidad and raised in California. Graduating from Stanford and the University of California's Bolt Law School, she has even better professional prospects than Carol Ann, and the same goals. She has also come closer to achieving them than most of the lawyers *she* knows, but not close enough. As she explained at the time of our first interview,

> Work is not my life. Some people live for their work. I'm determined that I'll just refuse. When I took my job, the partners assured me I wouldn't have to work marathon hours. I just had to give my best effort.

Leven, Meale, Bender, and Rankin seemed to her like the kind of small law firm where the four young goodwilled partners would support the associates. She was impressed that every associate they hired was a woman, and that they offered excellent on-the-job training. Although three of the partners are fathers, they all worked long hours and expected their associates to do the same. No "family is our priority" here. So Kemba's at the office at 8 A.M. and, without ever volunteering for extra work, rarely leaves before 10:00 P.M.

On one level, this firm is more appealing than Carol Ann's. It's certainly a hipper-looking place, without the hushed halls and archly traditional style. On the day I visit (dressed in my best Ann Taylor suit), Kemba and Niven Youssef, her colleague and housemate, greet me in jeans and running shoes. It's casual Friday and the atmosphere *is* casual. We have Chinese food at the mall next door, not at some six-kinds-of-bottled-water establishment.

I can see why Kemba thought she'd found a home of sorts. She has the right attitude, looking for a congenial place, trying to control her work. For example, whenever she realizes that she doesn't have the energy to get up at 5 A.M. in order to work out at the gym, she knows she's burning out and cuts back a bit. Once a week, she makes it a point to party or visit with friends. But once a week is all she can manage. That, and Wednesday night Bible class, which is sacred, so to speak. Only she usually heads back to the office afterwards.

Grueling work hours aren't confined to legal jobs, of course. For professionals, the 40-hour week died somewhere back in the greedy eighties when go-go workaholics in investment banking could pull down millions before they hit middle age. Follow their heroic-seeming money-is-all model with a high-speed, high-tech Internet business model, and 24/7 has become everyone's mantra.

In virtually every major newspaper on this past Labor Day, when I was writing this chapter, I found stories about the overworked American, as in the *Los Angeles Times* front-page headline, "With Labor Day Comes More Labor, Less Play."

The headline wasn't kidding: more than 37 fewer play hours a week on average, and fewer still for professionals. While the 40-hour week still exists on paper for most blue-collar and government workers, as you move up the private-sector professional ladder, people are averaging closer to 60-hour weeks. Given that one-third of today's employees are managers and professionals, the mean number of hours on the job has been pulled up to 47.1. And be aware, this trend is growing dangerously fast. Back in 1992, the mean was just 43.8 hours.

In a five-day workweek, 60 hours means 12-hour days. In by 8 A.M. and out by 8 P.M., on an easy day, then home by 8:30. Or later, given how few of us work within easy commuting range. "Just in time for a shower, falling down dead, and getting up to do it all over again," Kemba complains. And she doesn't have a husband or kids who would demand whatever spare minutes she might have. Niven, Kemba's coworker, told me that her boyfriend broke up with her because she had no time for him. Then, like a lot of young career women, she had no time to meet another guy. And wouldn't have time to go out on dates if she did.

Some 82 percent of 5,000 executives surveyed by a Cleveland search firm, Management Recruiters International, say they work on vacations—such as they are. In the global scheme of things, our average vacation time is a pitiful 13 days, compared to Italy's 42 days, France's 37, Germany's 35, Britain's 28, Canada's 26, and worker-bee South Korea's 25! What's more, a recent AT&T survey showed that more than half of today's travelers call their office on vacation, while 38 percent carry cell phones and 20 percent bring beepers. Almost half the workers questioned in a joint study done by Rutgers University and the University of Connecticut said they had to work overtime with little or no notice.

Add to this frantic pace the fact that many entry-level jobs at the most elite employers demand truly slavish hours. Erin Martin, who worked between 100- and 120-hour weeks at Morgan Stanley, shudders at the memory. She talks about "getting scutted out," or doing all the "grunt work" for her superiors, like distributing documents, which can take a precious hour or two a day. From her point of view, the 12-hour-a-day job she's considering at Star Media, an entertainment conglomerate specializing in Latin American programming, looks tolerable because at least her hours would be predictable. At Morgan Stanley, she never knew when she'd be off for an evening, so she could never plan to see her friends.

The entrepreneurial option might sound like just the ticket since *you're* in charge, but often is not. Consider 29-year-old Joe Minton, part-owner of Cyberlore Studios, Inc., a start-up that makes computer games. According to a portrait in the *Wall Street Journal*, he loves to travel but hasn't taken more than a week off in the past three years. He says he would like to marry, but doubts that he will have time to have kids. His girlfriend, Rachel Meyers, who makes $100,000 a year as a corporate recruiter, complains that working on commission is not any easier.

Part-time work seems a plausible alternative. A very few enlightened workplaces do offer part-time work with full benefits and the possibility of making partner or the equivalent. But usually part-time means a 40-hour week, no chance of promotion, no health care or pension, and low status. The average part-timer is paid 60 percent of the average full-timer's rate, even when calculated on a per hour basis. Yet, that's the choice many mothers now make. Sixty-eight percent of all American part-time workers are women, and most of those are mothers. Part-time work, in its current out-of-the-loop form, is more a symptom of an overworked culture, not a cure.

Most working parents say time pressure on families has gotten worse in the past five years. On the books, two-thirds of American companies do offer flextime, but also exert a lot of pressure not to take it. According to a study of over a thousand managers of large financial services companies done by Michael Judiesch and Karen Lyness of Baruch College at City University of New York, most executives believe working parents who telecommute one day or more are at a career disadvantage. Unfortunately, they seem to be right. When the Ford Foundation studied a group of engineers developing a color laser printer for Ditto, a Fortune 500 technology company known for its flexible work policies, they found that a gifted woman manager who took the option to work at home one day a week was taken off her project after eight months—though her staff thought she was doing a great job.

By the same token, don't assume legally mandated benefits are really there for the taking. According to another study, this one in the *Academy of Management Journal*, taking the 12 weeks of unpaid leave provided by the 1993 Family and Medical Leave Act posed "significant risks for managers." In the group of 100 managers they analyzed, those who took leaves earned lower salaries and were less likely to be promoted.

Just how far does 24/7 go? In companies without work-life policies, as far as a workaholic's imagination can travel. Deloitte Consulting in Pittsburgh boasts a sleeping room in the office. Netscape, now a division of AOL, employs a dentist on wheels who services busy Netscape workers in the company's parking lot. Companies routinely offer perks in the form of laundries and concierge services, which essentially means someone will buy Grandma a birthday present or wait at home for the couch delivery so that *you* can stay at the office.

People are literally getting sick from such long hours. While absenteeism eased a bit last year, stress as a cause has tripled since 1995, according to CCH, Inc., an employment information company surveying human resources officials. The National Institute for Occupational Safety reports that back pain is costing the United States billions of dollars a year in lost workdays. Dr. Ann Meyers, a psychologist at Johns Hopkins University who worked on the study, believes that the main cause of the back distress is high demand and low control at work.

The World Bank, with 5,000 employees regularly crisscrossing the globe, found significantly higher rates of health insurance claims filed by employees who traveled compared with those who did not. Three times as many of those travelers' claims were for stress, anxiety, depression, and other psychological disorders. And so were their families' claims. These are grim statistics when business travel is up 14 percent and rising, and most business travelers report that they never get a day off after a long trip.

No one seems to have time to sleep anymore. A Gallup poll found that four out of ten Americans average six hours or less of sleep a night. It seems the eight-hour night has been jettisoned along with the eight-hour day. Stanley Bing, pseudonym of "a real executive at a real Fortune 500 company he'd rather not name," titled one of his regular *Fortune* magazine's columns "Sleep Faster." "It's 6:47 A.M.," he writes, "and I'm already late." According to Bing,

> The meetings go late. The meetings start early. The cell phone is always on. Last week I got a beeper. It came in the interoffice mail. I didn't really ask for one, but they sent it anyhow. I put it in a drawer. One day, you know, I'm going to put it on. Then I can add a little ring in the soft cartilage of my nose, one they can run the chain through easily when they want to lead me around.

How long is he planning to live like this? Only "for now."

That's what a lot of executives say. Yet few of them actually fight the tide of overwork. I recently read about the early retirement of 58-year-old J. Gary Birchhead, the vice chairman of Fidelity Investment. "Thirty-five years ago I promised my wife I would work a normal work week in five years," he remembered ruefully, "and then every five years I would say only five more years." Now, after surviving prostate cancer (which apparently put him over the top), he's decided to spend more time with his family. One wonders what Gail McGovern, who has replaced him, will do.

Why are we doing this? Why do we consent? "World Class Workaholics" is what the *U.S. News and World Report* called us. In its cover story, business writer James Lardner asks, "Are crazy hours and take-out dinners the price of America's success?" Not really. While there will always be driven people who want to work that way, something's wrong when the majority toils into the night. Workaholism has crept up on us. Assuming that's just how work must be, we tank up on Starbucks and hurl ourselves into the whirlwind of our endless workdays.

Familiarity with long hours does not breed contentment. The Families and Work Institute study found that 63 percent want to work less, up 17 percentage points from just five years ago. Harvard University's Juliet Schor, author of *The Overworked American*, found that 20 percent of workers had purposely slowed down over the last five years. But, alas, the broad numbers suggest that others are filling their places on the Great American Treadmill. So why do we do it?

The Devil Drives: Debt, Pink Slips, Material Dreams

In part, the younger generation accepts gruesome hours because they were raised to believe that being a professional means a 60-hour week. That's why they call it work, right? Still, they might have rebelled against such oppressive norms if they didn't have strong incentives to accept them. That is, to accept the highest pay they're offered, at whatever personal price.

First among those incentives may be debt. Without the generous government tuition grants available to the boomers, today's generation is graduating college with an average debt of $10,000. Those who get through medical school end up $100,000 in debt, and if they take a surgical residency the number escalates to $230,000. As one doctor commented, "It's sort of like a big mortgage with no interest deductions." Carol Ann, you may remember, came out of law school $82,000 in debt, in spite of the fact that she'd economized by living at home a lot of the time. Niven Yousseff amassed $100,000 in debt by the time she earned her law degree.

We may be a prosperous people but a lot of the parents still can't come up with four (or six or eight) years' tuition or stake their children while they settle into jobs. That's one big reason why young people take the highest-paying jobs they can get. Not that most jobs pay all that well.

Those six-figure starting salaries we hear so much about aren't as widespread as you'd think. For example, the actual starting salaries for economics and finance graduates in the class of 1999 was $35,668–$15,000 less than the students said they expected. The average lawyer earns $60,000, while the average physician goes through residency inching up from $32,000 to $41,000 over six years before the big bucks roll in. Starting teachers make $37,000; engineers $38,000. Psychologists with doctorates begin at $35,000 and work their way up to $55,000 after five or ten years.

True, Kemba and Niven earn $140,000 plus $20,000 in bonuses, but they are both top flyers from top law schools living in a big city where two-bedroom apartments rent for $2,000 a month. And remember, as they both said, they haven't had the time to enjoy it. At least *they* are able to pay down their education loans. What do lesser luminaries do, and what if, God forbid, they have kids?

Jobs also feel less stable nowadays because turnover is greater. Downsizing can whack thousands of jobs in a day and tons of start-ups fail, leaving kids who traded competitive salaries for stock options with nothing but old pizza boxes as mementos. People worry a lot about losing their jobs and are very reluctant to say no when the boss calls for volunteers to work nights and weekends.

No workplace is exempt in such volatile economic times. Even top earners at the fanciest brokerage houses can get the ax on a moment's notice. In the wake of the Asian economic crisis and Russia's debt default, Merrill Lynch laid off 3,400—including some top executives—on one October day. It's not personal when Coca-Cola dismisses 6,000 in an afternoon. It's the economy, stupid.

Debt in the face of such instability seems unwise, but that doesn't stop this generation from blithely accumulating it. Debt comes from college loans, of course, but is also bred by the credit-card consumer mentality instilled in the young and the restless. Boomers had it easier in this regard. When I was in college, American Express didn't come knocking on dorm-room doors. Not that our Depression-generation parents would have let us use plastic, given their belief that we might be "out on the street" if we didn't budget and save. So we saw Europe on $5 a day, bought clothes in the army/navy store, and furnished our first apartments with a mattress on the floor and an Indian bedspread for decoration. Nor would we have had it any other way. The upwardly mobile were financially virtuous in those less materialistic 1960s and '70s. Most had their hopes set on good used VW Bugs, not their fathers' Oldsmobiles.

Now, everyone's a material girl—even the boys. Gen X spokeswoman and author, Meredith Bagby, says, "We learned from Wilma Flintstone and Betty Rubble that 'charging' was a great alternative if you didn't have cash." She notes that two-thirds of Gen X'ers who have credit cards carry more than $1,000 in debt. This is not to say boomers were better; just that it was easier for us to avoid debt without feeling embarrassed by not having things.

Today's generation *expects* to have nice homes, to drive SUVs, to fly business class. The kids in *Friends* aren't living in third-floor walk-ups or cramped studios in Brooklyn. They're not keeping up with the Joneses, they're keeping up with the well-heeled folks in the ads for Gap and Lexus. As the ad for Snowball.com, a start-up company, says,

> i am the internet generation.
> i am spending billions.
> i am changing all the rules.

Except with that much spending, young people *can't* change the rules; they've traded the power to remake work and home life for a whole lot of Nokia cellphones, Prada bags, and Jose Cuervo Jell-O shots.

In her new book, *The Overspent American*, economist Juliet Schor argues that most people who want to work less cannot afford to because of their spending. This credit-card lifestyle is so ubiquitous that the average young person often isn't even aware of its appalling outcome. One of them, Meghan Daum, describes her downward spiral in painful detail in her poignant *New Yorker* magazine essay entitled, "My Misspent Youth." At age 29, she had no savings, no pension fund, no investments, and owed $7,000 to Visa. How did this happen? The usual way. She graduated from Vassar and an M.F.A. program in creative writing with $60,000 debt, and that meant $500-per-month payments. But she only earned the normal entry-level publishing salary of $18,000. Rent for her Manhattan studio was $1,050. In order to live like her colleagues and friends, she bought coffee at Starbucks, ate sushi for lunch, and drank martinis at trendy bars after work.

Stopping a moment to look at the pressure to live well underscores the insidious materialism that sweeps young people into debt. Daum began with a choice to go to Vassar, accruing vastly more debt than she would have at a state school. She got a master's degree in fine arts, which, as she reflects, "was a rich person's decision." In both cases, she surrounded herself with people who could afford more than she. Her peers rented in Manhattan instead of Brooklyn, where rents are more civilized. She chose to work in publishing, where many rookies have trust funds to supplement their anemic salaries. Everyone seems to live rich, so it seems dorky not to. It might even have jeopardized her career.

Daum's overspent youth also illustrates the dangers of plunging ahead instead of designing the life you want to live. Creative writing is a courageous and exciting endeavor. But as I always asked my own M.F.A. students, how are you going to support yourself while pursuing it? Publishing offers deliciously interesting jobs, but you have to be able to live on less than it costs to rent a garret in Greenwich Village. One senior editor I know started out in the 1970s earning $6,000 a year when most of the rest of us earned double that. But she accepted the terms, which meant living with strangers she found through a roommate agency, eating soy nuts and apples for lunch, and hoping someone would give her a theater ticket for her birthday. But her peers didn't drink martinis or go to trendy restaurants, so she didn't feel left out. Moreover, her austerity was admired, not written off as pathetic. As Cornell economist Robert Frank argues in his book *Luxury Fever*, the cost of today's luxuries is spending more time at the office. It is as simple as that.

Glass Ceilings and Trapdoors

Debt and materialism support overwork. But for men at least it pays off in money, success, and power. For women, the payoff is far more problematic.

Unfortunately, most young women are in denial about the lingering residue of discrimination. With higher education today turning out near equal numbers of male and female graduates, half of middle management is now female. And since those early job offers are comparable for men and women, everything seems ducky. But listen to Kemba and Niven on the subject. Their first year at Leven, Neale, Bender, and Rankin, they both worked long hours but felt appreciated and equal. As Niven put it in a second interview a year after the first:

> We went through school, landed great jobs, and couldn't see the down side, except that we were working too hard. But at work, we felt like a family, so we worked till 11:00 P.M. and thought, "it's cool." It was even exciting. Except it's not so cool after a year of that kind of work. That's when we realized we had blinders on.

By year two, both Kemba and Niven wanted to normalize their hours. Kemba started to date a stockbroker whose own work left him with some time to play. He couldn't understand why she never had a break, even after a big case. That's when she saw how the pressure was an irreducible constant in her office; it would never let up. Niven took her first one-week vacation at a woman's yoga retreat where she had an epiphany. When she returned, she told the partners she was no longer willing to spend her life at the office. Before long, they made it clear that they weren't happy about her "lack of drive."

The next thing Kemba and Niven knew, the partners had hired a male associate "who would be there all the time." They paid him more than Kemba or Niven were paid when they began. Moreover, they both felt that the partners were treating him less critically than they treated the female associates.

When Kemba and Niven looked back over their first year's experience, they noticed that the highest praise had always come for the longest hours, not the success of a case. They remembered that the partners were so status-conscious that they told Niven to trade in her old Mercury Sable for something "more appropriate." Kemba and Niven understood that they were working too hard just to get more money in order to justify how hard they worked. Neither of them want to continue in that vicious cycle. Niven's now considering an offer to be in-house counsel, working 9 to 6; Kemba's got her ear to the ground. "Don't call us at this office a year from now. We're not going to be here," they told me. Wherever they are, I believe they'll have their eyes wide open.

Unless you work for that rare employer who believes in equal opportunity as well as obeying the law, you will feel the discrimination after a while. Men just don't see it, but most women do. A professor at the Graduate School of Management at the University of California at Irvine asked a hundred female and male managers if women were underutilized. The men said no; the women said yes. Catalyst, the leading nonprofit research organization studying women in business, asked 325 male CEOs why more women weren't at the top of their organizations. Eighty-two percent cited the lack of line experience (in charge of revenues); 64 percent said they weren't in the pipeline long enough, and 49 percent said "exclusion from informal networks of communication." When the same question was put to female executives many did cite the lack of significant line experience, but most cited "male stereotyping and preconceptions about women"—a category the men didn't even check.

The fast-growing numbers of women entrepreneurs indirectly attests to women's feeling of discrimination—at least among those who left their employers to become their own bosses. Dorothy P. Moore and E. Holly Buttner, two professors of management who studied a group of these women, found that they weren't starting businesses to accommodate family life, as is often thought. Having hit the glass ceiling, they started businesses to advance and to be in charge.

Typical among them was one woman who described the subtle, cumulative effects of discrimination, what Kemba and Niven might have felt if they had soldiered on in their current workplace or if they had not had each other to corroborate their experiences: "I had the overwhelming feeling of not fitting in. At first I thought this meant something was wrong with me, instead of with the situation."

You have to wonder how many more women believe it's them, not the situation, then accept their frustrations. Successful women often deny that discrimination exists. Remember Carly Fiorina, who, when she was appointed CEO of Hewlett Packard, pronounced the glass ceiling broken. Until the next day, that is, when she retracted the statement. As the *New York Times* editorial put it, "Ms. Fiorina's appointment reduces to 497 the number of companies in the Fortune 500 whose Chief Executives are men."

To arm yourself in what is still a man's world, take a short tour of the workplace. Only 11 percent of corporate officers are women, and only 6 percent of those are in line jobs like finance and product development rather than service positions like corporate communications or human resources. Less than one-half of 1 percent of the highest paid managers and corporate officers are women. Even women nurses earn 11 percent less than male nurses. And in a report to the president and Congress, The United States Merit Systems Protection Board determined that women in government white-collar jobs are promoted at a lower rate than comparable men and earn 25 percent less.

Discrimination against women turns out to be a constant fact of life, even in organizations that pride themselves on rationality and fair-mindedness. After a five-year investigation, MIT, the foremost technical and scientific university in the country, determined that their women faculty members had less money for research, less access to lab space, and less clerical support. They also had fewer and slower promotions and lower salaries. Another study, *Who Succeeds in Science? The Gender Dimension,* undertaken by two Harvard physicists, showed that among scientists who had received prestigious postdoctoral fellowships, men were a full academic rank ahead of women after a decade. One of the authors, Gerald Holton, was motivated to study the thousands of interviews and questionnaires in order to understand why the pool of female senior physicists was so small that Harvard had been unable to hire any.

To really understand the subtlety of discrimination, look more closely at one science, astronomy. Dr. C. Megan Urry, an astronomer at the Space Telescope Science Institute in Baltimore who did a study of women in the profession, found that while 25 percent of the new Ph.D.'s were women, only 5 percent of full professors in astronomy were female. One reason is surely that almost half the male graduates in astronomy got post-doctoral fellowships, while only a quarter of the women graduates did. Another is that men get more of the tenure track positions than women.

What do the male astronomers have to say about this lopsided state of affairs? An issue of *Status*, a biannual report on women in astronomy published by the American Astronomical Society (that obviously cares enough to look into the problem), contained an article concluding that "women clearly don't like these fields or don't excel in them." Not terribly scientific, eh? It goes on: "They're less prone to the intense, cut-throat aggressiveness that usually marks the successful scientist or engineer." But, as Dr. Urry points out, getting a Ph.D. in a very difficult discipline would suggest a liking for the subject.

In testimony collected for Dr. Urry's study, one woman described her very different take:

> At a conference I approach two male colleagues in my field, wanting to introduce myself to the senior astronomer whose work closely parallels mine. I hope to join their conversation about a science issue with which I am very familiar. After continuing their conversation for a few minutes, the senior astronomer finally turns from his counterpart and addresses me, saying, "Ah, but we are boring this sweet young girl. What can I do for you, dear?"

Remember what I said pages ago about professors as colleagues versus professors as educators. I rest my case. And if their uncollegial response seems unimportant, think about getting a dozen of those reactions in a month while also not getting the fellowships or the jobs.

One result of gender discrimination is a lot of discrimination cases—77,444 filed with the Equal Economic Opportunity Commission in 1999 alone. Impressive when you think how few women go to the trouble of filing a case or have the courage to do so. Famous cases make the news, but women often think about them the way I did when I started out—something is wrong with *her*. Think again.

Ann Hopkins was denied a partnership at Price Waterhouse in 1983. The case dawdled on for seven years. In 1990, she won. They made her partner and awarded her back pay. The case had established that Hopkins had brought in more business and billed more hours than the 88 male candidates for partnership during that time. But she was seen as "too aggressive." When she first asked the partners about her rejection one partner advised her to "take charge less often." She was criticized for being "overbearing" and told she would have a better chance of making partner if she wore makeup and jewelry and acted "more feminine."

More recently, on June 5, 2000, the EEOC determined that Morgan Stanley Dean Witter discriminated against 38-year-old Allison K. Schieffelin, one of the small number of women thriving at the near top of Morgan Stanley's chair of command and taking home over $1 million a year. But she didn't make their equivalent of partner (managing director) in 1996 or in 1997, having worked there for 14 years. By 1998, her boss just told her she'd never be promoted, although men who brought in less business had been. She claims that she was excluded from the male-bonding events like a five-day golf trip to Florida, hurting her chances of getting to know the partners well enough. She was also told that she was "snippy," although men were praised as "aggressive" for the same behavior. Sound a lot like Ann Hopkins? That's because it is.

Not only does Morgan Stanley still deny the charges against Schieffelin, but the EEOC had to get a court order to force Morgan Stanley to release files, suggesting a broader pattern of discrimination, which the EEOC found in the institutional stocks division where Schieffelin worked. And yet none of the four younger women I interviewed at Morgan Stanley thought the case had anything to do with their lives. Nor, my guess is, do the Gen XX'ers at Citigroup's Salomon

Smith Barney unit, which just settled a similar discrimination case out of court.

A working girl can't win? Well, she can, but unless she's lucky enough to be among the token few she's better off being aware of the prejudice she's up against. After examining a large number of sex discrimination cases, Deborah L. Rhode, a law professor at Stanford, found that women have been denied promotions both for being ambitious and argumentative *and* for being old-fashioned and reserved. They get you coming or going, so don't imagine it's something you said—or didn't say. It's probably both.

Where discrimination can't be measured, it can be even worse. In an essay entitled, "It's No Wonder Women Enter Politics a Decade Later Than Men," syndicated columnist Ellen Goodman talks about the prejudice against Massachusetts lieutenant governor, Jane Swift, a 35-year-old who took office three weeks after giving birth to her child.

> As one of the first women to run for statewide office in a maternity dress, she was taken to task by the right wing of her own Republican Party. One particularly irate citizen said that if she wasn't going to stay home with the baby, she ought to have a cat instead. That was the easy part.

Then they vilified her for taking a government helicopter home when her daughter was diagnosed with pneumonia and another time for using staffers to keep an eye on that same daughter at the office. Swift concluded that "we haven't made as much progress as my generation has been led to think."

We certainly haven't. Six months later, the Massachusetts State Ethics Commission found "probable cause" that the lieutenant governor violated rules by having two aides babysit. Was ever a man in office so scrutinized? Not unless he couldn't keep his hands out of the till or off his intern.

Radio and television, where we see and hear so many women now, offer the illusion but not the reality of equality. One *Los Angeles Times* piece reported that women television news anchors earn on average 28 percent less than men, even though women coanchor every single local newscast in Los Angeles. It's worse there in radio, where 15 of the local 19 radio stations have a male anchor and no women host any of the popular drive-time shows. No women are full-time talk-radio hosts.

Women's progress isn't as great as we hoped. But why not? In broad terms, that's the question addressed by Virginia Valian, professor of psychology and linguistics at Hunter College, in her book, *Why So Slow?* She undertook this study when she discovered an academic report proving that the same credentials are evaluated differently depending on whether a man or a woman's name is attached. Women, she concluded, are generally viewed as less qualified and competent than men, so that women must still meet higher standards than men for the same rewards. In one of her many examples, one, incidentally, that shows the universality of the problem, women were 46 percent of the applicants to the Swedish Medical Research Council, but only 20 percent of those accepted. "An analysis showed that females had needed 100 or more 'impact points'—a combination of productivity and journal prestige—for a rating equal to that of males with 20 or fewer impact points."

What makes discrimination so tricky to handle in this generation is that it's no longer "in your face" as it was in the famous discrimination cases discussed earlier. As Valian puts it,

> A woman does not walk into the room with the same status as an equivalent man, because she is less likely than a man to be viewed as a serious professional. Moreover, since her ideas are less likely to be attended to than a male peer's, she is correspondingly less likely to accumulate advantage the way he might. A woman who aspires to success needs to worry about being ignored; each time it happens she loses prestige and the people around her become less inclined to take her seriously.

In a test where women and men were trained to take leadership roles with a group of strangers, the group paid less attention to the women than the men, made more negative faces when women led, and gave women leaders less positive feedback. What should be understood, Valian argues, is that this lack of support finally affects women's self-images. Add to that the fact that women feel less entitled to the rewards of success than men, and you can see why women often accept lower salaries and rates of promotion.

Remembering Kemba and Niven's experience, it may not be surprising to learn that as of 1994, women comprised 35 percent of the associates in law firms, but only 12 percent of the partners; the dramatic increase in the number of associates over the previous decade didn't pay off in terms of partnerships. M.B.A.'s fare no better. They start out on an equal salary footing with men, but then a gap widens within a few years. Remember, too, that judging oneself critically as a woman goes along with judging other women critically. That is, women can be just as prejudiced as men.

The subject of discrimination is so important to me because I, who started out expecting to soar in academia, was "terminated" toward the end of my second year of teaching at Middlebury College. I was informed of this on the day after 2,000 people had filled Middlebury College's gymnasium to hear Gloria Steinem and Margaret Sloan on the subject of sex discrimination, part of a week-long symposium I had organized. As my chairman explained, I belonged at a more urban center where politics was welcome.

What follows is the short version of the usual discrimination story. Ask women who've worked for two decades or more and most will have one.

After students protested my termination, there was an internal review committee set up that, it came out in court later, voted to reverse my department's decision. But no one knew this because the review committee, sworn to secrecy, could say nothing when the president of the college announced that they had voted against me. When my termination was official, a lawyer practicing in the state capital—a Republican and a conservative at that—offered to take on my case pro bono. "You won't win," he said, "but only by making discrimination cases can we educate the courts." So we did.

By the time the case came to court, several years later, the woman who had been terminated before me (because she and her husband had a child) and the woman who had been terminated after me (because she was openly gay), and I all testified together. That was after we had a good cry when we met for the first time the night before the legal hearing. We didn't say anything much. It was just the catharsis of finally being with two other women who had experienced the same prejudice and embarrassments that we each had encountered individually.

In court, our lawyer rolled out our credentials, our student evaluations, our extracurricular activities, etc. Even we could see that the "terminators" were hardly objective, especially since we had all subsequently found jobs at other colleges where we were appreciated. And yes, as predicted, we lost the case. But the president of the college resigned and Middlebury, I'm happy to report, now has a Women's and Gender Studies program. At least we did not face debt and punishing work hours.

So where to go with today's triple threat of deadly work hours, driving debt, and discrimination on the job? The answer is not, as my mother believes, to find a rich husband. It's to know the playing field, including knowing the kinds of work most welcoming to women, how to negotiate, to protect yourself, and to recognize the danger signs, all of which we'll examine later on.

But even more important, it's critical to understand that women internalize societal impediments to success. If we are aware of our unconscious prejudices and weak sense of entitlement, at least we arrive at the workplace as our own best advocates. We cannot erase discrimination in the workplace if we don't eradicate it from our minds. To put it bluntly, discrimination begins at home. It is nurtured in those first love relationships, which all too often create the kinds of men who leave real life to their female partners while they mogul on. Keep relationships equal, and you'll have a generation that can bring equality—and sanity—to the workplace.

Rethinking Modern Romance

We'd all love to be loved by someone who thinks we're just as smart, worthy, admirable, capable, and entitled as he. Or would we? Anyone remember Paula Cole's 1998 best hit, "Where Have All the Cowboys Gone?" In a sultry voice, Paula croons to her "man":

Why don't you stay the evening
Kick back and watch the TV
And I'll fix a little something to eat
Oh I know your back hurts from working on the tractor
How do you take your coffee my sweet?
I will raise the children if you'll pay all the bills

OK, it's just a song. A tongue-in-cheek reminiscence of the perfect wife, circa 1950. But the depth of its haunting melody and wistful lyrics is also testimony to how old ideals can linger. When cowboys ride the range in our dreams, it's difficult to embrace egalitarian romance. By which I mean (before you gag on the term), lovers who each pull their weight in a relationship and treat each other's goals with the same respect they give their own. Consider that Paula couldn't actually live the life she sings about or she wouldn't have time to write her songs, no less perform them. And fortunately for Paula, she doesn't need someone to pay all the bills. But romance isn't about logic; it's about the heart and as we all know, the heart has its reasons that reason does not know. Well, that's not entirely true in our psychological era. We can reason out quite a few of the heart's reasons, even the reason for our conflicting romantic ideals.

Most couples don't live that 1950s homemaker/provider life anymore. Take a look at the newspaper's wedding announcements. The bride's work and degrees are listed along with the groom's, even in that last bastion of antiquated fantasy, The Young Royals. Under Prince Edward's wedding picture, the *New York Times* referred to his new wife as "the head of a public relations firm." That, I believe, is a first.

Reality ignored, however, a whole lot of music, movies, television, and magazines feed off of and into bodice ripper fantasies of the powerful male who takes care of his maternal woman, or just "takes" his woman. This passive female image is certainly one of the reasons why most young girls report having unpleasant first sexual experiences, a quarter of which are forced. The macho man, especially in music, is alive and admired. In July 2000, I caught a VH1 segment hosted by Carmen Electra, who licked her lips at all the "bad boys" on the beach and confided to the camera that she had a weakness for "bad boys" ("don't we all," she whispered). Consider it a variation on the cowboy theme.

The message is in the air we breathe; it's the dream life of the American entertainment industry. We just may not realize it's filling our hearts while our minds have another agenda entirely.

Most young women now feel so free that they don't worry about society's hidden romantic agenda. But that freedom lives in a limited time zone: that first young adult stage of life. Before children. While they're dating, living together, or married without children, lovers live similar lives. They're usually both in school, cramming for tests or climbing the lower rungs of the corporate ladder, *both* doing scut work for their superiors. At this stage, they very likely earn about the same income.

During this easygoing 50/50 stage it's hard to read between the romantic lines. For women, it's especially hard to distinguish between the generous impulses of love and the socially bred impulses toward female self-sacrifice. However, it's during this brief time of freedom that the seeds of an unequal future are sown. Later, when the world of work is moving him up the ladder, she may hit the glass ceiling at the same time as she realizes she's the one left holding the dust pan, the grocery list, the baby, the social calendar, and his mom's recipe for Thanksgiving turkey. It's best to examine the seeds that produce this often bitter fruit.

Take one small example from my own world a few years back. My nephew's then girlfriend came to visit during the last weekend of his summer of apartment-sitting while we were away for vacation. During those two days, his girlfriend did the entire summer's cleaning to ready the place for our return. Her rationale (I asked her about it): He's a terrible cleaner, so she took over for him, which she also did at their own apartment near the campus where they both attended graduate school. At that stage of life, she had enough time so that she didn't pay a price for her generous gestures. But most women who work and have children won't have the time later.

The truth is, she may have considered herself lucky to have a man as egalitarian as my nephew, who certainly respected her intelligence and her work. Unfortunately, even the most fair-minded guy has a hard time turning down the kind of service many women feel obliged to provide. Also, although his mother worked, she also did all that "woman's work," so it must have seemed normal to him, as it does to many young men. Household upkeep isn't something either of these 24-year-olds ever thought about. They just did what came naturally. Except it's not natural; it's learned. And, in fact, I'm happy to report, my nephew married quite a different kind of women who holds him to higher standards. He now makes great *pad thai*, his sister tells me, serves candlelit dinners, and keeps a tidy house. And, yes, the couple is flourishing.

Men who are less egalitarian, or simply more selfish, can often send their girlfriends a signal that they expect such service, even when they verbally espouse 50/50 ideals. These roles are almost automatic. They're what we've seen at home and on the tube. One recent television commercial shows a bunch of little girls bringing bowls of different sorts of Jell-O to the same little boy in the hopes that he will choose *her*. This in the year 2000.

Our Faulty Default

Know this: homemaker/provider, earth mother/cowboy, femme/macho man is our default mode. It's what's programmed in there, whether we like it or not. My nine-year-old daughter knows that in all her favorite movies, from *The Mask* to *Tarzan*, men rescue women, even the sweetest, most unmacho men like George of the Jungle. She knows *Men in Black* have hilarious adventures and men in armor do remarkable things and only occasionally can a girl like Mulan pass for a guy and have remarkable adventures too. By four, she knew that whatever animal we were reading about—the bear, the fox, the eagle (unless it's Mrs. Duck waddling by with her little ones)—it's always a "he" even though I said "she" half the time "cause half the animals are always girls," I told her. In school, she is learning a history of male rulers, inventors, and Indian chiefs because that *is* history. But it makes it hard for her to think of herself as a player in history or in life. I won't even get started on music videos, which are the absolute Neanderthal pits.

We're all up against the same hidden persuaders that suggest men make the world run in ways big and small, while women support their efforts. Men are out there; women are at home. And despite advances in women's rights, stereotyping has actually taken a step backwards from the "Free to Be You and Me" decade. Toys R Us has gone back to separating the "Girl's World" of dolls, bake ovens, and makeup from the "Boy's World" of trucks, action figures, and walkie-talkies. Fox Family Channels is starting up boyzChannel and girlzChannel. And let me just say that for every mom who tells you that boys and girls really do play differently, there's another mom, like me (who hosted a mixed-sex playgroup for four years), who'll tell you that little boys love bake ovens and kitchens while little girls get a kick out of action figures and walkie-talkies. And later on, when it's boys, not girls, who play death and destruction video games and mow down their classmates, we have to ask *ourselves* how they got that way.

So there we are, culturally primed to take on the old provider/homemaker roles though they are the farthest thing from our minds when we and our boyfriends are both cramming for exams in molecular biology or getting our first promotions. Psychologically primed as well, according to marriage and family therapist Carol Zulman, whom I interviewed on the subject. She explains that many women still believe in the old chestnut that if a man really loves her, he will take care of her. If he cannot, he's not man enough. That is, there are women who want it both ways. They want equality but they still want a man to be able to support them.

Zulman points out that many of these women had fathers who showed their love through gifts and protection; some may have low self-esteem, others may be ambitious but also want the American dream of staying home with their children, if only for a few years. So they seek men who can offer them that option. But Zulman also believes that women help turn men into providers. Most men, she feels, are comfortable with parity.

Studies bear this out. For example, a survey done by Prudential Securities found that "American men, for the most part, no longer care if their wives earn more than they do. But it seems their wives do care."

Many men are willing to do the "woman's work" it takes to have parity. But a lot of women choose to trade it for the option of staying home. A case in point is one of Zulman's own daughters, Tanya, whose husband used to come home earlier than she did in order to make dinner while she worked later as an account manager at Sony. When she had a second child, she decided to stay home because she was so harried by the 45-minute commute to work with two babies she brought to on-site childcare. That's when her husband stopped cooking and started seeing the house as her domain.

Zulman says that like many women, her daughter is moved by this dream of traditional motherhood, though in its flawed millennial form. Believing that women who work full time forsake family and parenting, "They want a career, then they want to stop to have children, then they want to go back. But they don't pause to think, who will I be in ten years? I will have lost ten years of professional experience. I may have lost my confidence, my self-esteem. They don't realize that money means power in a marriage by bringing a sense of entitlement."

And as we've seen, because work is harder for women who face more of a struggle up on the higher rungs of the ladder (while their husbands are getting reinforcement and rewards), they often take the opportunity to get out.

Tanya's life embodies the common trajectory from egalitarian to traditional marriage. Tanya is an accomplished professional who married an equal partner but

- she viewed children as her responsibility and
- she viewed staying home as her privilege.

At the other extreme, Zulman notes, are women with low self-esteem who marry a larger-than-life male in order to feel their reflected glory. They don't realize that their job is to make him shine and that he will step on them to make himself taller. By that time, the contact-high is gone, particularly when the reflected glory from children replace less satisfying glory from his achievements and power in the world.

Despite how little this sort of powerful self-absorbed man has to give, he can seem attractive in the beginning of the relationship because of his exciting plans and strongly asserted ideas. According to Zulman, the woman may believe he's going to take her needs into consideration and share everything with her. She's usually stirred by the notion of a beautiful home and taking care of a man, never realizing that her husband's inability to nurture or to respect her would eventually embitter her.

Think about the mogul who, once his power is secure, leaves the wife of many years for a younger woman or a business associate. Lorna Wendt, one such "dumped" corporate wife, made history recently when she sued her husband, CEO of GE Capital, and won $20 million of his $100 million fortune because, as the court concluded, her considerable efforts were necessary for his rise. Even so, she didn't get half the money. Her protective, powerful husband was finished with sharing and, according to the courts, her years of domestic service just weren't worth his years of professional work.

Some experts don't think you have to have particularly low self-esteem to accept an unequal marriage. Psychiatrist Ethel Person, who has written about fantasy, sexuality, and power, talked to me about how fearful wives can be of becoming single again, which in this culture often means being left out socially. "The world travels in couples," Person observes. "As singles, men have higher social status than women do; hence women put up with difficult or unfair men in order to be part of a couple, and part of the social world. Men don't have to."

However, staying married to a powerful, narcissistic man is clearly a tough row to hoe. But what to do about it if it seems like that's all that's out there, or that's what you're supposed to do, or the heart has its unsavory reasons? Let me offer a variation on the advice the female elders of my family often give to their daughters: It's as easy to fall in love with a nurturing man as it is to fall in love with a narcissistic one.

Whatever your romantic profile, it will undoubtedly seem as if you cannot possibly get there from here—here being lovers in one another's arms (choose your scene: strolling by the Seine in Paris, going down the Grand Canyon rapids in twin kayaks, lounging in bed with the Sunday papers, making love after a romantic dinner) and there being disgruntled housewife whose husband drops his socks on the floor and says he's too tired to "baby-sit" for his children. But again, the stats are all too clear on this point: Married women who work for pay still average two-thirds of the total household work. Just as important, most of the participants in the study saw the unequal divisions as fair.

Sociologist Arlie Hochschild theorized that women just can't admit to themselves that they don't have equal relationships, so they choose the last refuge of the deeply conflicted: denial. I would add that women today grow up with inherently conflicting dreams: of being a strong female with her "best friend" guy and of being some bad boy's bitch, of being an independent professional and a traditional wife. Instead of modifying (or modernizing) their two dreams, they hang onto both until the fantasy self-destructs.

From Lover to Mad (Read "Angry") Housewife

It can't be that everything starts out equal—as in best friends, 50/50, then we all turn into gender stereotypes. Yet when we look down the road that's exactly what we see. Let me offer as Exhibit A a joke e-mail that circulated last year.

> No Wonder We're So Tired
>
> Mom and Dad were watching TV when Mom said, "I'm tired and it's getting late. I think I'll go to bed." She went to the kitchen to make sandwiches for the next day's lunches, rinsed out the popcorn bowls, took the meat out of the freezer for supper the following evening, checked the cereal box levels, filled the sugar container, put spoons and bowls on the table and started the coffee pot for brewing the next morning.
>
> She then put some wet clothes into the dryer, put a load of clothes into the wash, ironed a shirt and secured a loose button. She picked up the newspapers strewn on the floor, picked up the game pieces left on the table and put the telephone book back into the drawer. She watered the plants, emptied a wastebasket and hung up a towel to dry. She yawned and stretched and headed for the bedroom. She stopped by the desk and wrote a note to the teacher, counted out some cash for the field trip and pulled a textbook out from hiding under the chair. She signed a birthday card for a friend, addressed and stamped the envelope and wrote a quick note for the grocery store. She put both near her purse. Mom then creamed her face, put on moisturizer, brushed and flossed her teeth and trimmed her nails.

> Hubby called, "I thought you were going to bed."
>
> "I'm on my way," she said. Then she put some water into the dog's dish and put the cat outside, then made sure the doors were locked. She looked in on each of the kids and turned out a bedside lamp, hung up a shirt, threw some dirty socks in the hamper and had a brief conversation with the one up still doing homework.
>
> In her own room, she set the alarm, laid out clothing for the next day, straightened up the shoe rack. She added three things to her list of things to do for tomorrow. About that time, the hubby turned off the TV and announced to no one in particular, "I'm going to bed," and he did.

At 21, you dismiss the portrait entirely as descriptive of your mother, not you. At 31, you know it can be you too (Dr. Beth Davis Phillpotts, thirty-something physician and mother of one sent it to me). Keep in mind, women don't become "moms" overnight, at least not that kind of mom, and actually you don't have to be a mom to do all the caretaking. It's a long way from lover to mad housewife, but most women grow angrier every time they do what they don't want to do in order to avoid a fight, or each time they do the "women's work" because it seems "easier," or each time they find what needs finding because they like feeling needed.

Feeling needed is good. But if you have to feel needed where the laundry and the lamb chops are concerned, you're probably more *needy* than *needed.* You might even be encouraging your boyfriend's dependency to compensate for an insufficient emotional connection. Or you might think that's what you have to do to keep him. If that's true, maybe you don't want him. Or maybe you think that's just the way men are—all men.

Erin Martin, the former Morgan Stanley associate, certainly believes that all men want power and prestige enough to accept only women who support their ambition. That's why she's trying to find a skill that she can sell anywhere and thus be able to follow her medical student boyfriend wherever he wants to practice. She doesn't consider that his medical degree might give him more geographical options than she has. But, then, she doesn't believe he would accommodate her, nor does she believe he would (or should) choose a medical specialty to maximize their time together. In Erin's view, men just don't do that. In other words, she's beginning a relationship on the premise that her life is not as important as his and that she has to make the compromises. Fertile ground for blossoming resentments. It's the shortcut to mad housewife, the one who works full time, less successfully than she hoped, and does the second shift at home while her partner is oblivious.

Even if you both agree on 50/50, your boyfriend may be so programmed not to do the work this agreement involves that he will automatically resist. Francine Deutch, a psychologist studying the problem, enumerates men's unconscious strategies for avoiding "women's work." Although she focuses on men as parents, the strategies are the same: passive resistance, strategic incompetence, and inferior standards. Remember my nephew who didn't know how to clean? Or the guy who thinks cleaning means doing the dishes every three days?

I'm not suggesting that men consciously dupe their girlfriends. In fact, it's so unconscious, it can be hilarious. One woman has called the problem, "Honey, where do you keep the ice cubes?"

The longer that men don't do the daily household upkeep that women do, the less competent they become and the more trouble it is for women to simply say, "your turn to do laundry." You can't say that to a guy who thinks Clorox is a brand of mouthwash. Women will rarely say, "you gotta learn to cook—go buy a cookbook," or buy them a cooking school course for their birthdays, as I did for my husband. Yet few women love to do all the cooking all the time. Often it just seems easier to do it yourself. It's not in the long run, though, not when you have no time left for yourself.

The Nurturing Man

Of course, the egalitarian man doesn't just do half the housework; he supports a woman's goals, just as any real friend would. At the dating or lover or even the childless young-married stage, many a man can pass for a 50/50 kind of guy—maybe cooking his famous spaghetti with canned clams for guests and making sure his underwear ends up in the hamper. He may even spend the occasional Sunday helping her with her new computer or her work. And, of course, he probably does believe in equality between men and women as most men today do, at least intellectually.

Unfortunately, none of that necessarily signifies a nurturing man, a true partner in love and parenting. If he is not, his wife will end up doing most of the emotional work in the relationship as well as most of the domestic work. She'll be getting her own work done on the side because, what does it matter, she's only earning half his salary anyway.

Nearly every successful woman I've read about or interviewed has the support of a nurturing man. "I couldn't do it without him," they say. Nearly every one has partnered with a man who has made life compromises to nurture her, just as she has for him. But most of these women had to ask for that support. It wasn't automatic. As one thirty-something CEO and mother of three put it, "My husband didn't say, how can I help here. I managed the housekeeper, bills, kids, then I said, hey, you've got to be a part of this and he responded 'absolutely.'" But this immensely successful woman, Hillary Billings, whom we'll meet in a later chapter, had ample evidence that he was the kind of man who *would* say "absolutely," then reduce his work schedule to follow through.

Well, even if you want a nurturing man, how do you recognize one? How do you know if he's nurturing even before the acid test? While people are capable of change, men who are nurturing are usually so inclined even before they fall in love. Remember Carol Ann Kalish, seeing Greg's home for the first time, noticed pictures of him hugging puppies, pictures of his family, pictures of his friends. Those were signs to her that this was a man with strong emotional connections. She also learned that he had no problem with her earning more than he did or being more ambitious. His ego didn't require her to be less than him. And, of course, he was in a nurturing profession (cardio-rehabilitation), which he spoke of with great enthusiasm. These may not be proofs, but they're pretty good indicators for the woman who's watching out for her future, and who believes men are capable of equality.

Remember Sarah Pearson, the freelance journalist who is now happily married to a musician but can't quite figure out how to work and have kids? She didn't always choose her men so well. Looking back at her first great (and too often painful) love affair, she can see wherein the difference lies. "Gabriel is more like my mother—supportive, free with me, accepting. We mother one another," she reflects. With her former boyfriend Bob, she believes she was working out a destructive relationship with her own overbearing father. Bob's strength, like her father's, was intellectual deftness. "He was the smartest man I ever met, like my father, with an unshakable sense of his own rightness and the verbal abuse that often goes along with that. With Bob, though, I could fight back, and did, so we fought all the time."

Because Bob was intelligent and opinionated, Sarah tended to take his word for things she was less sure about. She didn't realize that he blamed others for his own inadequacies, which meant frequent condemnations of her. "Because he didn't enjoy social connections and was socially awkward, he blamed me for being friendly, as if I were stealthily and pathetically trying to charm people to get them to like me. I came to believe that my strengths were weaknesses and selfish, that my openness, gregariousness, and warmth were just vanity and flirtation. He criticized my work, my thinking, my writing, tearing it to bits. Now I understand how competitive he was with me. I bowed out of the competition to let him shine. My writing got more and more obscure, my real thoughts buried somewhere no one could see. What saved me was a constant stream of people telling me something different about myself than he did."

Bob and Sarah stayed together for three years, even moving from college across the country to settle together. But Sarah says she knew from the beginning it wasn't a good relationship. She saw "the whole thing roll out in front of her" and still couldn't resist it. She was still in love with him when she left. By then, though, she knew she could never have children with someone so self-absorbed. She saw how her life with him was pinched, unkind, and cold.

The first time she saw Gabriel, playing the drums, he seemed completely different: warm, relaxed, happy. He was enjoying the music and people. "With Gabriel, I laughed for the first time in ages, as if I were physically retrieving my laughter." Reeling still from her relationship with Bob, she fully appreciated Gabriel's kindness and respect, a respect so fundamental, she calls theirs a "cruelty-free relationship."

Perhaps it takes a writer like Sarah to be so incisive about the difference between a destructive and nurturing relationship, but most women have some experience with both and can draw conclusions as well as she. Each bad relationship is bad in its own way, but generally there's a lack of giving, of trust, of honesty, of fundamental respect. Sometimes people just don't understand themselves well enough to see what they're doing, good or bad. Sometimes they don't leave a bad relationship because they don't believe a better one will come along. Sometimes they don't believe that giving, honesty, trust, and fundamental respect are possible.

This is a cynicism that Melissa Banks grapples with in her best-selling novel, *The Girls Guide to Hunting and Fishing.*

Discouraged about not meeting Mr. Right, Banks's protagonist, Jane, decides to abide by the "hunting and fishing" approach to mating outlined in a popular girls guide, which parodies the actual best-seller, *The Rules.* Jane won't accept a date less than four days in advance, won't have sex before marriage, won't pay her way, asks him questions about himself rather than talking about whatever she wants, and is never funny because, according to the guide, "humor isn't feminine." Jane, herself a very funny, irreverent, honest person who can easily pay her own way, recognizes *The Rules* as sheer manipulation, but tries this "reeling your man in" approach because she hasn't been successful before. Unfortunately, the man she tries it on liked her for the same reasons she liked him: humor, honesty, and irreverence. He doesn't want this new version who makes him go on "datey dates," and "earn or win" her. So she drops the act, choosing instead "to be a truthball in search of a goof."

The moral of the story is obvious, the more you are authentically yourself, the more you're likely to meet someone who's like you and who likes you. Honesty can still lead you into the arms of Mr. Wrong, as Sarah found out, but fortunately, there are some generalizations about nurturing men—guidelines, so to speak—which, while limited by the infinity of human personalities, can be helpful.

Family therapist Diane Gottlieb advises young women to seek out men who are aware of their emotions, especially fear and sadness, and able to express them. Not only does emotional awareness signify that he accepts his vulnerabilities, says Gottlieb, it also means he can be more empathic to others, particularly to his partner and to children. However, Dr. Gottlieb warns young women that they also must accept a boyfriend's vulnerabilities. The nurturing man might not be willing to empty the mousetrap. He might not be at the top of his class or be the toughest lawyer on the block.

May be he's just a nice, funny, loving guy or an introspective, poetic, earthy one—just not especially outstanding in the world. Maybe he's as insecure as you are, which in this society means his social status is less than yours. Women are so trained to marry up—marry stronger than or better than—they may find it harder to tolerate a decent equal than a version of the all-American hero. At first. But if you're alert to nuance, you may just begin noticing the emotional advantages.

The man whose success provides his real heat, who's always protecting his girlfriend, or who does not reveal his fears may actually fear his own "feminine" side too much to be an equal domestic partner. The silent type who doesn't want to talk things over may be impossible to negotiate with later on, which means the couple cannot grow together into new stages of life. The man who is so competitive that he's always asserting his superior virtues over hers will have to shine at her expense. The man who talks and never listens wants an audience, not a partner; approval, not truthfulness.

My college roommate Molly was so thrilled with her handsome boyfriend, a man from a wealthy and distinguished family, that she chose not to notice how intimate dinners à deux amounted to interviews with the great man to be. She was so pleased to have the financial support to paint that she accepted the paltry half-hour a day he allocated to her and their son. And she did achieve some success as a painter, which seemed to please her husband, although he did nothing to foster her talent. By the time her son was in high school, she realized that she was living with a stranger who gave little aside from financial support accompanied by humiliating controls over her household budget. Fifteen years after they were married, she got a divorce.

Most of the time, in spite of the social consequences, women initiate divorce proceedings. Most of the time, they get fed up with marriage as service, of living with a partner who neither nurtures them nor takes the trouble to know them. Nurturing is a subtle quality; the devil is often in the details. It's these relationship details that an equal marriage is built on. Take the example of the next couple.

Trini and Willie Quinn

Since Willie's considerably older than Trini, they might seem unlikely candidates for an equal relationship, especially since both of them came from traditional cultures and large traditional families. But 50/50 was as easy for them as falling off a log. Mostly, I think, because both are fiercely independent people who followed their own convictions.

Now, married eight years, they have two businesses (his, a construction company, and hers, a nursing home) and two daughters, Aoife, six, and Brigid, four. Both are hands-on parents, allowing each other enough alone time to cultivate their private passions: He sings in an Irish band; she is a belly dancer.

They couldn't look more different. Trini's Mexican-American and Willie is from Ireland. Yet they still look every bit the well-matched pair—both slight, thin and wiry, soft-spoken, gentle people with impish smiles. Willie immigrated to America almost 20 years ago, but his brogue remains as melodic as a Celtic lullaby. It's midafternoon in a chilly driving rain when I come to interview them at their home in Santa Barbara, California. Willie brings tea and cookies to where we sit by the fire. His skin and hair are so pale you can't see brows or lashes. But his cheeks are ruddy, his eyes Irish blue, and he has a sweet gap-toothed smile. With his gray woolen cap and work boots, he might have just walked off the dairy farm where he was raised.

When Willie met Trini, he was working on and living in a house next door to where she was taking care of an Alzheimer's patient. On the pretext of having a beer with Marv, the patient's husband, he stopped by often to see her. Not that Trini had much time for love. She was working two shifts and taking classes at the Santa Barbara campus of the University of California, where she eventually got her B.A. So Willie carved out time for them by having dinner waiting every night when she got off at 8:00 P.M. Afterward, she'd go home, grab a nap, and start again on the 11:00 P.M.–7:00 A.M. shift. Eventually (the only time he was ever bossy, Trini confides), he convinced her she shouldn't work herself to death.

To Trini, working hard meant working as many hours as possible. Petite and quite feminine, Trini nonetheless projects a palpable strength. There's a no nonsense look about her freshly washed skin, wire-rimmed glasses, short hair brushed back, and red lipstick to match her sweater set. No wonder, Trini was raised by her grandmother, who brought her to America and supported her by cleaning houses and working in the vegetable fields.

Willie interjects how extraordinary Trini's grandmother was. "A tiny woman with such character that nothing was ever too hard for her." She never learned English, Trini says, but she made friends with everyone, including Cesar Chavez, the farm labor union leader, to whose cause she was devoted. They show me a Chavez poster with her grandmother's picture, a wizened old woman in a kerchief, her profile against the sky. Above, the words "We fought for it. The Union Label."

With this legacy, Trini urgently wanted to better herself. But before she met Willie, Trini had given up on men. The ones she met in college seemed like exploiters to her, more interested in service than in sharing. But in Willie, she recognized a true friend, someone who cared about her deeply and accepted her. "I could be comfortable with him. I could be myself."

When Marv and his wife died, they bought the house and converted it to Trini's nursing home. Willie stood behind her throughout the long year of untangling the red tape needed for a nursing-home license. Her first two clients actually lived with them the year Trini gave birth. Now, she has nine clients and four employees and lives a few minute's drive away with Willie and the kids.

Her own father died when she was five and she never knew her grandfather either. But even without role models for men, she had the clarity of mind and self-confidence to evaluate her suitors, choosing one who loved her for her ambition as well as for her caretaking. When I ask him what attracted him, Willie replies, "For one thing, I thought she was gorgeous. I could see how kind-hearted and patient she was with the people she cared for. I admired how hard she worked."

Trini never asked Willie if he was willing to be a 50/50 parent. She knew he would be from the example of how lovingly he cared for her. For his part, Willie knew he'd love being a father. "I love little babies, probably because I took care of my younger brothers and sisters."

Now, while Trini picks up Aoife after school and takes her to the nursing home (where she does homework and entertains the clients with her singing), Willie calls for Brigid at childcare, takes her home, and makes dinner. "Brigid is the greatest kid I've ever seen. She starts up, plays all on her own," Willie beams. He's teaching her to sing, too.

When Trini and Aoife come home at 7:00, dinner's on the table; they all say prayers and dine. "There's none of this eating one now, the other then," says Willie, "I believe in meals together." Enough to get up early and have the family's breakfast ready, too.

Both Trini and Willie say that owning their own businesses means they can control their time. If the kids need to go somewhere in the day, lessons or doctors, Trini can just leave with them. She takes both Aoife and Brigid to their violin, ballet, and swim lessons. And Willie can end the day earlier than she likes to; they both have time to ride bikes with the kids, play music, visit their schools, and still do quite well in two expanding small businesses.

Their advice is: Don't get married until you're truly ready. Trini and Willie lived together for a year, so they knew it would work. They were both older and had formed their life plans. But obviously, relationships come easily for Willie and Trini, even when both partners are distracted by a myriad of work and parenting obligations. Notice, though, that when partners have the insight to choose an equal mate, they base their choices on tangible evidence: Willie's nightly cooking for Trini, his concern for her welfare, his respect for her entrepreneurial dreams. The harder question is how do you achieve the kind of mutuality Trini and Willie have when your emotional survival instincts aren't as strong?

Creating an Equal Relationship

Without Trini's determination to own something and "raise herself up," intuition wouldn't have sufficed to ensure an equal relationship. Unfortunately, intuition alone can as easily lead to a traditional relationship. Another determined woman we'll get to know later created so unequal a relationship that she ended up doing everything at home—a house, two dogs, and a daughter—on top of a demanding job. A successful stockbroker in the 1980s, when her job ran totally against gender, Carol Malnick was obviously an independent thinker, professionally. Socially, she was very much a product of her upbringing. As she explained,

> I was always the caretaker. Even for our weekends on his sailboat before we got married, I'd bring the food, invite the friends, and take care of David. It's what I was trained to do. It's how you please a man, I thought. In my childhood, I'd always been the little mother who took care of my much younger brother while my

> parents eked out a living. And I still am. I would never have dreamed of asking David to take our daughter to school or make her lunch, even though he was very proud of my work and we depended as much on my salary as on his. He didn't demand caretaking. I considered it my job. My mom worked but she was still the Girl Scout leader and the homework lady. I wanted to do the same.

Except her mom wasn't a stockbroker. Career ambition and traditional motherhood is a tough mix. Carol did resolve her conflict in a very creative way, as we'll see later. For now, suffice it to say that people do actually create their relationships, whatever their form. At the very least, be aware that the relationship you create is your choice.

How to transform the critical process of choice into a conscious decision? Talk. Talk about everything. Denise Thomas, a mother of three and vice president of a successful Internet business we'll see more of later, says, "You must ask questions before you marry someone. Don't be afraid to say how you want life to be and encourage him to do the same."

Denise's husband, a true partner, said he didn't want to be the only one earning money. She was glad to hear it. Not only wouldn't he be one of those men burdened by the need to provide and succeed at any price, but he would support her considerable entrepreneurial force. And he has. Also, note that it took courage for him to admit he wanted Denise to earn money. He was revealing his "unmanly" feelings, going against gender type. This is the sort of revelation Dr. Gottlieb referred to when she described nurturing men.

Joyce Abrams, a psychologist in Silicon Valley whom I interviewed, specializes in work with entrepreneurial couples. She thinks Denise Thomas's approach is on the mark. For her, the *key* is talking. "Women should start a conversation, say, 'Let's sit down and talk about our life, our values, where do we want to go and how do we get there.'" In her experience, even women who are executives can have traditional expectations. Often, they don't know how to assert their needs. They cannot take the risk of asking, "What kind of life do we have if I'm so harried and I'm so compromising?" Quite simply, they are insecure.

Abrams points out that many women who are very savvy about the world of making and earning are not savvy about themselves. High-powered women can be very vulnerable psychologically. At work, for example, they may feel enormously guilty about firing someone. Or they simply give up the work, like an MIT graduate she was seeing who had been a player at a major firm, then became a consultant after her kids were born. One female executive she worked with was angry when her husband took her to dinner for her birthday and only talked business, as if she had no say in what they talked about.

Abrams counsels women to ask themselves, "Do I have a voice? Am I shaping what we talk about or how we resolve arguments. Do I express my real feelings? Am I willing to get angry? Can I test the reality of my perceptions? A woman's voice, she believes, is the most important issue. Personal equality begins with voice. Think of Sarah, who lost her voice in her relationship with Bob and was reduced to watching their life together grow more and more pinched, antisocial, and unkind. Only by testing the reality of her perceptions with others did Sarah see how the relationship had distorted her, how much of her voice she'd suppressed.

Abrams encourages women to challenge their fears: Women give up their voice out of fear, she reflects. They're afraid they won't be perceived as feminine. They're afraid of abandonment, that their men will leave them. They don't have enough self to risk having a voice or, perhaps, they're so used to being ignored they don't try anymore. If they take the chance, says Abrams, they will discover that men don't leave because women assert themselves. They're just projecting their fears of what will happen. It's a fear of the unknown.

Of course, a man might leave. Bob might have left Sarah if she'd refused to accept his perception of her or if she had judged him objectively. But, then, losing Bob wouldn't really have been a loss. In Sarah's story, it's clearly her child-fear of her father that was rekindled with Bob. Now she no longer has the strong, authoritative, ego-crushing man, but as it turns out she quite likes thinking for herself. And she's terrific at it. Footnote here: when she left Bob, her writing took off. She even won a prestigious award for her journalism.

Think of Gabriel, of Greg, of Willie, of Garfield, of the "goof" Melissa Banks's protagonist ends up with. They're all egalitarian men. Might I say, men who truly love women as people.

Abrams reminds us that a man who desires a woman with a voice is a different sort of man. He's more mature and wants the richer relationship that comes from partnering with such a woman. Perhaps it seems like the odds of finding such a man in a culture where so many have been trained to win and to take control are small. But more and more men, even those in more traditional cultures, have been trained in more feminine values.

Studies in Scotland and Japan have found that people of both sexes now prefer feminine-looking men over rugged, highly masculine types—the alpha or more dominant male. Feminine men project the right personality for today: warm, honest, cooperative, and potentially good parents. Since nurturing men have become attractive, the chances of finding one should be better, even abroad.

In fact, the younger the man, the more likely they were raised to express their feelings, respect women, care about the planet, and resist the classic male work ethic. William S. Pollack, codirector of the Center for Men at McLean Hospital in Massachusetts and author of *Real Boys Voices*, makes exactly this point. Despite the rigidities of the macho "boy code," he believes boys "desire to be closer to other human beings and to be allowed more flexibility and tolerance in how they reveal themselves to the world. They want the doors open." What they want, as Nicholas Lemann concludes in his *New Yorker* magazine review of the book, is to be more like girls. The younger you are, the more nurturing men there are around.

But finding such a man isn't enough, Abrams cautions. Men and women have to cultivate awareness together, understanding the tendencies of women to fear anger and thus suppress it, just as men typically fear sadness and suppress it. The more conventional the male, the harder it might be to have the conversations that would lead to change. But the harder you try, the more likely you'll make some improvements.

Having a voice to shape a relationship into a fair one isn't a matter of keeping score. No relationship can survive a daily tally of he does/she does, he talked/it's her turn. But relationships that allow for a true work/life blend for both partners require a lot of flexibility, as in, when she's in a work bind, he takes over, and vice versa.

Partners need as much role interchangeability as they can comfortably manage so that neither is clueless about how to handle their mortgage payments or their kids' lunches. They have to be comfortable talking about money, about how to pool their funds. If geography comes into play, partners have to consider what's right for both of them instead of simply going where the man's job goes.

The *New York Times* documented one such collaborative move. Dan and Laura Rippy met when they both coincidentally returned home to Massachusetts for a vacation. A cofounder of HomeAdvisor.com and Sidewalk.com, she then held a fast-track job with Microsoft in Seattle. Once they married, their deal was that he'd leave his job at Bristol-Myers Squibb in New Jersey and join her in Seattle, but when he found something he really liked, she would move. He found a job in Dallas, so Microsoft arranged for her to work in Dallas, where she recently moved on to become CEO of Handango, yet another software start-up. Now both are settled professionally and personally in Dallas. Miss Rippy's counsel, "You and your partner need to clearly articulate your goals and expectations so that no one will feel like they're getting the short end of the deal."

Avoid the Jerks

That's the advice of Hillary Billings, the CEO of a San Francisco company and mother of three who asked her husband to cut back and share home responsibilities with her. Yet, while following her advice may be easy for women like Hillary and Denise Thomas whose fathers encouraged them to reach for the sky, women without such supportive backgrounds or great models may find it a lot harder to keep the jerks at bay.

A lot of men are still seeking a helpmate instead of a partner. A lot of men, fair-minded though they may be, are so driven to succeed, they cannot compromise enough to accommodate a woman who also wants to succeed at work. So women need to have good radar for the warning signs of a future patriarch or a workaholic husband. Zulman suggests that women assess how supportive her boyfriend is of her interests, whether she can influence him, whether he's considerate of her—reliable, keeping promises, finding time for her. Notice whether he only wants to see his friends, go to his movies, or make love to satisfy himself.

I would add that a man who is very critical or too free with jokes at his girlfriend's expense may be unconsciously competitive or have too weak an ego to really accept a woman's success. A man whose temper makes his intimates afraid to broach sensitive topics may be unconsciously using that temper to control those close to him. A man who places his girlfriend in his fantasy future instead of creating it with her may not be willing to pay the real price of an equal partner. What is that price? Caring as much about each other as you do about jobs, money, and success. Caring about the other's success deeply enough to support it with time, with home comforts, with enthusiasm.

Women who want a successful work/life blend have to ask whether very ambitious men make suitable partners or, if that's the kind of man they fall in love with, whether it makes sense to forego parenthood so that both of you can enjoy your ambition together.

Woman who want children down the line increase their chances for balance if they give up the cowboy fantasy of the powerful man. They have to face a newer, deeper challenge—of finding strength in themselves and sharing it with a companion. As Abrams puts it, the first order of change was women going to work; the second order—creating egalitarian relationships—is more profound.

The difference, she says, is analogous to going on a diet or, more effective and more difficult, changing to a healthier way of life. We all now know that women can do virtually any job. The second order of change will come about when this new generation of women raise their voices, each in her own home.

Designing a Life
Finding a Direction/ Choosing Your Work

It's a jolt, moving from the subject of romance back to the subject of work. But it's basically the same subject. Conflicting values, confusion, and vulnerability are just as much a part of choosing work as they are of choosing a boyfriend. The challenges are similar and the principles the same. Choosing work is like finding the right relationship with yourself, not an idealized image created from oughts and shoulds. Many people never understand how they ended up doing whatever it is they do. Sometimes it works out, sometimes it doesn't. However, the more you know about yourself and what you want, the more likely you'll find a good match.

In reflecting on her legal career, Kemba, the Los Angeles attorney working 12-hour days, offers a few provocative insights that apply to choosing any line of work:

> Most people hate being lawyers. In law school no one explains what it means. Students don't have a sense of reality. They don't know that law means mostly paperwork, long hours, endless worry about how the partners perceive you, and few of those exciting court experiences they see on television. Unless you're really lucky, you don't even work in a place where people like each other.

> Think about why you want to go to law school, or any school. Most of the people I met there were liberal arts majors, they don't know what to do, so they figure they'll get a useful degree. Find out what lawyers (doctors, social workers, teachers) really do all day. Spend days with someone in the profession. If it's law, go to a courthouse, interview lawyers, interview their spouses, interview someone who quit.

As cheerless as Kemba's words may seem, this is the soundest advice anyone can give to students who haven't yet chosen a career. Though simple, her two points are crucial:

- Know why you want to do the work you're planning on;
- Know what it means to live the life of someone working in your chosen area.

You're probably thinking that might be a lot easier if you had a clue about what you want to do, or even what you're good at. So it's there we'll begin.

The Psychological Moorings

The choosing years—from ages 20 to 30 (and sometimes later)—are all too often the most confusing. When the pressure is on, you can feel despondent trying to find something as grand as a direction for your life. It can seem as if the ship of life is sailing, leaving you to drown in indecision, that everyone but you knew from birth exactly where they were headed. Some people are lucky in this regard. They've wanted to be veterinarians or cartoonists ever since they got their first pet lizard or uncle Donald showed them how to draw a stick figure. Even if all people really know is that they want to work with little kids or are hell-bent on earning a million by the time they're 29, it's at least a direction. And that is enviable, if you don't have one. Desperate, some will grab at the life raft of the familiar, following a best friend's lead or a parent's profession. Or they'll go to work in Aunt Kate's public relations firm. Others respond to the first teacher who tells them they have talent . . . in anything, whether it leads somewhere they want to go or not.

Headhunter John Driscoll of Management Resources International, where he counsels people at just such crossroads, observes that 95 percent of the people he advises have not reflected on what's important to them. Is it money, a fun work environment, training, low stress? They only look at the immediate crisis: I need a job. I need to *be* something. His suggestion, "Empower yourself to step back and define your goals. You'll get where you're going a lot faster."

The key is reflection, but not when it's done in isolation from family. Dr. Diane Gottlieb, the psychologist and family therapist who commented earlier on the nurturing man, says that a major aspect of the job choice problem is a cultural mandate to separate from one's elders, particularly parents. Unlike in Europe and Latin America, young people in the United States are isolated from adults and rarely use their family members as mentors. And that is a big loss, since these are the people who know you well, care deeply, and have a lot of valuable work experience.

Gottlieb also points out that the cultural emphasis on economic riches rather than emotional fulfillment leads many young adults, particularly those with large college and professional school loans, to choose the lucrative over the satisfying. Current materialist values are a bullying influence. They are so pervasive, it's all too easy to assume they are your own. By contrast, when I was in college it was supremely uncool to want to make a ton of money. Business was considered crass, and lawyers (except for ACLU and legal aid do-gooders) were viewed as defiled. Our heroes were people who did "meaningful" work: helping the helpless, vanquishing political rogues, or tilling the soil. Those same people today might be working for a dot.com in Silicon Valley or leveraging an M.B.A. from Stanford into investment success. But it's no better to be growing organic tomatoes if the outdoors gives you hives than it is to be a CFO at a start-up if you don't like the money game. You've got to know your own values and personal likes, then respect them. This is hard. Very hard.

Amy Wu, a 23-year-old freelance writer, says that "the overnight success of the Jerry Yang's of America [cofounder of Yahoo!] has made them a symbol of my age group, replacing the goofy Adam Sandler image that once defined Generation X." Wu complains, rightly, that "it's hard to stay grounded when high-tech nerds are becoming poster boys for our generation and making it onto the most-wealthy lists. It's even worse when people who are old enough to know better look at us as if something has gone awry because we are not making six figures."

That's pressure. In spite of it, she and her friends have chosen lower-paying jobs as teachers, social workers, and even as extras in films. Amy left her dot.com job when she "realized that money, titles, successful initial public offerings, corner offices, and Porsches were important things, but not important enough to sustain me beyond my 40s if that wasn't where I wanted to be."

Amy took the time to assess her values when she didn't like what her life looked like at the dot.com. That kind of reflection has to happen if you want to wake up in a life you like.

How to begin? Dr. Arthur Kornhaber, a psychiatrist specializing in the problems of adolescents, offers a useful approach. Borrowing from our currently ubiquitous business vocabulary, he suggests young people consider the "spiritual currency" of their decisions if they want to "get paid" in fulfillment and happiness. If we don't, we go on to live partial—even empty—lives. Those alpha-type, driven people, he says, are often just frantically filling their time. "When they stop, like sharks, they fall to the bottom of the sea."

Of course, Kornhaber is hardly alone in his belief that spiritual currency, which he defines as our place in the universe, our feelings of love and connection with others, counts a lot. But it might surprise him to learn that two economists, David Blancheflower of Dartmouth and Andrew Oswald of the University of Warwick, have actually quantified that the value of happy marriage, estimating from survey data, brings as much joy as an extra $100,000.

Most people are convinced, but not all are able. So how do we become people who are good at connections and relationships? Through cultivating our contemplative and connective sides. For example, Kornhaber suggests writing down the topics your mind talks to you about; that is, record your internal conversations. Note the positive, life-enhancing ones that make you feel good. Build on these through spiritual pursuits, whether they be romance (yes, even romance is spiritual in that it connects us deeply to another), or fighting a local injustice, or spending time each week helping others. Meditate. Enjoy something beautiful in your environment. Start a reading group in your office. Be with people, not to network, but to discuss life. In these activities, one finds life; one creates "the vital balance," says Kornhaber, quoting the late psychologist, Karl Menninger. Taking his own advice, by the way, Kornhaber, who had just moved to a new town when I interviewed him, had recently joined a philosophy book club.

Contemplation might seem like an oddball activity in what Kornhaber calls our "businessified" culture, but it's actually the classic advice for living a fulfilled life. In her book, *The Working Life: The Promise and Betrayal of Modern Work,* Joanne B. Ciulla reminds us that the Greeks and Romans believed that studying liberal arts—for their own sake—was the correct preparation for life in a free society. She notes also that in his classic book on our business society, *The Lonely Crowd,* David Riesman argued that business breeds "outer-directed" people who "belong to the company first" rather than "inner-directed" people who belong first to themselves, their communities, families, and churches.

As for connections, the more you have, the more mature your level of coping. Pat Raskins, a psychologist and director of Columbia School of Education, was part of a research project that looked at what made some women more successful at coping in our high-stress culture. Connections made the difference. Raskin also noted that women who attempt the superwoman style, doing everything at home and at work, don't really have a voice. "People who have an identity or voice say what they want and no one wants to do it all," says Raskins. In other words, it's not just any old attachments that fulfill people, but authentic ones, where we are honest and sufficiently ourselves to speak our minds.

The admonishment to cultivate an inner and a social life is the core of the immensely popular book, *Tuesdays with Morrie,* which has been on the best-seller list for more than three years as I write this. In it, a young workaholic sportswriter learns from his dying friend and former professor:

> So many people walk around with a meaningless life. They seem half-asleep, even when they're busy doing things they think are important. This is because they're chasing the wrong things. The way you get meaning into your life is to devote yourself to loving others, devote yourself to your community around you, and devote yourself to creating something that gives you purpose and meaning.

The sportswriter knows that this vital balance is what sustains Morrie himself, who always made time for discussion groups, walks with friends, dancing, and volunteer projects. Ironically, although Morrie never "wasted" time watching television, Ted Koppel devoted three television shows to the final months of his enviably full life.

Actually, this new generation, as fed up with workaholism as it is enticed by the fast track, often gives itself this advice. In one of the chat rooms of a Web site called chickclicks, the topic of the day was a woman who lamented her inclination to measure self-worth by her salary. Most responses went something like this first one:

> Ummm, just stop moaning about how meaningless your life is. And do something. Go for walks, check out museums, write poetry, start silly office games with miniature footballs and oddly named pitches. If you tie your self worth to the amount of money you make, when you make 90K you'll end up thinking that 120K means more, etc.

Knowing your values, interests, and talents comes from cultivating pleasures both in work and outside. It also means protecting both with strategic thinking. This might take more time and somewhat more risk than just following the herd.

Take the example of 28-year-old Sasha Gottlieb, the daughter of psychologist Diane Gottlieb quoted earlier. Sasha holds a $58,000 a year job as an environmental specialist at the Organization of American States in Washington, D.C. During high school, she had loved her student exchange visits to Latin America, and became fluent in Spanish, then majored in Latin American studies in college. Not knowing quite where to go with an interest in South America and a talent for languages, she took an M.A. in Latin American studies at Stanford. Once there, however, she realized she wanted to be politically active in North/South American relations, and took a second master's degree at the School of Advanced International Studies at Johns Hopkins, this one in international relations, paying for her graduate education with a combination of fellowships, loans, and parents' help.

Meanwhile, she interned, then worked in various OAS offices, did fellowships in Chile and Argentina, and got to know a lot of people in the field. She also realized that environmental issues were her central political interest. During this long process she was able to determine just where she wanted to work, and how. As she says, she could have gone into corporate America, but she chose instead the less well-endowed office she works in—and still earns a good living. Though she doesn't make a fortune, she lives well enough to have just bought her own apartment while also paying back her school loans. She works hard, but manages to leave the office at 5:30 every day, to cultivate friendships, and to spend time with her parents. During the week I wrote this account, her mom is meeting her in Puerto Rico, where Sasha is attending business meetings.

Not that it's been easy. All Sasha's mentors were men who work 100 percent of the time, or older women who had to fight so hard to get where they are, they too devote everything to work. She's had to ask, "Who in my office do I respect?" When she realized they were the colleagues who work efficiently and then go home to coach their kid's soccer team, she modeled her work life accordingly. Her outside interests not only provide the contemplation, discourse, and connection to others that Sasha needs—all the things Dr. Kornhaber suggests you build in from jump—but, as she herself says, these activities also protect her from falling into 24/7 work.

Although Sasha has had periods when she's had to work much more than she likes, she's always been a person of balance and spiritual values. She was brought up that way by parents who each worked half-time so they could have enough personal time for her and the other interests in their lives. However, even if you weren't brought up that way or even if you didn't start out thinking about "spiritual currency," it's never too late to start acquiring.

I recently read about 29-year-old Liz Steele, who exchanged her $120,000-a-year job as deputy director of the Brussels office of an important lobbying group in order to manage a refugee camp in Nicaragua, where she earns a stipend of $9,000 a year. Granted, most people couldn't live on so little money for more than a year or two, but that year or two might change your life. It did for her.

Watching a TV news report on aid workers in Kosovo, she realized that "that work seemed much more satisfying than just making money." Her revelation came in a flash, which can happen if you pay attention to your reactions. Then she had to figure out how to change jobs. Since she'd heard of Doctors Without Borders, an eminent aid group based in Europe, she took their two-week training course (not a huge commitment just in case she didn't like it) and went with one of their teams to Nicaragua. With her considerable administrative experience, they soon put her in charge. Humanitarian groups are, in fact, wisely looking for M.B.A.'s, accountants, and business people these days. And often, you can be given much more responsibility than you would in the private sector, which translates into a better job later on if you want to return or perhaps a foreign service position if you don't.

If you're already in that fast-paced world, follow the advice of Dr. Ben Carlson, a pediatric surgeon at Johns Hopkins. Carlson, only 33 and one of the few African-American surgeons at the medical facility when he began, actively cultivated balance. In the morning, he mediates or reads the

Bible. He follows the advice he gives others—to do things for people. The scholarship fund that he and his wife started looks for students with academic excellence and a commitment to help society. He's definitely the doctor I'd want to see, one whose soul is there in the room with him.

Financial Moorings

Dr. Carlson is another exception in the balance story. Discussions of values and balance usually turn on stories about people who moved from the materialist fast track to "meaningful" work, or who had a heart attack at 38 (just after their IPO), and then learned to cultivate a richer perspective. And they are usually men: Although a lot of women are bitten by make-it-big-fast fever, most are raised to value spiritual currency. (For most women, "ConnectionsRUs" often leads to the neglect of the professional part of the equation.) They will often put their relationships, their families, their desire for kids, and their volunteer activities ahead of their work. If they do, particularly if they do so unconsciously, they may wake up in a life so overwhelmed by personal obligation that they can't do the work they love. More commonly, they can't support themselves. For women, professional ambition and the desire for money are more likely to be what they fail to cultivate early enough. Higher education and training aren't enough. Women need money-smarts along with perspective and assertiveness.

Susan Rietano Davey, a partner in a cutting-edge employment agency we'll learn more about later, argues that women sell themselves short. She observes that small thinking about money traps women. All too often they're thrilled at the prospect of making $40,000. They don't feel entitled to more. They hesitate to advertise their credentials to recruiters or bosses because it feels like boasting. Instead, Davey coaches, women should aim high and promote their accomplishments, which is what men do. "When you don't self-promote," Davey says, "'they' don't know what you're worth."

"Whenever possible," Davey suggests, "explain your achievements, approach opportunities aggressively." She suggests observing what successful people do, and then do it. Sit down with them, pick their brains, find a mentor, or several mentors. If there's a peer who's doing better, sit down with him or her and ask for help. Negotiate for what you want rather than asking or complaining about what you don't have. Explain how what's good for you is good for the company.

A case in point: our previous female model of balance, Sasha Gottlieb. Recently, she went to her boss and told him that she would like to be in charge of one project rather than just assisting the directors, which she'd done for over a year. She got what she asked for. Trading in spiritual currency doesn't mean forfeiting the green stuff.

If this were a book for men, I'd skip the part about money. Most men feel such pressure to be good providers and are so inclined to measure themselves by their paychecks that they need to save themselves from a life of lucre. But women need to be as serious about their financial futures as their spiritual futures, lest one make the other impossible. Think of all the divorced mothers who have to work long hours (or two jobs) and thus can't spend enough time with kids and friends.

Meaning isn't the only part of the balance equation. You have to make a living, too, and acknowledge just how well you want to live. Often, women have a hard time thinking strategically about money, as if dollars-and-cents smarts automatically means giving up all the spiritual currency. As if financial independence means that you won't have a partner, since you don't need one.

Of course, nothing could be farther from the truth. We're talking about harmony and balance here, not celibacy. Financial independence gives you the leverage to cultivate all those other things, on your own terms. That is, not being dependent on one job, one boss, or one man to have the life you want. So if you do choose one of the low-paying professions like early childhood education or social work, you have to calculate how you're going to pay the rent and still have the financial room to maneuver.

Early childhood education as a career is a case in point. Women entering the field obviously haven't chosen it for the money, but they may not have fully considered hard questions about how dependent on a man—or any partner—salaries of $30,000 a year may leave them.

Karen Hughes, who has higher degrees in special education, left a public school job to open her own childcare center in New Milford, Connecticut. But after a decade of operating one of the best in the area, Karen had to close Over the Rainbow.

In lean years, Karen earned $20,000 a year. But she says even the $55,000 she was able to earn in a good year wasn't enough.

> I have no choice, really. I'm a single parent now. I'm forty. I have to go back to public school teaching. It's the only way I'll get a pension, health benefits, vacations, and enough money to take care of my family. It's not just the money, either. You don't go into this business for money. But here I work all the time. On weekends, I'm collecting materials; on days off, I'm calling in, writing curriculum, helping families with problems. I'll miss this terribly, but I can't keep doing it.

When I interview Karen, we are sitting on knee-high plastic chairs in the converted barn of an old chicken farm that is now filled with shelves of toy cash registers, tea sets, and yellow dump trucks. On the corner stage, kids were dressing up in feathers, boas, pirate hats, and capes. One little boy sat patiently waiting for Karen to play Yahtzee with him. Over the Rainbow is one of the cutest places I'd ever seen; I'd certainly have sent my kid there. But Karen is teary as she talks about closing, about the families who depend on her and the children she's watched grow for several years. With her arm around the little boy, she whispers, "Childcare asks so much and gives so little."

Karen organized her life around her devotion to education and the spiritual enrichment that gave her. But she made the mistake of counting on her former husband's salary and didn't investigate how to make more money from her center, perhaps by growing her business larger, as a group of women did with Country Kids Farm, a childcare center in a neighboring town.

These six women formed a collective to run their center in Brookfield, Connecticut. They don't work such punishing hours and they've been able to expand enough so that they can each count on the $55,000 a year Karen only made in good years. Nor was Karen aware of Connecticut state-funding initiatives in childcare that saved another center in Hartford, by coincidence also named Over the Rainbow, which was then able to pay top dollar, benefits, and offer vacations to their employees. Ironically, the professions with most heart and spiritual value require the most business savvy to survive.

These grim facts are in no way an argument against pursuing people-loving careers. They are an argument for making informed choices that can make the difference between success and disappointment. You may still choose to be, say, an artist. But, like my niece Jessica, a fine dancer who performs regularly, you might not mind waitressing to finance the calling that you love. Unlike me, who spent four years earning a Ph.D. in comparative literature, you won't end up surprised to be in an oversubscribed profession. Although you can always find out the information for yourself either through a career counselor at school or directly from the Bureau of Labor Statistics on the Internet, let me offer a bracing look at median salaries in various professions:

Teachers	$37,000
Dentists	120,000
Social workers, B.S.W.	23,000
M.S.W.	40,000
Physician, resident	32–42,000
Private	160,000
Surgeon	225,000
Reporter, beginning	23,000
Experienced	40,000
Engineers, B.A.	38,000
Ph.D.	59,000
Psychologists, beginning	35,000
Ph.D.	55,000

It is also worth noting the differences in earnings linked to where you went to school: There's a big gap between starting salaries out of MIT compared to the average state university. It's also a good idea to investigate which of the professions are especially hungry for recruits, like accounting. Right now the Big Five accounting firms are so desperate for women, they've turned to high schools to find and create future accountants, offering kids generous scholarships and perks.

No surprise, computer science may be the biggest winner for women. the *New York Times* interviewed one woman majoring in product design engineering who will earn $60,000 starting out with a software company in San Diego, plus stock options and a signing bonus. America needs computer techies so badly that companies have pressed the oval office to double the number of annual visas for skilled foreign workers.

The problem is that few women are biting. A national report from the American Association of University Women says female students account for only 17 percent of high schoolers who take the College Boards Advanced Placement in computer science. Women make up only 20 percent of information technology professionals. In fact, fewer women study computer science now than did in 1984. Apparently, women are uncomfortable enough at the computer that in classes with men, they simply quit. However, in all-women's classes, women excel at a level equal to men, both in engineering and programming.

With an open mind and an eye to financial security (as well as getting in on the ground level of the computer revolution), women might consider computer science, even if it means running the gauntlet of a male-dominated profession. They might also keep in mind that leadership opportunities for women at the dot-coms are greater than in established bastions of corporate America. In 1999, women were chief executives of 6 percent of Internet companies (compared with 1 percent among the Fortune 500s), and held management posts in 45 percent, almost doubling the numbers of the previous year. Not only is this a wildly growing area, the need for skilled workers is so great that qualified women can easily negotiate for workable lives.

Since a lot of women do shun the idea of working in high technology, it may be worth noting that at tech firms, lots of the jobs fit conventional management or marketing categories. William Schaffer, head of International Business Development for Sun Microsoft, majored in French literature. By no coincidence, he coauthored *High Tech Careers for Low Tech People.* Maybe this isn't your cup of tea, especially hearing from some of the dissatisfied former dot-com'ers like Amy Wu. But women do profit enormously from thinking out of the box, going where they've never gone, and balancing money against heart and soul.

Consider the career of Jamie Rubin, a 35-year-old stock analyst who first covered the pharmaceutical industry for the Shroeders Bank, a major New York investment firm, then for Morgan Stanley. Her job was to follow new developments in big companies, rate stocks, and make investment recommendations to her clients.

Graduating as a history major from Vassar, a degree that doesn't lead to anywhere special except teaching, Jamie spent a year traveling around the world. When she returned, feeling refreshed and open, she was flexible enough to consider work outside of her specific training. Although she wasn't numbers-oriented, when she saw a job listing for assistant to a stock analyst, training program included, she gave it a try. To her surprise, she found she was quite good at it. Actually, many of the basic skills involved in analyzing historical data applied to stocks as well. Deciding to stick with stock-picking, Jamie then worked round-the-clock for five years in order to get the experience she needed. But she knew that when she became a senior analyst, she'd have control over her time.

Jamie also modeled herself on the only other woman she knew in the profession, and shrewdly chose a job at a small, nurturing firm. As she explained, "A place like Morgan Stanley is so well known, analysts gravitate there. But Morgan Stanley is the investment banker for major players. If they tell you to fly to Tokyo tomorrow to check out a firm, you do it." Note too, that on the research side of investment banking, work was less intense than on the deal-making side.

At our first interview, while Jamie was still at Shroeders, her management-consultant husband had flexible enough hours to get home in the afternoons to be with their 19-month-old son. Jamie would usually arrive by dinnertime but often had to travel to conferences to learn about new pharmaceuticals. No problem, she said. Her son was used to it and her husband could "man" the house. She also earned enough to lighten his burden—to take her family on holidays to Italy, to buy a weekend home, and, generally, to live well.

After several years at Shroeders, Jamie was sought out by Morgan Stanley. She told them she was pregnant with her second child, which was not a problem for them. (In fact, she soon learned that they had a better family leave policy than Shroeders.) With a staff of 20 and a willingness to delegate responsibility, Jamie maintained the same hours, home by dinnertime—though she admits feeling guilty walking out of the office when her staff stays late. However, as she points out, they're all twenty-somethings and none has kids, so they accept the hours just as she used to.

The big difference is that because Morgan Stanley is in the major leagues, Jamie occasionally has two or three very intense work weeks during a live deal. But there are compensations. At Shroeders she had to attend a 7:30 meeting three times a week, which meant missing her son's waking. Now her workday typically begins at 8 or 8:30. Meanwhile, she's better poised to move up the career ladder. "At Morgan Stanley, I'm not just a stock picker," Jamie notes. "I can work with bankers offering my mergers and acquisitions ideas."

Consider the planning that went into Jamie's career choice. She took a year off after college, an excellent choice if you have the money and inclination. But you can always work instead. After graduating from Brown University, Dr. Beth Davis Phillpotts moved to New York City and worked at a bank. This gave her time to live the high life in the Big Apple, which was one of her dreams, and do some useful thinking. There's teaching English abroad, internships, and plain old work to build some life experience before making big decisions.

Jamie also calculated that a career in history wouldn't lead to jobs, money, or control over where she lived, so she branched out. She also found a woman mentor—a tremendous help—and chose a small, personal firm over a larger one. She traded freedom up front for the prospect of having it later in the form of control and flexibility.

What's interesting is that Jamie is still planning and still flexible. As she explains, her current work is very exciting but very, very hard. She thinks that a lot of people stay with Wall Street in order to support the lifestyle that it allowed them to create. She doesn't want to be backed into that corner, however. Her move to Morgan Stanley was, in part, to get to know about venture capital and investment banking so that when she's ready, she can become a corporate planner or join a start-up as CFO. (Chief financial officers work fewer hours than the bosses, she explains.)

Jamie's calculations reflect her refusal to be a wage slave and her determination to live her values. Note that she chose work that provided a royal income, which she very much enjoys. Not everyone cares about having a fat paycheck, but it's well worth bringing money into the picture when choosing work. It is also worth repeating that money doesn't mean you have to lose out on the spiritual side of life.

The Brass Tacks of Life Design

One obstacle to finding out the spiritual and financial underpinnings of any kind of work is that career counselors and placement offices focus on the nuts and bolts of the job or the graduate school, not on what kind of life you'll have. That's because they are under pressure to show that a significant percentage of students go on to graduate schools and/or get good jobs.

Another obstacle is that students, champing at the bit just to get out on their own, to earn money, and to prove they have the right stuff, don't pursue lifestyle questions with their counselors. Those offices often have (or can get) the information on work hours, income, or the degree of competition within a profession, even on parental leave polices, etc.—if you ask.

Internships are a great introduction to a profession. How better to know what it's like than to spend a summer or even a couple of afternoons a week working for the people who do what you're thinking about doing. Even browsing books like *America's Top Internships* or *The Internship Bible* can provide career ideas. If you are aiming yourself at a specific newspaper, corporation, or agency, it's often possible to find the name of the internship director there. Or check the Internet for internships for sites like *www.internshipsininformation* technology or *www.feministmajorityfoundation* listing internships in women's leadership.

Internships are generally very competitive. You have to apply by December because the good ones are gone by March. Also, most don't pay—and, therefore, require subsidies from parents or earnings from work during the school year. Although an internship usually means a lot of xeroxing and answering the phone, it's an opportunity to get to know the people who do the work, to ask them whether they like the work, what kind of balance they have, and what advice they'd give to someone interested in doing it.

Another great source of information is the job interview. When I was job hunting it was considered too feminine to ask anyone about lifestyle. You were supposed to be able to work like a man and more so.

Now, many men don't want to work like a man. And fortunately, the work-life buzz is so strong and unemployment so low that companies accept employees' right to a personal life, at least in theory.

Asking about time on the job is no longer a taboo. In fact, it means you know yourself and you can protect yourself from burning out. It means you know your worth and can pick and choose the best place to work.

Rest assured, you're not alone in asking. As we'll see in the next chapter, the demand for trained professionals is so great, companies are now turning their policies upside down, offering signing bonuses, and letting recruits write their own job description in order to get and retain them. Remember how Carol Ann Kalish took a look at the parking lot during the weekend when she was considering a certain law firm. Well, others are catching on. *Wall Street Journal* columnist Sue Shellenbarger writes:

> Welcome to recruiting in the New Age. Eyeballing the parking lot is just one of many new job-hunting tactics used by recruits. Weaned on working-parent lifestyles and raised reading Dilbert, they're heeding some sophisticated signals of corporate culture regarding work hours, deadline management, and work/life balance.

Shellenbarger informally surveyed 13 big employers on campus recruiting and 11 of them said students are asking about work hours. According to Keven Renahan, director of recruitment marketing for Johnson and Johnson, recruits ask, "Is this job going to suck the life out of me."

Top dogs ask too. The vice chairman who made Ann Mulcahy the president and CEO of Xerox said she made sure he understood her concerns about balance before she would accept.

So go ahead and ask. Also assess how honest the recruiter is. Ask for examples. Perhaps you'd like to talk with someone doing the job you're interested in. See how much discretion the employer gives you. Assess how difficult it will be to just say no to extra work. See how important "face-time" is to your prospective employer. Be shrewd. The only thing you have to lose is a job you don't want.

Then there's the issue of gender discrimination. This takes some keen observations and inquiries: How many women work in the field? How many at the particular place? How quickly do they move up the ladder? Are any in charge of anything outside of human resources? Is there a woman whom you can interview who might tell you what it's like to work there? Is mentoring available? Are there female career development programs within the company?

The answers don't have to all be "yes." But just take note, and know, too, how valuable every "yes" can be. Shaunna Sowell, a single mother of three who is now a vice president at Texas Instruments heading a division with 750 employees and a budget of $275 million, was able to rise because of networking and leadership opportunities, management-training workshops, and mentoring programs. "I don't believe people succeed on their own," Sowell says. "If you don't have people recognizing your talent and opening doors for you, your career won't accelerate the way it could." A Catalyst survey of women in senior management found that every one of them could point to a mentor who was crucial to her advancement. They also point out that the bigger the company's revenue, the greater the likelihood it will have women on its board. That is, the first Fortune 500 companies have more women on their boards than the second 500 companies.

Carly Fiorina's 1999 appointment as CEO of Hewlett-Packard is relevant here. In a male-dominated corporate world, Hewlett-Packard was an anomoly with more than 25 percent of women managers, including Ms. Fiorina's rival for the job. But they had corporate programs and an aggressive woman-promoting corporate mentality. Why? Because Hewlett Packard's chairman, Lewis Platt, was a single parent after his wife of 16 years died just at a crucial point in his rise to senior executive.

He learned that he "couldn't cope any better than the women did," which humbled his sense of male entitlement. When he became CEO, he encouraged flexible schedules, telecommuting, job sharing, sabbaticals. He sent memos about the importance of work-life issues to his managers. The result was that the gap between the turnover for women, which was twice that of men, closed. And, by the way, Fiorina's former employer, Lucent Technologies is also a woman-friendly place. Its new CFO, Debby Hopkins, left the "phenomenal male dominance" at Boeing for Lucent, where 4 out of the 16 top executives are women. The point is that how women fare in any one place is rarely unique. So find out about the work culture you're entering.

Choosing strategically, then, means assessing your values and talents. It means knowing the kind of lives lived by those in the jobs that appeal. It means knowing where the opportunities are for women, knowing how you'll cope with the lack of them, the lack of money in a field you passionately want. It means thinking out of the box, as Kimber McKenzie has plainly done in an occupation that continues to excite her after 20 years.

Colonel Kimber L. McKenzie

Although I meet with 42-year-old Kimber McKenzie—Kim, as she introduces herself—during her recent one-year stint as a Senior Military Fellow at the Council on Foreign Relations in New York City, the interview feels anything but military. At her suggestion, we lunch at a French restaurant near the council's townhouse offices on Manhattan's tony Upper East Side. I expect a uniform, but she's dressed in a handsome gray suit accented by a silk scarf flowing over her shoulder and a pretty pin in her lapel.

She claims to be enjoying her "Seinfield experience," as she referred to her first extended stay in the city, although she's actually a VIP. Every year, all of the military services compete to send one senior officer to the Council on Foreign Relations, the brain trust for the foreign policy establishment. Not only does that officer bring a military perspective to the table, s/he gets a year away from the urgent pace of military command to cultivate a more contemplative perspective on policy. Kim, a colonel in the Air Force, chose to work within the Council on the Commission on National Security for the 21st Century, chaired by former senators Gary Hart and Warren Rudman. Les Gelb, the council's president, also asked Kim to set up a Task Force on Relations with Columbia to be cochaired by former National Security Advisor, General Brent Skowcroft and Senator Bob Graham of Florida.

At the end of her year at the council, Kim will become commander of the 91st Space Wing in North Dakota, responsible for the safety and readiness of the Minuteman III Intercontinental Ballistic Missiles and the 5,000 personnel who service the weapons delivery systems. In fact, Col. McKenzie is the highest-ranking female officer on the military operations side of the Air Force; those women who outrank her are in the service sectors, such as medicine or intelligence. Not that you would immediately picture her leading the troups, not until she begins to talk. Then her authority, sense of purpose, confidence, and on-her-feet strategic thinking make it quite credible indeed.

Growing up in Oklahoma, then Virginia, Kim was "in every sport imaginable," earning an athletic scholarship in track and field to Virginia Tech. After graduating, she returned to her hometown to teach, but didn't love it the way she expected. With a degree in health, recreation, and phys ed and an early love of travel, she decided to be what an awful lot of undirected women decide to be . . . a stewardess. But a friend of her mother's made an intriguing suggestion: If you're going to fly, you might as well command the plane.

The military life appealed to her, enough at least to commit to four years. She liked the idea of an immediate community of people who were living the same life and would therefore be more likely to support one another. Changing jobs and locations every three years promised new adventures and new challenges to learn and grow on. She liked the feeling that, in the military, she was making a contribution, working for something larger than herself. But she also chose carefully on the basis of where she would have most control.

Unlike the other services, the Air Force allowed her to choose her career and plan ahead where she would serve. She also found that the Air Force was committed to advancing women and was light-years ahead of the other services on this path because it had integrated women in many more fields.

The only time she felt discrimination was when they opened AWACS (Airborne Warning and Control System) to women, who numbered only 8 among 800 officers. "It took us one three-year tour to figure out how to make it work. We learned to be competent, to speak out about harassment, and to make our weight felt. With more time and more women, the problem was solved," she tells me. Working with the AWACS in Saudi Arabia, where she was responsible for training Saudi airmen to operate complex command-and-control systems, her senior officers let her know she'd get all the backup she needed if she had gender problems. But she never did, even there.

AWACS duty meant directing pilots where to go, where to bomb, where to confront the enemy. It gave her an overview of how air campaigns are run, which captured her imagination, and held it, for the next 11 years. She had mentors—all men—who sought her out, cultivated her, and guided her. Then, when the military space program opened up for commanders in communication and navigation satellites, she saw another unique opportunity. Again, high-tech work helped to level the playing field. As a woman, she believes she was at no disadvantage, which sounds a lot better than the majority of corporate jobs.

Strategic planning is not only crucial to Kim's work, it led to her work. It also led to her work/life balance, which is apparent from the moment she tells me that she had a limited time for lunch because she wants to get home to see how Katy, her two-year-old, was doing before going back to the council for a dinner meeting. When Kim had left that morning to join me, Katy had a fever and Katy's daddy had taken her to the doctor. Mark, Kim's husband of nine years, is a retired pilot and a house dad. Kim offered to switch roles, but he loves his and is looking forward to more kids to raise. Both of them want a large family and their timing is impeccable.

"We got pregnant," Kim explained, before her last assignment at a Montana base when Mark was ready to chuck his postretirement job and take over at home. But that doesn't mean Kim just walks out the door. "We've learned how to share the load, take turns, and give each other time to rest."

In Montana, with 1,200 people in her command, she worked a 12-hour day and was always tied to the job by beeper and cell phone. But she was able to go home to nurse or to see Katy when she wanted, home being quite nearby at the base. When she had Katy, she was already at a level where she could avoid the heavy travel jobs, which, she says, are for the young people. The Air Force's joint-spouse policy is designed to keep couples together and also lighten stress on the family. What helps, too, are Kim's and Mark's strong extended families, who keep them connected despite their peripatetic life. Kim's family is so supportive that the first time she was "on alert" and couldn't go home for Christmas, her parents packed themselves, her sister, and their grandkids into the Winnebago, driving from Florida to the Midwest to surprise her. Kim also never has to hide her motherhood. When she went on convoy in Montana, she took her breast pump and had the troops step away from the truck while she pumped. But could a general do the same thing? Is there work/life balance at that rank, which is the next for Kim?

With that question in mind, I show Kim a recent article from the *New York Times* on how all the army colonels who were mothers turned down promotions because they needed more time for their families. As one woman put it, "I certainly would have kept going if it wasn't for the family. I loved being a commander. But I found myself saying I would be a better commander if I wasn't a parent and a better parent if I wasn't a commander." The women refer to the Pentagon's "brass ceiling"—the military's indifference to the stresses that prevent military mothers from rising in the ranks. In 1999, when the article was written, 37 women were generals or admirals, but the only mothers among them are three admirals in the special medical or support branches. One problem is that military salaries aren't enough to cover the cost of a nanny, which is a necessity for most mothers in command positions.

As usual, Kim has thought about this carefully. Her view is that the military isn't different from any other job. Each promotion means you weigh the balance between personal needs and professional growth. The jump to flag command means you're responsible for thousands of lives; she feels she would be capable, given her parenting and extended family support. None of the women interviewed by the *New York*

Times had what Kim has—a husband who mans the home front—though every married male general has a wife to do the same. Also, as Kim explains, the air force has special troops whose job it is to look after the families. "If your people are too stressed out because of family problems, you can't rely on them." The first sergeant, or "first shirt," as they're called, has to know each individual in the unit, and to know their families or personal life. If there's a problem, it is the first shirt's problem to solve it by providing health services, schools, home aides, whatever.

In Kim's view, the higher your rank, the greater the responsibility—but the more support you have as well. Also, she believes that the Air Force is working hard to mitigate family stress. The Air Force has introduced an operations concept that gives families planning time and predictable cycle rotation, even set vacation times. Kim explained that each commander has the power to issue flexible schedules to ensure that one parent is home or to lighten whatever burdens military parents, especially single parents, feel.

As of the year 2000, the Army's highest-ranking woman is three-star General Claudia Kennedy, the deputy chief of staff for Army intelligence. In the work-life balance department, she has this to say: "I don't attempt to get balance. I don't believe it's possible when you're working at a level as high as I am." In March of that year, she also filed a sexual harassment complaint against an army general who groped her. Quite a setback in military image. But just maybe, Colonel Kimber McKenzie will prove the military can change its spots. Just maybe, determined women can stop the groping and change the way work gets done.

Understanding the Workplace 2000

As people flee unremunerative people-friendly fields for the high-paying ones, they run straight into the time crunch. Business types, accepting that business means long hours, sign on for a life of office slavery, then either lose themselves in it or quit when they can't take it anymore. Those who choose the people professions usually trade money for quality of life. To avoid either extreme, you need a clear overview of different industries and professions and a good sense of what power you have within them to carve out a niche of work sanity. The second step in plotting a balanced future (after wisely choosing a career), then, is knowing where you can find or create the kind of work life you want.

As we saw in the last chapter, some professions are in disastrous shape. Welfare caseworkers have killing workloads and earn a pittance for what can be a dangerous, thankless job. Ph.D.'s in the humanities, another traditional female enclave, face underpaid, scarce work because universities now economize by using adjuncts instead of full-time professors. Grade school teachers are paid so poorly they sometimes can't afford to live within commuting distance of the schools they work in. Yet universities rarely tell students about such realities. From their point of view, your life is not part of their job.

If job candidates simply avoid professions that don't pay a living wage, the market is likely to force a change in the conditions of employment. That's what happened after World War II when teachers were so scarce that legislators voted large increases in salaries. It's starting to happen again because many areas can't recruit enough teachers. Some school districts have had to offer the extra incentive of signing bonuses.

In California, Governor Gray Davis proposed to exempt public school teachers from the state's personal income tax, which would mean the equivalent of $1,000 in spending power for a teacher earning $50,000. Governor Davis also wants to spend $500 million to reward teachers with $5,000 bonuses when their schools show improvement in student performance. Why is he making these radical gestures? Simple supply and demand, though I'd like to believe that Davis means it when he says teaching "is the most important profession to us in the year 2000."

In order to attract women and families, the military also made radical changes when the civilian economy became successful at vacuuming up potential male recruits. Some of those changes have stuck. Linda Smith, director of the military's Office of Family Policy, says that "every department had to make a choice to take money from other operations and put it into childcare," for example. The Navy recently created a new troop carrier to accommodate women: The controls of all key systems are lower, within reach of the shorter sex, and require less force to operate; shipboard washing machines have a gentle cycle; and the "heads" have plenty of outlets for hair dryers. Mercifully, employers do change when they cannot otherwise attract the good employees.

Simply avoiding the dinosaur professions sends the strongest message. As Sue Shellenbarger, "Work & Family" columnist for the *Wall Street Journal* notes, "The inhumane demands placed on physicians (long hours on call, rising patient loads) and lawyers (2,000-plus billable hours a year) are one reason applicants to law and medical schools are declining among workload-wary Gen-Xers."

Currently, senior executives, heart surgeons, and trial lawyers put in longer than 16-hour days. But it doesn't have to be that way. Most of the hard-driving professions have operated with the type-A competitive personality in mind. They were able to evolve into such demanding workplaces because they could fill the slots with uncomplaining warrior types. Quite a few are still available. If you don't mind forfeiting personal time, then you might make the choice to become a woman warrior and maybe you can advance the cause of humane work from inside the legal or medical establishment. Just understand what you're getting into. For the men and women who don't want to give up their personal lives, there are alternatives.

The Power of a B.A.

In this booming economy, employees have tremendous leverage. According to the *Wall Street Journal*, executives now rank getting and keeping qualified employees as their top priority, above keeping up with technology.

With turnover at a 20-year high, employers have to be concerned. Replacing an employee costs on average one to three and a half times the position's yearly pay. Which doesn't factor in the drop in office morale when employees leave, particularly when they leave often. "Never mind finding good workers: Try to keep the ones you have. In a tight labor market, with raiders lurking, it is easy for employees to leave but costly to replace them," says Bruce Pfau, a research chief for Hay Group, Philadelphia.

Whole industries have had to hire "retention experts." At the top six accounting and consulting firms such as PricewaterhouseCoopers and Ernst and Young, for example, it was common to lose 2,500 women a year, and along with them productivity and client goodwill. What client wants to have his or her personal accountant changed every six months?

Now, they have reduced those numbers drastically by giving women what they asked for: flexibility in when and how much they work. Anyone can choose compressed workdays and part-time work with no loss of benefits or diminished prospects for promotion. They've also made a run at decreasing the 60-hour workweek by cutting back on meetings and freeing consultants from administrative duties, as well as permitting people to not answer e-mail or phone calls on weekends. Deloitte and Touche, which had an annual turnover rate of 33 percent among women in 1993, now has no turnover gap between women and men. What's more, woman making partners increased from 8 percent to 20 percent, saving the company an estimated $38 million annually in hiring and training.

College graduates can and should keep demanding as much as they want. Another *Wall Street Journal* article notes that

> This spring, 1.2 million college seniors will graduate with bachelor's degrees into the strongest U.S. job market in more than a decade. Competition is so heated that companies are going after young undergrads with tough hiring tactics normally reserved for M.B.A.'s and law students.

Mostly, they're offering signing bonuses and promises of year-end bonuses in addition to sky-high salaries. But their eagerness means that new graduates are in an excellent position to find the company that promises not to work people to death. They can simply state their terms. Period.

When students talk, recruiters listen. One of the directors of Stanford's Business School's career management center says, "Fun is the big ingredient," these days in job decisions. That wasn't a consideration a decade ago. And balance, even family friendliness is now on the list of Stanford's students' top ten priorities in a workplace. Two years ago, such considerations weren't on students' radar screens. Recruiters know it, too. Xerox, for example, has taken to setting up colorful vans at campus sporting events and rock concerts, hoping to send the message that they know recruits have a life beyond the office.

Keeping the larger job market in mind, college graduates can and should interview the potential employer to determine

- realistic work/time expectations
- how much control they will have in doing their work

- flexibility available
- what the future could look like
- how respectful of employees the firm is

People are nervous about appearing "unserious" by asking such questions. Seriousness, however, is in the attitude and conviction that you can do a good job on your own terms. Stating those terms means giving the employer a chance to accept who you actually are, how you work, and how you intend to live. It's hard to resist big signing bonuses and top salaries, but as we saw in the *Fast Company* reader survey, a lot of the top candidates aren't going after the biggest buck.

Once they have offers, they negotiate for more important things. One savvy candidate won a completely outfitted home-office in Malibu from which he telecommutes to his Boston-based employer. A Harvard M.B.A. with an eye on buying and running her own company chose a job in the leveraged buyout department (rather than the more typical consultant position) because it promised invaluable networking and training. Thinking strategically, college graduates can pave the way for a livable and sufficiently (if not wildly) lucrative future. They can even trade off 24/7 work now for better hours later on, like Jamie Rubin did, if they know their value in a full-employment economy.

Perk Smarts

Desperate businesses are offering perks galore to entice graduates. But this stuff is usually pretty shallow. Consider, for example, the two-year leases on BMW convertibles offered to engineers at Interwoven, a California software company. Or, more commonly, the discounts on everything from cell phones to massages to mortgage loans.

The hidden meaning of such perks is often, you'll be working all the time, so you'll have to shop (and consume) on the job. Andrew Grey, cofounder of Perksatwork.com, one of the companies that provides perk packages for employers, actually says, "The average American worker now has a longer work week than even the Japanese worker. That means a lot of the errands we once did off the job have to get done at work." Thanks a lot. As *Business 2.0* columnist David Batstone comments:

> Getting a better shopping deal. Is that the 90's meaning of "life" in the work-life balance? The equation once figured in the employee's family relationships, emotional stress, recreational activities, and spiritual development. Now a work-life benefit means getting 15 percent off a bouquet of flowers.

Netscape, you'll remember, provides a dentist-on-wheels to service their employees. Well, yes, it's a real convenience, but like many perks it smacks of "maintaining the machinery."

These kind of perks should sound an alarm that leads to other pertinent questions about hours, turnover, the numbers of people in a department who have families or outside interests. They should drive you right into the cafeteria, the ladies' room, the parking lot, wherever, to get some frank feedback from employees about life on the job.

Companies can and should understand the difference between perks that create more work hours and those that create a better work environment, which includes reducing stress. A *New York Times* article that tracks this newer trend notes that

> Unlike the last wave of corporate initiatives aimed at helping employees balance work with their personal lives—flexible hours, telecommuting, and concierge services—new programs address the fundamental problem of how much time a job demands and how to build a life beyond work.

They cite a sales division at Hewlett-Packard in which the manager realized that her professionally successful division was rife with divorces, bickering, and a 20 percent attrition rate. When asked, most said they felt excessive work pressure. So she volunteered her department for an experiment to reduce and redesign workloads. Employees were asked to set annual goals for productivity and for leisure. They are expected to meet both. If they fall short their supervisors have to answer for it. Now that's a valuable perk. And, though the manager admits that "expectations have been lowered," she points out that productivity hasn't suffered where it counts. The fact that no one has left in the last year, except to take promotions, suggests a contented staff.

Of course, you can take the fancy job, the BMW, and enjoy it for a while. Everyone I interviewed knew someone who, like Erin, took the high-paying consulting job with the promise of travel, fancy restaurants, and the fast lane, only to quit when they woke up stupefied and lonely two years later. Feeling good where you work matters. It's where you spend most of your working hours. It leads somewhere, though that might not be obvious, so try to calculate where. You might be willing to work 16 hours a day for a while, but it should be time well spent, and happily. If not, the trade-off has to be worth it.

Negotiating Time: Full, Flex, or Half

The interview is your first chance to negotiate for what you want. In a large company the benefits and perks are in writing; they're part of the corporate culture. In a small company, where they may not be, have your deal put in writing unless you really trust the place, advises Joan Bowman, from Management Resource International, an executive search firm. Specify hours, vacation weeks, benefits. "If they want you, they'll write a contract." She says that all the way up the ladder equal numbers of men and women are now demanding limited travel, no relocation, help with school fees for themselves, and college tuition for kids if they have them. Executive placement companies will tell you if it's an old-fashioned hard-line company or a new-economy flexible one. "Expect a cultural fit," she tells people.

Time, it turns out, is the biggest factor in negotiation, next to income, and you can negotiate both. One person might work long hours but insist on one month's vacation. Another may want to work four days a week but will settle for two weeks vacation. The engineer coveting the BMW might not care at all. Time is an even bigger issue in the negotiations that take place at the promotional level. Then they can make the job over in their own image. And why not? What stops most people is confidence.

Lisa Alecci, a field manager at Agilent Technologies, formerly a part of Hewlett-Packard, told me that even though she had cut back to 30 hours a week after her twins were born, she still did the same number of field reports she'd produced working 60 hours a week. Why didn't she just say no? Looking back, she feels she didn't have the confidence to believe her contribution was important enough. She was "filled with shame" for not playing by the fast-track rules she started out obeying. She knew her manager didn't want to hire someone else for the other 30 hours, then have to pay another benefits package. Finally, she created a new job for herself as diversity manager. It's a job she can do in 30 hours a week, though, as she points out, she doesn't do errands, go to the dentist, shop, or do anything else but work in those hours, so she's much more efficient.

While Lisa's solution was clever, she might have gone to the manager and said:

- This is what I need to do my job better.
- Here's a plan to divide my salary and benefits package.
- Here's the resume of a candidate to job share with me.

Given the labor market, she had the clout. She simply lacked the confidence. Whether kids are the reason or just plain life, the lesson here is how much power we really have to shape our jobs and change the workplace in doing so.

A whole other approach to work in today's round-the-clock workplace is part time, which no longer has to be a stigma, if it's negotiated well. And it's not just a mommy track as it used to be; now it's considered a lifestyle choice. People just may not want to work so much or they may have their own personal work they do as well, like serious athletic training or writing a book. Flexible Resources, an East Coast employment agency, specializes in part-time placements. As Susan Rietano Davey, one of the partners, explains, "employees expect to be handed a flexible schedule or part-time arrangements. But often you have to create the workable plan for the manager and make the business case." She suggests that people anticipate the difficulties for the employer and show him or her how to resolve them.

In placing part-timers, she will first educate the employer, even explaining how to measure the productivity of someone on reduced hours, how to deal with problems of coverage, or coworker resentment. She argues that if, for example, a company is offering $50,000 a year for a starting position, they might instead get a more qualified part-time person for the same money who, because of her experience, can do the job in less time. A small company may be creating a new position, say, a marketing director, for the first time. Rietano Davey might argue that the job can be done in 30 hours. After all, the company really doesn't know what it will take.

Part time, she reminds us, can be 10/4 or working 8:00 A.M. to 2:00 P.M. daily. It can be working long hours during tax season, then half-time or not at all during the slack season. If the problems are resolved beforehand, these are enormously successful solutions for employers who cannot afford or haven't managed to keep top quality full-timers. Flexible Resourses' business is mostly repeat business; the companies where they've created part-time positions—and they include Aetna, Dannon, General Electric, Calvin Klein—come back for more because they get quality people for less money. For example, one woman left a $250,000-a-year job to work part-time at $60,000 just so that she could work in the town where she lived. She had decided the salary cut was worth eliminating a daily two-hour commute. At Aetna, where they weren't getting the talent for managing investment funds, Rietano Davey suggested they break down the job into smaller caseloads. They did and it worked. Any employee or candidate can educate his or her employer just as Rietano Davey does.

If you're on the job and want to change it, she counsels writing a flexible or part-time work proposal for your boss, including your accomplishments, present responsibilities, schedule requested, how you'll meet performance goals, how you'll communicate on off-days, how daily issues will get resolved. Have a plan for the occasional work emergency and salary request commensurate with the reduced hours. Don't make work for the boss. And don't settle for 60 percent less than the proportional share of your salary, which is, remember, the norm. Your personal reasons don't matter, though it may help to point out that part-time prevents turnover, burnout, and is good for business. And, in car-clogged cities like Chicago, Houston, L.A., Philadelphia, and D.C., each telecommuter means a tax credit for the firm, a reward for reducing rush-hour traffic.

Another solution to the time crunch is consulting (as opposed to working for a consulting firm). There are some 12 million "free agents" or independent contractors, as they're now called, who work how and when they want, as long as the companies will buy their skills, which they will if you're a computer programmer or graphics designer. Michael Lewis, author of *The New New Thing,* a book about Silicon Valley, believes that in this labor market everyone can negotiate for similar freedoms. "Authority," he writes, "has not exactly vanished from corporate America, but it isn't what it once was." He cites Vault.com, for example, where employees of places like UPS and Boeing and many more can exchange information about superiors and company policies. Nonconformity is king (queen?) now. A lot of companies today look like college campuses, and call their sites campuses. Coffee stations are everywhere, people wear jeans, men have beards, and employees may be slouched on couches talking. But don't be fooled—it's still a battleground for time. Make sure you win.

Good-bye 24/7

The workplace isn't a monolith, nor is the 60-hour week written in stone. Because it is in transition, suspended between the frantic grow-or-die pace of the technological revolution and the backlash of people refusing to work all their waking hours, the office of today is highly idiosyncratic. But it's also easier than ever to find—or help create—a sane office culture.

It's not just *Working Mother* that reports the 100 Best Companies to work for, it's *Business Week* and *Fortune* as well. The buzzwords of business are work-life balance and work-life integration. Most business magazines and business sections of newspapers have columns on work/life or work and family—both of which were nonexistent 20 years ago. These columns generate the latest attitudinal changes, such as "secular humanism" and "high touch." As Colleen O'Connor, "Get a Life" columnist for *Business 2.0*, explains, "The humanistic trend is mainly a response to the crisis of retention." She notes that "employee happiness is the key to retention strategy, according to consultants whose top recommendations are (1) asking employees what would keep them, (2) supporting their professional growth, (3) supporting their lives outside the job."

Not only does a humane, sensible workplace save enormous costs in turnover but the companies that make employees happy show "sensational improvements in stock performance, outperforming the norm by 20 to 30 percent higher returns," according to Michael Moskowitz, the man who creates the leading-best-companies-to-work-for lists. And those outcomes are true for privately owned and publicly traded companies. Moskowitz also believes that the workplace is responding to employee demands now that competition is so strong. But it's not because business is good-hearted. It's because it's good business. At Boston College's Center for Work and Family, they've been studying how much money companies lose because of errors and additional medical claims that result from long hours. Mindy Fried, one of the researchers, says that it's "pretty clear that as people work over a certain number of hours, productivity goes down, stress goes up and work isn't as good."

An enlightened CEO is the best predictor of a humane workplace where employees' professional and personal lives are respected. Given gender discrimination, it is particularly important for women to know how interested the CEO is in work/life balance and promoting women, the two being inextricable, given that most working women do become mothers.

Hewlett-Packard, according to Moskowitz, is the granddaddy of gender-friendly, work/life balance companies because, as mentioned earlier, former CEO Lewis Platt, a single parent, understood that balance was a business issue. As soon as he became CEO, he not only instituted flextime, job sharing, telecommuting, year-long leaves of absence, he personally lectured managers about supporting balance and wrote memos saying, "Work/life issues are a business priority." Since two out of three male managers still have stay-at-home wives, they may not get it, but at Hewlett-Packard, they were more likely to do it because the CEO said so.

Since you won't generally meet the CEO for a personal cross-examination, you have to draw conclusions from company policies, from asking questions about CEO support, from talking to the human resources department as well as employees. It's also helpful to know what's possible in order to judge the place you're considering. To that end, let me offer a smorgasbord of policies and places so successful they've become the new industry standard.

Begin with the best, SAS Institute, the largest privately owned software company, presently valued at $5 billion, earning $850 million annually. It's been called "Sanity, Inc." (by *Fast Company* magazine) and "Utopia Ltd." (by the *Wall Street Journal*). CEO James Goodnight, who still bristles at the memory of working for the time-clock-punching General Electric Company, enforces a 35-hour workweek by shutting down the switchboard at 5:30 and the doors by 6:00 P.M. Even executives go home. Employees get an extra week of paid vacation between Christmas and New Year's (when no one works anyway). The company also offers year-end bonuses and profit sharing, though no stock options.

The 2,700 employees at the Raleigh, North Carolina, campus each have their own office (not a cubicle) and get to use the 35,000-square-foot recreation facility, free health clinic, on-site childcare, and the subsidized lunchroom where a pianist plays daily. There's an ergonomic specialist on staff as well as an artist-in-residence to create the right aesthetics. As one employee said, "I could make more money elsewhere, but money isn't everything."

One result is a 4-percent turnover instead of the industry average of 20 percent. Stanford University business professor Jeffrey Pfeffer, who studied SAS, concludes that "it's an enormously effective business model." The $50 million it saves in turnover pays for all the perks. Even the free medical clinic costs less than insurance for visits to private doctors. He also points out that SAS gains by having more alert, less error-prone programmers. In fact, SAS is so successful that 20 other companies, some really big ones says David Russo, vice president of human resources, have come down to Raleigh to study what SAS is doing.

But SAS is only number 6 on *Fortune*'s "100 Best Companies to Work For" list. Among their top five, perks include: sabbaticals of employment for everyone after 10 years (Xerox and Container Store) and two weeks of paid personal time after two years of employment (TD Industries). Many others offer on-site fitness centers with volleyball, basketball, and tennis courts (Qualcom); unlimited paid time off for charity work and help with kids' college tuition (Finova Group); fully paid insurance, including coverage for two massages a year (Granite Rock); free car loaners when needed, ready-to-heat take-out meals, dock spaces for kayaks (WRQ); coverage for laser eye surgery (Merck); a "life cycle" account to cover self-development and wellness, such as guitar lessons or a personal trainer (American Century); on-site dry cleaners, car wash, and fitness center (First USA, a Wilmington, Delaware, credit-card issuer).

Some well-known companies are famous for their humane policies. Goldman Sachs is known for being so democratic that when they went public, everyone benefited, including janitors. They pay their secretaries the highest salaries in the industry, offer limos for anyone working late, and back-up childcare for emergencies.

These perks may sound like unnecessary pampering to the dependent-free. But when you're trying to run a home and stay fit, too, it will be music to your ears. And if you'd like to have a full life before you get to that stage, they help.

Even if you feel you'll never be interested in family-friendly policies, they are often a good indicator of the workplace climate. Johnson and Johnson, the largest health product manufacturers in the United States, offers paid time-off for family emergencies, unpaid 12-month leave for men and women, and meals to go at closing time. Family-friendly policies at other companies include: $1,500 a year for childcare during nonroutine business trips, including flying in grandparents (Bramoco); on-site childcare for children or grandchildren (Aflac); 52 weeks' parental leave at half-pay (Lucent); three years off, unpaid, for mothers or fathers (IBM); 24 weeks' paid parental leave (Ridgeview, socks and hosiery manufacturers), bring-your-baby-to-work policies (San Jose National Bank).

You get the picture. Right now, there are plenty of wonderful workplaces. As *Fortune* magazine summed up their 2,000 list, "The story isn't about money, it's about balance." A company's assets are rarely steel and wheat any longer; they're people—who want time for their lives. So why work at a place with a long commute, long hours, short vacations, and a lot of business travel if you can work at a place nearby that offers reasonable hours and personal time?

Of course, many policies look great on the books, but aren't practiced. Either it's frowned upon to take advantage of them or the individual manager just doesn't enforce them. Several times, when I cited some of these company policies during my lectures, someone would come up to me afterwards to tell me The Truth. One woman, a lawyer at Aetna, told me the six-month maternity leave policy I touted had been rescinded, returned to the former three-month leave; another, a lawyer at Deloitte and Touche, said that everyone in her office still worked late into the evening, like it or not; and you already heard about how the field supervisor at Hewlett-Packard was expected to produce as much in her new half-time job as she had in her full-time. That's why it's so important to talk with employees—and listen—better than I listened when the woman I replaced at Middlebury College told me they treated women terribly.

See if there's a Web site where people discuss their particular office. Ask about turnover, which in itself will tell you about employee satisfaction. Find out about a company's charities or the political groups it gives money to. All these generally ignored factors can help to distinguish a disappointing work match from an exhilarating one.

Keeping in mind just how much a CEO influences the workplace culture and that it's possible to find a humane workplace, no matter how different each of those may seem, let's look at one young executive who has helped to create a sane workplace—in the dot-com world no less. What's so interesting about Sarah Vickers Willis is that she formulated her profoundly humane values so young and helped to create a business based on them.

Sarah Vickers Willis, UBUBU

Sarah Vickers Willis, 27-year-old vice president of business development for a wildly innovative hi-tech start-up called UBUBU (say the letters), works with the speed, grace, and focus of a thoroughbred, as you might expect in this frantic gold-rush valley. But she's got as much soul as any M.F.A. student I ever taught.

To look at her, "taller than everyone" as she says in her emphatically flat Australian accent, you don't think, "executive," not even in the boyish Bill Gates mold. Rather, she gave me the impression of a waterfall—beautiful (in a natural no makeup way), powerful, and calming all at once. Her silky hair, flowing to her shoulders and flying where it wants, is almost as animated as her face. Her old sweater and tiny skirt hardly contain her willowy frame. You wouldn't think she has three years under her belt at the prestigious Boston Consulting Group or that she opened this start-up with three fellow Harvard Business School graduates just six months before. But the differences all symbolize a cultural revolution.

Of course, Silicon Valley's known for its laid-back style. Excite, one of the original search-engine companies, has a slide from the second to the first floor. All the coolest start-ups have toys in their conference rooms. But UBUBU is zanier still. In the loft they share with a knitting company whose rainbow skeins of wool line one wall is "Norway," as they call the reception area for no particular reason: cushions on the floor round one of the many Home Depot doors that serve as tables. A "Welcome Joanne and Leo" banner festoons the room strewn with cups, plates, and stuff from that morning's Dr. Seuss (green eggs and ham) family breakfast (followed by *tai chi* lesson from one of the engineers) to make the new employees feel at home. How could they not feel at home?

Enter into the workplace: one open-space light-filled space, sheets for window curtains, each of the Home Depot doors for desks painted and decorated by its occupant. The first one I see has black-and-white checked legs with fur slippers and action figures glued to the top. Sarah's desk has a painting of a house and some grade-school green trees. Along its roof, a message: "Remember to Go Home."

Home is Oakland, about half an hour away, a small basement apartment she shares with Dave, her boyfriend of one year, who's running an educational technology start-up. When she speaks of him, it's almost with reverence. "Without Dave," she reflects, "I'd be terribly lonesome." Although they both work too hard, every month they sit down and ask themselves: "Is it worth it?" "Where are we going?" "Are we on the right track?" So far, the answer's yes. Partially because they've put enough brakes on work to nurture a relationship they love.

"However late we get home," Sarah says, "we make a meal together. David shops, we grill something on the barbecue, and we sit down—even if it's 11:00 at night." Monday is their evening. They both leave work early and go to a movie or walk around the lake near their house. They "absolutely" don't work Saturday, though they agree to both do e-mail three hours on Sunday morning. They never miss a friend's wedding and they go away for occasional weekends. "If you don't set boundaries, you'll always be there at midnight. Every day, critical calls don't get made. That's life." On the other hand, if either of them has to work, they forgive one another. "We really understand what the other is doing all day. And it's just for now. We're not going to live like this forever."

A lot of kids think that, then get sucked into the workaholic or material life. Not Sarah. She's entered into this gold rush wisely, and with a strong sense of self. Most important, perhaps, she has a personal life, including an inner life. Over lunch at the local Thai restaurant, Sarah tells me how she nursed her mother, who died of cancer at age 46 when Sarah was in her early 20s. Before she died, Sarah's mother told her children, "My death will be the making of you three," and it was true, Sarah says. "She gave me this massive set of wings," inspiring Sarah and the others with the model of herself made over into a highly successful real estate agent after a divorce left her economically bereft. And with her absolute belief that they could do anything.

However, such an early death of someone so beloved sends a powerful message, and Sarah got it. Her eyes misting with grief, she tells me, "I've seen the worst there is in her death. It made me fearless, but it also taught me that work doesn't matter. It's just work, nothing more. You have this fear of the 1987 crash where people made huge sacrifices for work, but when they didn't win, they wanted to jump out the window. I want to make money for the investors and employers, but if the business tanks, I'm enjoying the process. It's not the goal."

At the Boston Consulting Group, Sarah enjoyed parts of the job, but ultimately she was working on projects she didn't care about, such as making dairy farms more efficient and shoring up one of Australia's major mining businesses. She saw how so many of her friends in consulting or investment banking weren't enjoying themselves. "They're proving they can make it. They're smart people making exciting deals and names for themselves in the business elite. But I want to care deeply about what I do. And I do."

Which she has every right to. UBUBU is creating an entirely new interface with the Internet, so that teens and young people can have fun creating a relationship with the sites they use. As Sarah explains, "User interface is so boring. It's done by engineers. We're going for graphic and entertaining ways of going through the Web." Instead of lists of favorites, for example, they'll have planets with related sites—for schoolwork, for shopping, for games, whatever—and whimsical ways to link with others. In other words, their home page will be a gorgeously designed interplanetary universe. Sarah believes this will appeal to many 13- to 24-year-olds who aren't comfortable with just functional processing. UBUBU is an idea with legs, and with loads of merit. So how did Sarah find it? How did she get from there to here, so to speak? Strategy, good decisions, and staying true to herself.

Sarah didn't start out in business. With Eastern Europe blowing up, she studied international relations. But to get experience before going to graduate school (her first good decision), she took a job at Boston Consulting Group's Australia division, and was the only one hired with no business background ("I couldn't even read a profits and loss statement"). Even so the bosses put so much trust in her, she leapfrogged into the big time, doing the most important consulting for them and learning that she was great at the work, mostly because she was so good with people—a characteristic the numbers crunchers often lack. If she made a mistake at a meeting, the bosses would support her. "The partners set me up to win. They introduced me as an expert way before I was." Which is why she stayed four years—traveling most of the time, often living in completely isolated places (once, with 400 miners—all male, of course), gaining invaluable experience. Now she trusts her employees and sets them up to win in the same way. She makes sure they know they're appreciated and encourages them to learn on the job, as she did.

Knowing she needed the financial background if she were going to find or found a business she could care about, she applied to Harvard Business School. You would think that being from Australia, working four years with a premier consulting firm, and getting high marks would be enough. But no. The competition is every bit as qualified. The next year she applied again, and got in, she believes, because in her spare time she had started an innovative YWCA organization called GirlStory to attract young women to educational programs. That is, she distinguished herself with a successful project she genuinely cared about.

Sarah had determined her goals. "Work had to reflect who I was. I wanted authenticity. I wanted to promote economic independence of young people." Just as she'd done at GirlStory. Then she had to work toward them. At Harvard, Sarah found out about Independent Means, a company we'll learn more about later that creates programs to teach teenage girls how to become entrepreneurs. Wanting to work there, she raised the money to pay her salary for a summer's internship. Another summer, she worked with Concepción Lara, a former HBO and Fox executive who was trying to start Centropia, a spiritually focused cable channel. Back at school, Sarah got a team of students together to write Centropia's business plan. Another summer, she taught at "Citizen Schools in Boston," a "totally revolutionary after-school apprenticeship program."

Mind you, many of Sarah's schoolmates were making fortunes taking internships at the money companies courting them. But Sarah had her eye on *her* goal. So when her chum, Brian, came up with the idea for UBUBU, she "signed immediately." After putting together four Harvard Business School students and four MIT engineers, they raised their first round of funding between final exams. That was last May. Six months later, at the time I first interviewed Sarah, they were on their second round of funding and had signed deals with Fox.com, USA networks, and with Patrick Stewart of Star Trek fame to do their publicity. They've also grown from eight to 28 employees.

Sarah really practices what she preaches. She wants the employees to enjoy working at UBUBU. "The output has to be high," she says, "but this isn't a face-time culture. If you want to work from 10:00 P.M. to 5:00 A.M., fine. We're not a sweatshop either." Sarah believes the CEO, the leader, can make a sane workplace. "Most younger people don't want to go home at 5:00. It's too corporate. But they do want lives. For our part, we want interesting people and you can't have interesting people who don't have a life, so there are no meetings on weekends, no calls."

Sarah also supports her employees' personal needs. She offers examples: Abby, who just started six weeks ago but is on a two-week holiday with her "mum" because it was that important to her; Josh just got married and was given the space to focus on his wedding; Ari used all the office staff in the last independent film he made. "You just work it out," she says matter-of-factly.

The principal's salaries are low-$50,000, which doesn't go far in San Francisco, particularly when you're paying $1,000 per month on your business school loans, like Sarah is. The staff salaries are barely competitive, but they offer, well, authenticity, friendship, fun, and a chance at something important.

The question for Sarah is how to have both her start-up and a meaningful relationship with Dave. Her face illuminates with the answer. She's been thinking about this a long time.

"Back in B-school, I took a course in women entrepreneurs. One woman said, 'Think of your life as a series of five-year plans. You can have it all, but not all at once.'" Sarah feels she's on the second in her series. After three more years of this intense pace, she wants to transition to something different: maybe only work three days a week or six months a year, then spend the other six in Australia. Have kids, too. And Dave wants the same thing. He's not a corporate type, she assures me. He loves doing home things.

Sarah may not get exactly what she dreams of but she certainly knows her values and where she's heading. "My work vessel is full," she concludes, "my personal family and friends part of life is only three-fourths there. I don't see my friends. I miss my country. It's OK for now, but I'll change that."

As a woman, Sarah has an advantage, at least in creating this plan. She remembers how most of the men coming out of B-school had such a heavy sense of "I have to provide" and "at the end of the day, I cannot fail." Sarah has her mother's model and the latitude extended to women, "If I make it, it's extraordinary. If my twin brother does, it's expected." On the other hand, Sarah believes women's values will change Silicon Valley for the men as well. Her values helped create this nurturing workplace. "It's not competition anymore that's driving the market. It's cooperation. And women are great at that, great at relationships." Sarah has monthly meetings where she asks her employees how she can support their work better. "You have to be able to admit you're not perfect to hear their responses. And women are generally better at that, too."

Is her plan just a pipe dream? Well, she cites John Milone, the CEO of TCI who spends five months a year in Martha's Vineyard and talks on the phone only a few hours a day. How does he do it? He hires great people, then delegates. "If John Milone can do it, I can do it," Sarah proclaims. "This is the new economy. Flexibility is our option."

If You're Considering Medicine, Business, or Law

The big three graduate degrees can be shortcuts to power, income, and exciting work. But they are also magnets for workaholics, which means that the majority of your peers will be work warriors who feel compelled to succeed, on whatever terms. Such competitors are themselves an impediment to normalizing work, but in medicine and law, there is an additional barrier. Unlike the life-friendly businesses enumerated in the last chapter, much of the "unfriendliness" of medicine and law is institutionalized in tradition and bottom-line myopia.

Life on the Medical Track

Medicine is a tough nut to crack. From internships on, doctors are expected to practice their life-and-death work for more hours straight than has ever made sense. I mean, would you trust a mechanic to replace your spark plugs if he'd been on duty for 36 hours? Would you get in a taxi with a driver who'd had a 36-hour shift? When my dad had an operation, his (female) oncological surgeon didn't even send him to the operating room until 8:30 P.M. We held our breaths until he was released into post-op at 10:30 P.M., when presumably the surgeon went home. Though, you never know.

The insane hours doctors work made headlines when New York State passed a law reducing medical residents' shifts from 36 to 24 hours and limited them to 80 hours a week. That was after a powerful lawyer, Sidney Zion, won a case arguing that his daughter's hospital death was a result of negligence on the part of exhausted interns. However, 80 hours a week is no picnic either, and, anyway, as any doctor can tell you, only medical, not surgical services follow the New York State mandate.

If the law hasn't changed the entrenched work madness of medicine, what can? Women—and the men they influence.

Medicine does offer some sane work choices, but mostly women are taking them. Although women are now half of the medical school graduates, they rarely rise to the top ranks of the profession. Instead, they join multiphysician practices or work for managed care companies or hospitals so they can have 9 to 5 and part-time jobs. Twenty-five percent of female doctors work less than 40-hour weeks; only 12 percent of male doctors do the same. Even in the same specialties, women doctors earn far less than their male counterparts because they see approximately 300 fewer patients a year and spend more than the male average of 10 minutes with each. Obviously, a lot of women want to practice medicine differently, and do. Every one that I interviewed was trying, with greater or lesser success. Let's start, though, with some of the harsher realities.

Internship and residency can be the hardest part of a medical career. Samantha Kaplan is a 29-year-old second-year resident in obstetrics-gynecology; her husband is a 34-year-old resident in internal medicine. Both have five more years of training to go at the University of Rochester medical school, which they chose because they got full scholarships.

"That was my second lifestyle decision," Samantha told me. "I didn't want $80,000 of debt, which would force me into a certain kind of practice." Her first lifestyle decision was to take two years off before medical school to work at a foundation raising money for Native Americans. During that time, she realized that she wanted to stay close to her family, so refused scholarships to medical schools on the West Coast.

Samantha's problem is that his-and-hers residencies are much more demanding than she thought they would be, keeping them at work on incompatible 12-hour-a-day schedules with only two weekends off out of five. That adds up to 60 to 120 hours a week, with rotating duty they can't control. "My husband and I never see one another," Samantha lamented. "Even though we want children, I don't know how we'll be together enough when we're not too exhausted to make them, no less raise them. We don't even have time to litter train our cat."

Samantha believes in planning. She's already invited her father to live with her and take care of her future child. She's hoping that if she and her husband excel, they'll have more choices. Despite their planning, however, both are choosing very demanding specialties. He wants to go into critical care medicine because he likes the intensity of life-and-death decisions. She wants ob-gyn and will be on call for births. In an off-moment, she sighs, "People who aren't in medicine live better."

Yet it could be different. "The 80-hour-week residency madness is completely unnecessary," says Dr. Elizabeth ("Betsy") Kavaler, a 33-year-old urological surgeon spending a year working with Dr. Shlomo Raz, an eminent surgeon, author, and expert in the field who is now head of the urology department at UCLA Medical Center. Before winning the prestigious fellowship, Betsy was chief resident in urology at Mt. Sinai Hospital in New York City. In her estimation,

> it's neither efficient or cost effective to have residents working from 4:30 A.M. to 10:00 P.M. They order too many tests, they don't know what they're doing, and they're spending precious time drawing blood, sitting with patients at the cat scanner, wheeling stretchers, all of which physician's assistants could do far more effectively. Residents do have a lot to learn but they could learn it better between the hours of 9 and 5, without the exhaustion and anxiety they now endure.

Why is residency structured in this exhausting, wasteful way? Betsy says it's nothing more than a hazing ritual to create the exclusive club for doctors: "Residency breaks people down, then you build them up to receive this exalted status at the end. When you're chief resident, then you can be the victimizer."

Not all doctors are victimizers, of course. Not Dr. Shlomo Raz, Betsy's advisor, who is that rare exception to the rule of machismo in surgery. When I first interview Shlomo for this book, he's delighted to talk and does so with a charming Uruguayan accent, ready laughter, and twinkling eyes. He used to have only "fellows" in surgery, he tells me. But now that many of the best are women, he's coined a new name for them: "fellas." And they've taught him a lot about work/life strain, as has his own daughter, a new mother of two and also chief resident in neck and head surgery at Johns Hopkins Hospital. "In a five-hour operation, when can she pump her milk?" he asks, worried. "So many issues make her life difficult."

Determined to make it easier for women, Shlomo has given Betsy the unprecedented luxury of every other Monday off so she can visit her family in New York. When they've come to visit her in California, he's invited them to his weekend home. He is immensely empathic. As he points out, he lives with strong women: his wife, a talented sculptor, and his three daughters—a doctor, a lawyer, and a writer. They have taught him.

However, like most surgeons of his stature, Shlomo offers a model of utter devotion to work. In his 26 years at UCLA, not only has he created new techniques in reconstructive vaginal and urological surgery, but he teaches these techniques around the world. He's written numerous books on the subject, trained 39 fellows and fellas who will now be heads of reconstructive urological surgery at other hospitals, and has created computer imaging for urological surgery. Plus, as he points out, he has to see a lot of patients in order to get the input to create new surgical techniques.

Twelve-hour days have always been the norm for Shlomo. His hospital rounds start at 5:30 A.M. and he does surgery three times a week, finishing around dinnertime. Between office visits, rounds, and operations, he's writing his books, talking with doctors who seek his advice, answering e-mail, planning his lectures. Forget lunch. As for family, he's quick to admit, his wife did the sacrificing.

Well, he says, that was what wives did when he married. But he, too, was devoted to family. Evenings and weekends, he was only with them. He never played golf or did something for himself. But academic medicine, in his view, must be practiced this intensely or you cannot make medical progress. He also believes more and more women will take this road. But how so, I wonder, when few of them have the kind of support at home that Shlomo had. Most will have to sacrifice family entirely. Though next year, the husband of one of Shlomo's "fellas" is coming to live in Los Angeles to take primary care of their child during that year.

Fortunately, you can practice medicine—even surgery—and also have a life. Medical care might be better if more doctors did. Betsy points out that studies have been done to prove that this residency tradition isn't in the best interest of the hospital, the patients, or the insurance companies. Private hospitals with permanent staff are more cost-efficient than teaching hospitals with residents. But the tradition goes on because that's how it's always been and because Medicaid pays hospitals about $125,000 to train a resident, whom the hospitals then pay about $25,000 in salaries. And they'll squeeze every hour they can out of each of them.

As Chief Resident at Mount Sinai, Betsy gave the annual dinner address in which she appealed to everyone to make residency livable. She told the audience of doctors that she had a child during her residency, and just like the men who became fathers, she deserves some time with her family. After all, if someone had to take off six weeks because they broke a leg, there's no problem. It's only when they want family leave or family time that the refusal is absolute. In a final flourish, she argued that with this punishing residency regime we are creating doctors whom no one wants to go to. The next day, she lost her job.

The chairman said that although she worked hard and had done an excellent job, she had offended a lot of people by being too confrontational.

Unfortunate though Betsy's dismissal was, the difference between it and my "termination" at Middlebury College more than 20 years earlier is the sign of significant progress. Betsy has real market power; I did not. Urological surgeons with her expertise are highly sought after. Two jobs await her: as clinical instructor in urology at New York Hospital, Cornell Medical Center, and attending in urology at Lenox Hill Hospital. When she becomes a department head, which she eventually will, *her* residents will have time for family life. She, herself, will begin surgery at 9:00 A.M., not the traditional 7:30 A.M., so that she can take her daughter to school. And unlike my father's surgeon, I doubt Betsy will be operating at 10:30 P.M., except for the rare emergency. She will stop the madness and create a fleet of residents with an entirely different model of surgical medicine. She is one of the women warriors determined to get to the top of the professional ladder where she will make a difference. But Betsy's work has involved enormous personal sacrifice, only because the system was so strict and because she didn't design her life well.

By her own admission, Betsy is a perfect example of the strengths and weaknesses of her generation. She truly believed she could be anything she wanted, but had no idea how to combine her goals with a personal life. With little support or planning, she and her investment banker husband agreed that Betsy would leave him with their four-year-old daughter in New York City while she pursued this fellowship at UCLA. With her extra Monday off, she would visit them once every other weekend. The outcome was a disaster. Embittered, her husband demanded a separation, telling her that next time he'll marry a traditional woman. But there's an important story behind the story.

For our interview, Betsy and I meet as strangers in a fashionable dimly lit restaurant near the UCLA hospital. She's reserved at first, speaking impersonally in what sounds like a defense of men in general and her husband in particular.

Women always controlled the home, she argues, and now they're gaining control at work too. Women undermine men at work and in turn men undermine women at home. Her own husband, she says, is incapable of running a household and tending a child—"he can't, he doesn't want to, the house is chaos, our daughter watches television all day." And because she is a straight-talking, somewhat austere person, lean as a post, her eyeglasses her only adornment, I believe she truly subscribes to this harsh battle-of-the-sexes theory. Yet the more we talk, the more personal she becomes. As she does, her theory melts away and she begins to look tinier, even childlike, with her strawberry-blond curls pulled back and her eyeglasses too big for her face.

In response to my questions, I soon learn that

1. Even as a chief resident in New York, Betsy had done everything at home as well, including take care of her husband. When she left, he couldn't function. He hadn't been an equal parent before, and suddenly he was expected to be a primary parent to a child who, in addition to being needy, as four-year-olds are, was surely upset at her mother's absence.
2. They had no emotional support. Every colleague of her husband's has a traditional wife; they couldn't understand why he was "Mr. Mom." The nanny and cleaning lady both left, unable to deal with the new household stresses.
3. Angry and cut off from his own parents, her husband refused to accept help from her parents, which they were willing to give.
4. Betsy has no models. Only 1 percent of urologists are women. All her female doctor friends went part time after their children were born. They think she's crazy.
5. She and her husband's deeply different values clashed when he was infuriated by her accepting a relatively low salary ($125,000) in her post-fellowship job, though she doesn't care a jot for money and would do her work for free. Finally expressing his true values, he

> told her, "My worth is measured in money. If I don't earn I have no status." In his eyes, her status had fallen with her pay-cut.

Clearly, when this couple created a commuter marriage, reversed their parenting roles, and reached the power (fork in the road) stage of their professions at the same time, they put an unendurable stress on their marriage. Not too many couples could survive such a year. But those who could would surely have discussed the plan in more detail, had more support from extended family and friends, known one another better, had reliable help plus backup, and had more flexible professions.

After all, women in *his* position often make such a plan work. They are experienced and secure in running a household. They accept the need to sacrifice for their husband's career. Their children are not as upset because the now-missing parent wasn't the primary one, and they generally visit as often as possible—to support him, to facilitate the father-child relationship, and to make the marriage work. Betsy didn't have any of that. Which brings us to the tragedy at the center of Betsy's story: her generation's isolation.

As Betsy and I talk about her predicament, she suddenly interjects, "You know I have women friends, but I'd never tell them any of this. We don't talk intimately." This comment leads to her own description of her generation as so individualistic and competitive that they are terribly alone. Lonely. Success is so important that no one wants to talk of anything that hints of failure, like a marriage coming undone. "Most of us are very shallow," Betsy states flatly. "We've never lived through war or economic depression. We've never had to think about anything but ourselves and our comforts. There's no challenge to making money. The challenge is in making a ton of money." Betsy agrees absolutely that this combination of materialism and isolation is the Achilles heel of her generation.

Betsy became a urologist to help women. Gynecology training just isn't that good, she feels. With urology, she can make a difference in woman's health. But her friends think she's some ridiculous Joan of Arc. Her motives aren't lauded, the way they would have been in my generation. Nor does she have the self-confidence to be comfortable with her uniqueness. Believing that she achieved all she has by hard work, not talent, Betsy says she never did have much confidence and never did feel great about herself. Raised in the shadow of her brother and ignored by her father, she chose a narrow-focus profession so she never had to consider the larger issues in her life. Nor did she have the self-esteem to try. Successful though she is, I believe her when she says, "I don't have a sense of self-importance." Her lack of self-importance causes her a lot of personal pain. On the other hand, as she says, "it makes me a better doctor." It also makes her a relatively unique one.

All Betsy's girlfriends are physicians working part time. Their husbands are often furious because their wives have no power in their offices, no partnership track to follow, no say in the insurance the office uses, and little money. Don't get me wrong. Medicine is not necessarily a disaster area. In fact, my guess is that Betsy's a fast learner. Once she gets more analytical about her personal life, she'll find a more kindred spirit for a companion and will plan her life moves more thoughtfully. Some women doctors, hell-bent on doctoring and living well, have managed a successfully blended personal and professional life. It's true, they don't have the power in medicine that Betsy has, but as one of them says, they're changing the face of medicine one patient at a time.

Dr. Beth Davis Phillpotts, for example, has managed to carve out a lovely life—though not without careful thought and significant compromise. When I tell her about Samantha and her husband's residency choices, she responds, "With those specialties, they'll have no control over their lives." She, herself, gave up ob-gyn for that reason. When I tell her about Betsy Kavaler's choices, she says that she would never have left her family for a year. Period. Training be damned. But Beth is as grounded and wise as any 34-year-old I've ever known.

We're in my backyard, where they're visiting. Basically a relaxed, contemplative person, Beth always takes the time to reflect before she acts. Lazy she calls herself, but that's not a jot true. Her clothes are perfect: a simple tangerine linen skirt, beige shell top; her hair in a close cropped natural with a pretty headband. Earrings and silver bangles. "I like jewelry," she says sheepishly, having converted to her husband Garfield's church, which frowns on adornment. You can tell she enjoys sitting with him on a lounge chair while they watch their two-year-old run around on the grass. The baby has her father's copper skin, her mother's dimpled smile and button eyes.

"Without a boyfriend, everything was great, even residency. I'd come home, read a bit, then sleep and go back to work," Beth tells me. But once I met Garfield, I realized I was seeing him after four hours sleep, exhausted. I looked around me and saw attendings who were in the hospital on Thanksgiving and Christmas and I thought, I can't do this." That's when she switched residencies from ob-gyn to family practice, which was shorter as well as easier. As she explained to me, she also had an easier time than most because the residents at Cook County Hospital, who were unionized, had negotiated better hours than usual, such as only being on call every fourth night.

Medical school was fine, too. She chose the University of Illinois because it cost only $8,000 a year, plus they would cancel her loan entirely if she worked for four years in an "underserved" (minority neighborhood) Illinois hospital, which she planned on doing. (Although when it was better for her and Garfield to live in Detroit for a couple of years, she did that, despite the price.) As far as earnings were concerned, she was doing well enough. Back in Chicago with a baby in tow, Holy Cross Hospital paid her $125,000 per year for working 32 hours a week—four days—no matter how many patients she saw, or didn't. She needed more time because her baby needed a lot of special care. And Holy Cross, offering three months' paid maternity leave in addition to a paid five-week vacation, was clearly trying to attract women.

Although her salary went up to $132,000 after two years, she now has to work on a capitation basis. Because of the new hospital policy, doctors will now get a percentage of what they bring in, which for Beth is more like $75,000 for 26 hours a week since her patients are all on managed Medicaid, which pays relatively little. She still loves the job because the compensation is adequate for her needs, because she has control over her time, and because she is largely her own boss, though she admits that she couldn't have made that choice if her husband wasn't earning good money. Together, they take home about $200,000, which, in today's cities, does not mean extravagant living. They did buy a nice house in the Chicago suburbs, but, unlike their more extravagant friends, they have one car, no credit card debt, hardly any new clothes, and Dr. Beth takes a bag lunch to work. Is it a good life? She thinks so. So do I.

Being a small-town doctor has always been a lifestyle choice doctors could make, and still is. Dr. Tamara Sachs, a 41-year-old graduate of Mt. Sinai Medical School, did her residency in emergency room care at a hospital affiliated with Yale. As she explained, more women than men do emergency room care because the hours are controllable. You work two-day shifts, two evenings, two nights, then have four nights off. There's no beeper, no patients calling at home. But Tamara felt that she was seeing too many "nasty things." They were turning her cynical and hyper. So she rethought her life design.

Turning down a chief residency in high-stress New Haven, she moved to New Milford, Connecticut, in pursuit of quiet, a garden, and a gentler practice. Overcoming her own snobbery and her supervisor's contempt about working at a non-teaching hospital, she accepted an offer to work with a small professional group affiliated with the town hospital. As one of five physicians sharing office space and coverage, she had the benefit of support without the expense of buying into a partnership or the stress that goes into maintaining it. It was here she first learned the business of running an office: payroll, taxes, insurance, workmen's compensation, supplies. Most important, she could spend longer time with patients, which was something she cared deeply about. She'd always wanted to practice "down to earth" medicine, which is hard to find in the big city. As she quipped, "At teaching hospitals, it's not about did the patient die, but did you get a diagnosis."

Like Samantha and Beth, Tamara also took time off. Before going to college, she moved to France, lived with relatives, and tried lots of different things before returning to live with her psychiatrist father—her mentor, she calls him—and beginning college at Hunter in New York City. In France, she learned alternative medicine, which she now incorporates into her practice. For her medical mentor, she found an excellent model, a pediatrician in France who worked out of her home where her two children were always running loose and her whole family lived upstairs. "I loved that image, and I knew I wanted to practice like that."

By the time she married, at 36, she'd already set up her work with balance in mind, so the baby she'd have the next year wasn't a career shock. But as a parent, she wanted even more control and more independence. So she started her own office, bartering and bargaining for furniture from the hospital. She went on call on a fixed date instead of rotating, then stopped doing hospital care altogether. While she admits her patients to the hospital, they're covered by another doctor. She works three days a week, from 9 to 5, and a fourth until midnight doing callbacks, reading, and going over lab reports. In order to practice this way, she created a coverage group, though the (male) doctors who cover for her often comment, "I would have loved to be home more with my kids, too, but you're a primary care doctor. You just can't."

As Tamara's life proves, you can practice medicine in a new way. Perky, with an ample figure in a silky print dress, her curly cropped hair in what we used to call a poodle cut, Tamara doesn't seem tired or rushed the way doctors often do; her office is calm, never jammed with patients in the waiting room, the receptionist tells me. On the Saturday I visit their home, she and her husband, an oral surgeon, are more relaxed than most families, although they're leaving for France in two days. Her husband Joe also works four days a week, taking Thursdays off along with Tamara. If their sitter can't come on a work day, they each take off half a day to stay home. "Three days a week, Margot's all ours," Tamara says.

They take great pride in their airy Adirondak-style home with porches all around and woods surrounding. Their three-year-old daughter, Margot, shows me their golden retriever's new puppies. We all sit back on comfy chairs. "The house is a mess," Tamara says. But the truth is, she and Joe clearly don't care much.

Tamara and Joe feel their relationship thrives because they had such clear directions before they met, and they had the maturity to know what they wanted and to see beyond the infatuation. With the latitude they had at work, they could set up their lives to suit themselves. Joe is a more conservative person than Tamara. He never thought he'd marry another doctor or leave his child with a baby-sitter. But, as he says, "I'm a flexible person. I'm open to things." One of the payoffs for him is that they understand each other's work so well and help each other resist living for medicine alone. Together they breed dogs, explore nature, travel, hike, and garden. When they get back from their month-long vacation in France, they're starting tennis lessons together. But like Beth and Garfield, they're careful about money. They don't go to restaurants, they don't go into debt, they haven't bought one piece of new furniture, and Margot wears shoes from K-mart.

Samantha, Betsy, Beth, and Tamara will all change medicine, in their own ways, by providing new models and by being the kind of doctors people do want to go to. My hope, however, is that they'll change medicine much faster by somehow finding a collective voice to promote their common goals. Then, whether through unions, through power in the AMA, through groups like Women in Medicine, they'll take back medicine from the obsessive-compulsives.

The Business of Business

A majority of B-school graduates go into investment banking, consulting firms, or information technology, all of which have created the models of work madness we now follow.

While most people in these fields accept the life, not all do. Enclaves of sanity exist—even in Silicon Valley, which has the most frenzied work pace in America.

Silicon Valley is the place where "geeks" sleep under their desks when they sleep at all and people network on the Starbucks line. It's the place that gave us the horrifying term "drag coefficient"—points for each appendage that will slow a potential employee down, such as kids, hobbies, marriage, a vacation home, an aging parent—in short, a real life. If a workplace revolution can happen in Silicon Valley, it can happen anywhere. Anywhere, that is, if people have the guts to refuse business as usual. Let's look at some who have, in all three fields, in the infamous valley of the workaholics. Investment banking first.

High Finance/Low Stress: Carol Malnick

Carol Malnick, 41-year-old partner in Nelson Capital, a financial investment firm in Palo Alto, California, started out as a stockbroker in 1983, training at Drexel Burnham under the legendary Michael Milken. Finally, she landed her "dream job" at Harris, Bretall, Sullivan, and Smith, a leading San Francisco investment firm. "I made it," she thought, "I'm cool." Of the seven women whom she started with, she alone remained after five years. There are still very few women in investment management, she tells me. And there are some good reasons why. Carol, for example, worked 70 to 80 hours a week and traveled 40 percent of the time. Which was fine for a while. When she met her future husband, a product liability lawyer, they contented themselves with weekends on his boat. Condo living made life simple. No problem.

That, however, was a single person's life, Carol says. "Try doing the same work when you have a baby, a house, a yard, two dogs, and an hour's commute each way."

Carol admits that she was also doing everything at home because she was trained to be a Jewish mother. Despite the power suit, Carol looks utterly motherly, her round face glowing from within like Sabbath candles. "I was always the caretaker. It's what I was taught to do. It's how you please a man, I thought (his mother loves me!). I would never have dreamed of asking David to make our daughter's lunch. I considered it my job.

Carol says she would have had a nervous breakdown had she continued at that hysterical pace. But changing her deal with David wasn't an option. Instead, she set out to find a real "dream job": "I wanted a local firm, equity, socially responsible investment, control over my work, and no commute. And I wanted to work with people, not corporations."

And there was Nelson Capital—ten minutes from her home—a company with a 25-year track record and no pressure to grow, just a mandate to take care of its clients. With one woman partner already in the firm, a single mother who worked from dawn to 2:30 P.M. so she could pick up her daughter at school, Carol felt immediately at home. In fact both partners in Nelson Capital, male and female, balanced work and life. So she sat down with them and listed her goals along with the personal assets she could bring to the firm. "They gave me everything I wanted."

It was perfect but, alas and bravo, Nelson Capital became too successful. "We exploded last year from a $250-million business to a $600-million one," Carol explained. So once again, she's working too hard. At least now she's close to home, has afternoons with her daughter, and works with socially responsible investors whom she loves. "I'm the Walter Mitty character, living through their good works. That's why I can't stop working, too. These people fulfill me in the ways they give back to society."

So does Carol. Community work is a major part of her personal life. She and her daughter work in their Jewish temple's soup kitchen (it's their only home-cooked meal, she jokes). She's very active at her daughter's school and in causes promoting women and girls in business.

In Carol's view, the solution for Silicon Valley is social responsibility and stopping the madness. She believes you can definitely still have growth and innovation at a slower pace. "These kids think they want to work 80 hours a week, but they don't know the options—falling in love, exercise, travel, friends. Their thrill is in the widget, the office. They have no other life. But what do they end up with? Heart attacks. If our values don't change, we all lose." At least Silicon Valley has Carol as the new model 2000 woman.

Is There Life After Consulting? Yes, at Scient

Consulting, too, can be normalized. One high-tech consulting firm that set out to do it differently is Scient, Inc. This San Francisco-based "e-business systems innovator," *is* the new Silicon Valley Culture. Call it consulting with a heart. Yes, the staff works like demons to bring their clients' businesses up to electronic snuff, and yes, they've grown from a ten-person office in 1997 to a global group of 1,200 with branches throughout the United States, in Singapore, and in London. And yes, the company went public in a little over one year (with a current market cap at around $4.2 billion). But they've managed all this without losing track of human values, employees' needs, and, as they officially call it, "a fun environment."

All of which is obvious the minute you step off the elevator in the otherwise ordinary financial district office building and gaze down the chartreuse entrance hall festooned with a row of bright-red fire extinguishers. Or hear the merry din of "colleagues" (their preferred term for "employees" in their "non-hierarchical meritocracy") at clusters of desks spread out in a light-filled open office floor. Moving past conference rooms and "quiet" rooms named after heroes like "Nelson Mandela" and "Marie Curie," past the snack room with its free goodies, I make my way to the recruiters, who are all dressed in Hawaiian shirts for the party they're having later to welcome a bunch of prospective colleagues.

Ebullient, sincere, and brimming with efficiency, they tell me that "almost all of their recruits refuse higher offers because the environment at Scient is so great." Just what are they seeking, I ask? Courtney explains, "They want to have a balanced life, they want to work at a place that puts people first, they want to have fun, to belong." She says all the recruiters tell them straight: programmers working as consultants for Scient's clients average 55 hours a week and travel 55 percent of the time. "But we don't send someone alone to Iowa for three months. They'll always be in teams. Everyone goes out to dinner, goes to the theater together. If they want to be based in an office near their family, we arrange that. If they work a weekend, they get a day off. We really recognize people's efforts and give back with bonuses, sabbaticals, vacations. We encourage them to actively participate in their communities. We offer four "floating holidays" in addition to vacations, so people can just take off." It's obvious to me that she's genuinely charmed by where she works.

And Scient's recruiters don't just recruit, either. During the summer orientation they help new colleagues relocate. They work with their families to make sure they're adjusting. "These are college kids," Courtney tells me. "They may never have lived on their own, so we help them to learn how. We don't just say, 'be here after Labor Day.'" The result, she says, is that they have one of the lowest turnover rates in their industry.

But they choose the right people, too. "All recruits pass a values screening to be sure they are people who we *want* to work with. And they've turned down number-one techies because they're not people-oriented enough. We're team-based. People have to enjoy working with others."

Scient's managers are also committed to working out whatever work/life problems people may have. Twenty-nine-year-old Adriana Hartley, the Knowledge Services Leader, for example, helped to create their maternity policy when she became the first colleague to have a baby while working on salary (colleagues' average age is 26, so few are starting families yet). Scient worked with her to create a policy she was comfortable with. For her, that meant three months' maternity leave, then working three days a week for this first year of her son's life, then reevaluating. And they let her work part time while maintaining her stock vesting schedule! Scient's flexibility may be especially laudable since her job is "keeping people connected within the company rather than having them work in isolated little silos."

"They really try to work with you, no matter what the circumstance," Adriana told me, commenting how supportive they are of one of their colleagues who was diagnosed with cancer, insisting he stay out till he's strong enough, working with his family to help out. "They're a very family-oriented culture."

Incidentally, Adriana's husband, Jeff, who is the practice director of technology at another start-up, e.piphany, told his future bosses that he was about to become a father and wanted to be an active one. They gave him a flexible schedule and now, Adriana says, they're both primary parents.

Wendy Chin, another case in point, is an ex-engineer with a business school degree who manages Scient's training program. She and her husband take turns "doing mornings" with their two- and five-year-old boys. On the days she can go straight to the office, she's home by 5:30. Her late days are more like 7:00 P.M. Everyone's fine with her hours.

As for her job, she likes overcoming the gender odds, surprising the guys by fixing machines and teaching them about the technology. And Scient likes having a woman in charge of technical training.

These two women are studies in opposites Adriana—big, casual, with brunette hair falling out of its clip; Wendy—pencil-thin, a utilitarian look. Both adore Scient. Both fit in. Probably because Scient embraces all kinds of people. Then, too, there are the best reasons to work there, which they list on their Web site. Among my favorites:

- 3. Imagine the "Big Five." Now picture having fun.
- 7. Your mentor works here.
- 9. It sucks to keep losing to us.
- 19. Become a legend.
- 20. We have a sense of humor.
- 21. Who says the inmates are running the asylum?

Scient seems to be doing well by having fun. And its unique culture is making it stand out. My guess is Scient culture will stand up to business as usual. As they say (reason #14), "You keep noticing everyone is copying Scient."

. . . . .

Mind you, Scient isn't the norm in the Valley. Everything you read about tech culture makes it seem, in the words of journalist Jon Carroll quoted earlier, like "the Stepford economy"—all work, just work, and more work. Magazine articles quote (male) techies saying they're bored by dates. If a girl doesn't want to talk about technology, they're not interested. Not having a life is a badge of honor. A former Apple employee told me that they used to have T-shirts emblazoned with "80 Hours a Week and Loving It."

In *Nudist on the Late Shift*, Po Bronson's book about Silicon Valley entrepreneurs, he concludes, "Few of the people who work there are remembering to enjoy themselves. Too much is at stake, and time is too short." But as Bronson describes the soul-grinding, lonely lives of these guys, you realize he's only interviewing the Valley's "manly men"—the socially handicapped ones who give everything to make it big, then only want to make it bigger than the next guy. Like Netscape founder Jim Clark, featured in Michael Lewis's *The New New Thing*, whose "neurotic restlessness" drives him from one project to the next, all of them are bereft of the idealism that began the quest. Now, competition is the only motivation: "Once I have more money than Larry Ellison [$13 billion], I'll be satisfied," he says. But will he?

A lot of twenty-somethings make their first few million either by inventing a new Internet widget or with the stock options they get working from day-one for the right start-up. Both are dizzying prospects that can easily cause people to lose their grounding. And with the median income in information technology around $83,000, no one's suffering in the meantime.

But work is usually crazy. For one thing, job mobility is tremendous; average turnover is 50 percent a year. If someone's been at a company for five years there's a "what's wrong with him" attitude, says Professor Jan English-Lueck, one of the three anthropologists at San Jose State University studying Silicon Valley culture. "Knowledge work," she says, "requires so much communication, the volume is overwhelming. Three-quarters of your day is taken up with e-mails. You have 3,000 e-mails piling up during vacation."

Also, as she points out, so much of tech work is about networking, not only to find the next job or project, but as in, "Do you know anyone who has the answer I need."

Exciting, but frantic. Exciting, that is, if you're a winner. No one talks about the reality that a lot of people lose in this high-risk game: that is, they work for start-up after start-up that goes belly up. A venture capitalist at Sequoia, one of the giants, says that they get 50 business plans a day and fund about 20 a year. That boils down to about one chance in 650 that a business will get funded. Analyst figures are even lower: Only 6 out of 1,000 business plans get funded. Of those that get the backing, half will fail. Fewer than 10 percent of the funded start-ups ever go public.

Risk of failures aside, people in the IT industry are simply getting tired of this frantic pace and Stepford existence. More and more are becoming freelancers in order to avoid the problem. Even some of the "uber geeks," as Po Bronson calls them—supercompetent programmers and engineers—are forfeiting their stock options and $150,000-a-year salaries in order to work 18 hours a week and have some fun. They're so good at what they do, they can work however they want. Many more people would do just that if they could, and management has noticed.

In a survey of 1,400 chief information officers in IT, RHI Consulting of Menlo Park, California, found that 53 percent believed that offering flextime is much more important today than it was five years ago as a means of getting and retaining staff. And they've always had alternatives, according to Jan English-Lueck. She explains that a lot of the large corporations cannot dangle the prospects of overnight riches that the start-ups can. Instead, they attract an older group of employees who want more regular work hours and less travel. However, these flexible 9 to 5 types constitute the Valley's silent majority: They're the timid townsfolk in a land where cowboys rule.

Fortunately, while so many of Silicon Valley's hearts are beating cold and fast, there's a new start-up culture emerging, one run by people who care as much about the process as they do about product or money. Those who don't want to wake up 20 years from now with no life and a lesson in how little happiness a few million can bring. Sarah Vickers Willis, vice president of Business Development and cofounder of UBUBU is certainly one of these. So is Hillary Billings, CEO of the widely advertised RedEnvelope, Inc., another recent start-up. She's the one, remember, whose advice to the lovelorn was "avoid the jerks." There's a lot more to learn from Hillary's example.

Hillary Billings

When the *New York Times Magazine* chose RedEnvelope, a Web retailer in gift items, for a feature article documenting business at the speed of light among Silicon Valley's start-ups, they chose well. In six months time, CEO Hillary Billings put RedEnvelope on the map and sucessfully readied it for the Christmas rush. Yet, in the dense four-page article outlining Billings' strategies, only one line notes that when she took the job she was four months pregnant (with two young sons at home). To me, *that* is the story. Not that some automaton CEO pulled off this start-up miracle, but that a pregnant mother of two did it! So here's the story behind the story.

This 36-year-old mother of three (four years old, two and a half, and nine weeks) is living proof that the life most college girls dream about definitely is possible. And she looks like she's enjoying it. At our 9:00 A.M. meeting, she's perkier than I am and bubbling with pleasure in her favorite breakfast place, relating how much fun the kids were this morning and how great it is that her mom is visiting. No baby dribble on her clothes. She's neat as a pin, slender, has a fresh-washed face, and straight hair sliced at her shoulders, with bangs that make her look 12.

So how do you do it? I ask. Her answer is simple. "You work your tail off, get established, and make a reputation before you have kids. Then you write your own ticket. I was a crazy woman for eight years before I hit 30, but that enabled me to control my work environment."

Like a lot of girls, Hillary graduated an art history major, ready to devote her life to high culture. Fortunately, perhaps, given the scarcity of jobs for art devotees, her father convinced her to go out into the world before she committed herself to such "monastic work." So she took a job at Macy's that began with a training program for college graduates in humanities. "It was ideal experience," she feels. Three years later, she was managing home products, then buying them, and finally designing them, traveling around the world for ideas.

When she met her future husband, Bill, she was traveling most of the time. But as a doctor, he was working long hours too, and accepted her schedule. What made it hard was that they lived in different cities. They weren't together enough for the relationship to grow. So they both moved to San Francisco, where she took a job at Williams Sonoma to create their Pottery Barn catalogue. Talk about being in the right place at the right time. Plus, and very important to Hillary, her boss there was a terrific mentor. With his backing, she grew the catalogue business ten-fold in four years. Then she did product design for two years.

Of course, there was the matter of getting on with life. Bill, a few years older than Hillary, wanted to have kids before he was forty, so she slowed down and took two maternity leaves. She simply announced to Pottery Barn that she would now work three days a week, but she was so successful they accepted it for the next two years. "It was a perfect balance. And when Bill saw that I could demand that, he realized he could too, and did. That way, we each had full days with the kids and I could see a friend on Sunday or have alone time. We always had time to go out with each other, too."

Then, in 1997, she got a call from Barry Starwood, whose company bought Westin and Sheraton Hotels, then created the W Hotels. He wanted Hillary to create a style and personality for them. And Hillary saw an opportunity to create "style hotels that would cater to business people with faxes, modem hookups, and business service. It was a raging success."

And so was her family life. At that point, Bill was doing the real parenting. In their eight years together, he had always supported her. He was always willing to sacrifice for something important to her. "I wasn't the easiest person to be married to—I traveled a lot still, had high-powered jobs. But he was a great parent. Even so, she had to *ask* him to share parenting with her. "My husband didn't say, how can I help here. I managed the housekeeper, bills, kids, then I said, hey, you've got to be a part of this and he responded, absolutely."

At this point in their lives, she and Bill have even more in common. He was a doctor; she was in retail. Now they're both at Internet start-ups. A year ago, when Hillary was pregnant, she was offered the RedEnvelope job. She'd turned down three other jobs, choosing RedEnvelope because they said "We're hiring you for the quality of time you're giving me, not quantity." The other places essentially said your kids are your problem.

Although her team does work all the time, she does not. She's home by 7:30 to spend two hours with the kids and work a couple of hours after she and Bill have had dinner. Whenever there's a hole in the day, like after our breakfast meeting, she runs home to nurse the baby. Nursing does put you in a bit of a fog, she admits (not that it shows), but she has good people to back her at work.

Bill founded a medical software company, Adam.com, and now has been able to cut back to four days a week by doing more work from home. So he's the main parent while she has a heavier schedule. She says she wouldn't have accepted the CEO position otherwise.

For Hillary, family, friends, and personal goals are the basics of life. "At the end of the day, what is life about?" she asks herself every few months. "I check in. OK, will I be happy with the direction my life is going? Bill and I check in. Right now, we talk about making enough money to live in Italy for a few years. That's our family goal."

What gives Hillary the perspective so many people lose in this driven economy? She thinks about her father and what he taught her. About how he retired early when her mother began earning more than he did, both of them enjoying life more and more. Also, she was raised in Tanzania, where her father was an engineer. Spending so much time without television, toys, even other kids, meant learning to think alone and to create your world. It certainly gives her a constant global point of view to prevent getting caught up in any local madness.

Hillary saw a lot of other women at the top who were resentful for having given up their families. But that's changing, she feels. The change is coming from both women and men who are disgusted with this out-of-control work ethic. The backlash, she predicts, will be dramatic—and Hillary Billings is a great predictor. I certainly read a feature a week on some CEO who has sworn to live and let live.

Overwork in Nine-Tenths of the Law

Kemba and Niven are typical of most law associates, working 12-hour days and weekends. That's because the collective structure of legal partnership—in which profits and risks are shared—means that partners choose associates in part for their willingness to work long hours. That way, they are fairly certain that this future partner will pull his or her weight in the collective. Also, associates' long hours support the partners' high incomes that serve as a kind of payback for the slave hours they themselves put in before making partner. A "we worked that hard, therefore you have to also" mentality prevails.

Because law firms are usually pyramids, with many associates vying for a few partnership positions, competition is intense; more so with the present glut of lawyers on the market that is predicted to last through year 2006. (Have you heard the one about why they're using lawyers instead of rats in laboratory experiments? There's more of them.) That glut may be one reason why billable hours have increased in the last decade from 1,800 to 2,000 per year.

Galia Swetschinski is a 27-year-old lawyer working in an eight-attorney San Francisco firm that represents banks and leasing companies in corporate finance issues. She knows it's a "good" place; associates feel valued and are treated with respect. In fact, the firm was started by two women who left large law firms, presumably to elude the glass ceiling and punishing hours. And still, instead of just cutting back on her hours, one of those original partners retired in her mid-40s to spend more time with her teenagers. The other, a mother of two small children, works 60 to 70 hours a week. Galia routinely puts in 12-hour days. She knows she's lucky, yet from where she sits, partnership doesn't look any easier than life as an associate.

Galia feels that in many ways the remaining woman partner is a "model 2000" woman, a successful lawyer and mother. But Galia doesn't want to work so many hours—not now and certainly not when she has kids. The pressure to do so, however, is palpable. Not long ago, when some of the big San Francisco firms increased associates' salaries, the partners asked the four associates whether lifestyle (translation: time) or money was more important to them. Although the associates *felt* that lifestyle was more important, they *said* money because they knew that was the right answer. As Galia put it, "Even if I had said I want the time, they couldn't give it to me. If they work weekends, we work weekends. If they stay late, I have to stay late in order to work with them."

Like most partners everywhere, Galia feels the work ethic in her office is revenue driven—both because lawyers want the high income and, even more, the prestige that comes from earning it. In law as it is practiced today, money is status. But as soon as you set that goal, you're putting in grueling hours and you can't say no to a client—who expects you to be "on call."

Although graduates can earn more in business, if they go into law, they're more or less guaranteed a high income. Wages for first-year lawyers in New York's 25 biggest firms ranged from $101,000 to $111,000. Of course, in the city's district attorney's office, the range is $30,000 to $40,000, clerkships average $35,000, and government lawyers earn about $72,000. So while the median income for lawyers is actually only $60,000, they can earn much more. Most of the senior lawyers Galia knows want to. "Money," she says, "is the one common denominator among an otherwise diverse group." In fact, she just read that law schools are having difficulty getting professors because newly minted graduates can earn more than tenured professors.

The problem is that Galia sometimes finds herself beginning to act on those values, even though she doesn't share them. Usually, she likes earning $150,000 at age 27, feeling as if she's proving herself. But, recently, when she found herself resentful of the two paralegals taking vacations at the rush time at the end of a fiscal quarter, she wondered if she, too, wasn't becoming a workaholic. Especially since one of her bosses refused to cancel the paralegals' vacations on the principle that we have to respect each other's lives. Galia also noticed her resentment of the office newcomer, a man who had been an in-house counsel, one of the few legal jobs with regular hours, who still maintains those hours, leaving by 5:30 to make dinner with his kids. Even though he never dilly dallies and is a hard, productive worker, Galia found herself annoyed that she cannot do the same. Hence, the vicious cycle: Workaholics create a workaholic life for those around them.

Although the killer work ethic is alive and well in Galia's office, she believes that "at the end of the day, the partners here make the right human—not money—choice." When one of the married associates told the partners she was trying to get pregnant and would be wanting to work part time when she had a child, they told her they would work that out with her, that they would promise not to take the interesting cases away from her, and they would support her.

Money isn't Galia's goal, but she pays $1,000 per month on her law school loans and the two-bedroom apartment she rents with her fiancé costs $2,800 per month. In the Bay area, life is very expensive. She has to plan carefully, especially since her fiancé wants to leave the law, precisely because it's so money centered. He doesn't want to work so hard or be on call all the time. He's not alone, either.

As Galia says, I don't see my friends making that choice. We don't want to live for money. We do want "lifestyle." We do want meaning. Her best friend from George Washington Law School just left a fancy Washington, D.C., law firm to be a public defender in Denver. Galia herself wanted public interest law but found only one position in the Bay area, and it paid $28,000.

It turns out that most law associates, even well-paid ones, are unhappy about their hours. One study of what economists Renee M. Landers, James B. Rebitzer, and Lowell J. Taylor called the *rat race model* of the legal profession found that "nearly two-thirds of the associates indicated they would prefer to reduce hours." Worse, a poll taken by *California Lawyer* magazine in 1993 found that over 70 percent were sorry they chose law. They don't find the collegiality, honesty, and security that used to characterize law.

Even a surprising number of graduates of the sacrosanct Harvard Law School are unhappy practicing law. The current directory for the class of 1990 shows fewer than one-half the graduates working in law firms and a quarter who don't practice law at all according to Robert Kurson, one of those defectors who is now a magazine editor. In an article he wrote about this for *Esquire*, he describes his former classmates as largely overworked, discontented lawyers or escapees, like himself, who experience daily relief. Back in the 1960s, he laments, in the fanciest firms where Harvard Law School grads inevitably land, an associate could expect to bill 1,500 hours a year and make partner if he didn't drool or stutter. Today, associates bill 2,200 to 2,400 hours a year and have only a one in eight chance of making partner. Even then, "if his revenues or hours drop, he will be invited to resign."

Back in the old days, apparently, lawyers had time to become Renaissance men, going to the theater and traveling. Now, they're drones. Kurson notes that about 80 percent of incoming Harvard Law School students express a desire to practice public interest law, but fewer than 5 percent do. How bad does the practice of high-powered law get? He refers us to an article in the *Vanderbilt Law Review* on overwork, depression, suicide, and the law. One of its authors is a Harvard Law School graduate.

These surveys give new meaning to Kemba's warning about knowing what you're getting into before taking the LSAT's, and to Carol Ann's choice to bypass the big firms for a small place with decent values. Some lawyers can practice law and live their lives. More will be able to if lawyers change the practice of law.

Changing the Law

Obviously, the practice of law has to change both from within and without. Change from within is like the former in-house counsel lawyer who simply gets up and leaves Galia's office at 5:30 P.M. The more lawyers do that, the more everyone will accept that it is done, and the more law firms will have to limit their client service. Most clients can accustom themselves to a more limited kind of service, just as we've all gotten used to, say, mechanical options instead of telephone operators and receptionists.

Why more don't do this is the problem of the type-A personality that often scales the professional ranks. The authors of the "rat race" study of the legal profession argue that the kind of person who accepts grueling work hours is often clinically depressed and, therefore, unable to get much pleasure from personal life. Essentially, this is the theory that workaholism comes from within, either because of a personality disorder or because people feel obliged to work that hard. Despite the inducements women have to resist it, workaholism can affect women even more than men because women often feel less entitled to enter the aristocracy of prestigious work. As Galia said, she felt she had to prove herself; a man in her position might have felt he wanted to do things his way, make his mark on the firm.

A lot of overdrive lawyers also convince themselves that they are working this hard out of love. That is, being a 70-hour-a-week attorney has got to be a very important job because no sensible person would do this just for money. Though as Galia remarked, neither she nor her friends ever understood just how money-centered the practice of law actually is.

An ambitious lawyer generally does want money and perks, first to pay back school loans, then to keep those BMWs and beach houses coming. As one male attorney told me, "I can't work fewer hours if we're going to live in Manhattan in a six-room apartment and take great vacations." His decision is motivated by values that trade time for luxury, which is a choice.

Lawyers do have choices. Niven, Kemba's colleague, was always volunteering for that extra case. When she started out she would often work all night, then shower and go in again—and still she blamed herself for not being fast enough. Nor would she quit because, as she says, she's not "a quitter."

Yet, even a driven person can make different choices. If you're aware of your predilections, you can strategize to make sure you have a life before it's too late to get one. Peter Van Tol, another compulsive type, left a major New York City law firm of 500 attorneys where he was an associate working "round the clock." "I thought I could deal with it," he said. "I didn't realize you need down time, psychic time. Plus, it was ruining my relationship. The only fights my wife and I had were about my never having time to be together."

He took a less prestigious job, negotiating reinsurance at another large firm of Rosenman and Colin, where he leaves most nights at 5:30 P.M. Knowing himself to be the kind of person who just cannot refuse fascinating cases, he put himself in a place where such cases don't exist. "I took myself away from the banquet because I knew I couldn't control my appetite," he allowed. His income declined only $20,000 and he still loves his work. But now he gets to have a thriving relationship with his wife and two-year-old daughter. Once he had a child, the desire for connection outweighed the ego gratification of working on the most compelling cases, at least at the price he paid for doing so.

Choosing those niches within law where an attorney can live a less pressured life will change the law from without by limiting the supply of overdrive lawyers. Knowing about them is a first step.

A litigation-only firm will have a harder time with flexibility and part-time arrangements because of trial schedules, court appearances, and depositions. A transactions attorney—broadly speaking, one who negotiates deals—can control his or her practice more, although that's not Carol Ann's experience. Her experience, however, may be particular both to the kind of law her firm does and her town. Speak to most small-town lawyers and you'll find a far more relaxed pace. My dentist's husband, an attorney in Ventura, California, works only four days a week now that they have a child.

Another possibility entirely is choosing those public interest jobs that do pay a living wage, though you'll have to get past the peeling paint. New York City's Office of the Appellate Defender (OAD), which provides 16 attorneys to represent indigent defendants in criminal appeals, is a far cry from the hushed leather and chrome offices of Rosenman and Colin and their ilk—places that clearly spare no expense to display their wealth and put the wealthy at ease. The OAD looks more like some spare workroom in a New York City subway terminal or the Bronx division of the Board of Education: poor lighting, old metal desks, small crowded spaces, peeling paint, and the ever-present clatter in halls with no padding, pictures, or carpets. Yet, of the four attorneys I interviewed, all loved their work.

Like Galia, 40-year-old Daniel Warshawsky graduated from George Washington Law (with high honors), and knew just what he wanted. After a stint in New Jersey's Public Defender's office, he became director of the volunteers in the OAD—those are the associates who come to them from the fancy law firms to do their one mandatory pro bono case a year—many of them pushing paper all the time and getting their only trial experience as a volunteer. Unfortunately, many of the largest law firms have cut back sharply on their pro bono work, which now averages 36 hours a year instead of the American Bar Association recommendation of 50. Daniel gets to do it all the time.

"I've always been a public defender type, not the driven type. All my driven men friends from law school are always lamenting their choice. No one's happy, except for the money. Me, I want the time and I like what I do," Daniel reports. He looks the type: granny glasses, mussed hair, oxford shirt open at the neck, and a scholarly intonation in his speech. Interestingly, though Daniel only earns about $60,000 and is home by 6:30 every night to be with his three babies (all under four), his wife works for a fancy corporate law firm and rarely gets home before the kids are asleep.

Risa Gerson, also 40 years old, is a supervisor of volunteers in the same office, having wended her way through various public interest offices since graduating Brooklyn Law School in 1984. To Risa, her $60,000 public interest salary seemed quite comfortable, particularly back when her husband was a freelance journalist who could really do half the childcare and you could happily live your life in Bohemia, as she says. Now, when no one over 30 seems to live in a garret any more, Risa, like Daniel, supplements her salary with her spouse's much higher one. Her once free-lance husband became a rock columnist for *Newsday*. While Risa loves her work, their combined incomes and a relatively modest lifestyle make it possible.

The practice of law will change, eventually. It has to. According to the National Association for Law Placement, some firms are losing a quarter of their associates a year and most lose three-quarters within seven years. The first-year cost of hiring a law associate fresh out of school is about $100,000. Firms can't afford to continue losing those associates. They're much better off making accommodations. And some are starting to. As a perk, Shearman and Sterling sends their associates and families to one of their European offices for three months, has them take time off to learn a foreign language, and assures them that they can work fewer billable hours without losing ground. Most of the legal perks are money: bonuses for staying more than a year, more than five years, or stock in some venture capital firm. But many more are offering part-time and flextime work. Some, according to the *National Law Journal*, are even offering the unheard of luxury of paternity leave.

Keep up the pressure and law may become a civilized profession again. Or defect. Take advantage of the myriad books now counseling attorneys about alternative ways of using their skills (see Notes). The more who do, the more quickly the practice of law will change. Or start your own law firm.

Can you imagine starting a law firm that would work differently? I ask Galia. "Yes," she says immediately. The two women who started the firm where she works improved on the former cutthroat model. Galia thinks she can go a step beyond. Why not, especially if you're willing to forego the biggest bucks?

And if supply and demand fail to change the practice of law, the government could actually mandate a limit on billable hours, just as the Canadian Bar debated doing in 1999. Imagine.

Striking Out on Your Own: The Entrepreneur

For a lot of young women, starting a business may sound like a monumental step, a financial impossibility. It's not; even teenagers do it.

Jenai Lane started a business when she was 20. Though no longer technically a teen, her planning began while she was in high school. Taking a shower one day, she decided that her bath stopper and chain would make a cool necklace. So she went to the hardware store, bought some ball chains, a few O rings, and wore them to school. When everyone asked where she found her necklace, she made some and gave them to friends, then sold others to acquaintances. Next, she was selling to local stores. So many orders came in that she had to get help. But five banks refused her requests for a loan to create working capital, as often happens to women.

Luckily, she found a mentor who connected her with a "micro" lender, someone who makes small—$25,000—loans to high-risk firms. With that seed money, she rented a windowless space in the back of a shop, hired a helper, and was in business. She did OK, but her enterprise didn't really take off until she came up with a second creation: leather thong necklaces with astrological sign pendants and explanatory cards attached. While Jenai isn't rich yet, she's doing very well, has ten employees and a client list that includes Neiman Marcus, Macy's, and Nordstrom. Oh yes, and a window for her workshop.

If teenagers can start a successful business, so could a lot of women—especially older, experienced, educated ones. The idea has obviously occurred to many of them. In 1972, only 5 percent of businesses were owned by women. Now, half of businesses are. The real growth happened in the last decade, with the number of women-owned firms increasing by 100 percent. Women are starting businesses at four times the rate of men and employ 35 percent more people than the Fortune 500 companies do worldwide.

The story of why and how is nicely illustrated by Joline Godfrey, a visionary who is doing well by doing good—helping hundreds of young women get their start.

Joline Godfrey, Entrepreneur

At 50, Joline, a woman with more bounce in her step than most of the teens she enlightens, is the CEO of Independent Means, a company offering a variety of programs, products, and sites for the financial novice, particularly Y Gen girls. Not only do they franchise programs that women can use to teach girls the fundamentals of finance, they work to foster girls' economic development at schools like Miss Porter's in Connecticut and The Archer School in California.

As she changes the lives of girls, Joline also changes the way women will think. And she is just the right person to bridge the generations, with a baby face and soft blond bangs that almost make her seem more contemporary with her teen clients than her peers. And because she created a financially viable business to build women entrepreneurs, her story illustrates more about the subject than any dozen tycoon stories I could easily summon.

When Joline was 36, she built a business by creating games to help corporate managers spark creativity in their teams—something she'd already done for Polaroid, where her degree in social work originally led her. This was a long way from the small-town dairy farm in Maine where girls rarely strayed from convention, much less to start their own businesses. Intrigued by her own experience in breaking gender barriers, she wrote her first book, *Our Wildest Dreams: Women Making Money, Having Fun, Doing Good.* However, while Joline was heartened by the stories of her sister entrepreneurs, she was also struck by how hard they had all struggled with their projects, most of them undertaken in middle age and out of frustration with hitting corporate glass ceilings. None had reached the big leagues of American business; few were movers and shakers, even in their specialized fields.

At that point, Joline asked the right question: Why are we coming to business ownership so late in our lives? If we started earlier, wouldn't we be more successful, just as we're more fluent in a language the earlier we learn one? Nobody ever said to these female entrepreneurs, why don't you start a company, go get rich. Most, in fact, were told they were crazy. Yet they, like Joline herself, all were natural entrepreneurs, by which Joline means someone with lots of "initiating behavior."

Joline didn't want to change women. She wanted to change their perception of themselves and give them options they would not otherwise have considered. It was then, in 1992, that she began a nonprofit called An Income of Her Own to develop educational programs and products that counterbalance the anti-entrepreneurial messages girls generally get. But a few years in, frustrated with the usual fundraising hassles of nonprofits, Joline had to ask herself the question: Why had she taken the typical nonprofit nickel-and-dime "girl" path? Why hadn't she started a business of training female entrepreneurs?

After all, in her four nonprofit years, Joline had proven the market wrong. Girls *were* interested in financial independence. They *did* come to "Camp $tart-up." They *did* compete in her "Teen Business Plan Competition," an annual competition that she publicized through schools or articles in magazines like *Seventeen.* Schools and girls groups *did* buy her training kits and they flocked to her conferences.

Fortuitously, the world out there had just taken notice of this gap in female education. Welfare reform had suddenly made female financial independence the subject of the day. Coincidentally, in Australia, Melbourne's Women's Commission had just published a signal study on personal economic development proving that the "apprenticeship" stage—between the ages of 8 and 18—was crucial to creating *homo economicus.* Now Joline had the research to convince her market (parents, educators, girls, and businesses) of the importance of her products for creating "economic woman." And she did.

She approached the finance "angels," a term for individuals who make investments to start-ups. One woman, unwilling to risk her own cash in such an unheard of (and, let's face it, female) venture, arranged for Joline to present her business plan to Investors' Circle, an informal group of angels. Once several initial investors signed on, the first woman followed.

Joline soon landed her first two clients: a business in Australia, and IBM, which saw in its future a new, more entrepreneurial kind of employee of both genders. IBM saw Joline's company, rechristened Independent Means, as a way of creating them.

Early on, Joline realized that the Internet was an important new vehicle. Repackaging her business for the Web, she created a Web site for Independent Means and Dollar Diva, a fun financial site for teen girls. Dollar Dude's coming soon.

The business has grown enormously. Independent Means' "partners" include Charles Schwab, Fleet Boston Bank, Home Depot, Guardian Insurance, and Prudential, all of which sponsor programs in exchange for cobranding. They developed "Hot Company," a financial game for teens; they run six Camp $tart-ups (two weeks), Club $tart-ups (four days), and ClubInvest (four days), along with one-day conferences throughout the country. And they've produced a fleet of teens who have become entrepreneurial models for girls and women.

There's Meghan Ellwanger, a home-schooled 15-year-old who, with her own herd of dairy goats on her mother's Somerset, Wisconsin, farm, created a line of body lotions and gourmet cheeses she now sells to Chicago's upscale shops and restaurants; Allison Beckwith, a Belleview, Washington, teenager, tired of the dorky products for Christian kids, created Flare.com, with "cool" products for her religious sisterhood; and one of this year's Teen Business Plan competitors, a 14-year-old who designed a handbag with a light inside so you can find your keys (or calculator or mace) in the dark.

These teens started like Joline did, step by logical step, opportunistically, and with a lot of hard work. Maybe the most important ingredient, says Joline, is having a model. That's why she constantly brings together young and older women and counsels anyone interested in starting a business to meet with women who have done it.

(Almost) Any Woman Can

America's 9 million female entrepreneurs employ some 27 million people and generate $3.6 trillion in revenues. What's more remarkable is that although women own 40 percent of American businesses, they have access to only 2 percent of the available venture capital and 12 percent of all credit provided to small businesses. However, they have paid a price for their lack of capital: two-thirds of women-owned businesses have annual revenues of under $50,000. Of course, most small businesses fail within a few years because of undercapitalization and only a small minority of entrepreneurs ever earn six-figure incomes. But female entrepreneurs clearly face a greater challenge than most.

As of 1998, just over half of the women and men who owned businesses did have bank financing. However, the scale of borrowing by women is much smaller—and women of color receive even less than white women. One problem is that women set their sights too low, applying for the smaller loans of the type banks consider to be money losers. They establish small, local, low-collateral enterprises that have trouble getting start-up money. Without sufficient loans, many women have had to start businesses on their credit cards and scrounge for support among family members.

Kathleen Allen, the coordinator of the undergraduate Entrepreneur Program at the University of Southern California and author of *Entrepreneurship for Dummies,* says that women entrepreneurs often come up against the skewed gender perception of the bankers. One female-owned Houston plumbing supply company, for example, approached the largest local bank and was told it would need the women's husbands to sign for a line of credit. The women walked out and, luckily, did find another lender. Few men have these hassles.

Professor Allen points out, however, that women do often lack the financial expertise that bankers and investors look for because of a history of putting financial matters in the hands of others. Among her M.B.A. students, Allen says, the women take the managerial and marketing seminars instead of the number-crunching ones. To build financial confidence among women, Allen holds special seminars with women role models and, as she describes it, she also does a lot of cheerleading. With good results: In the last three years women students won USC's business plan competition, which is judged by outside venture capitalists.

Role models and mentors can help the female entrepreneur immeasurably. But according to Allen, she must have money-smarts and a clear understanding that investors are looking for growth potential—ideas that will scale up, proprietary technology and patents.

Allen's views resonate with other experts on the subject. Jennifer Kushell is the 27-year-old head of the Young Entrepreneurs Network, a group she started at Boston University in the early 90s. She's also the author of *The Young Entrepreneurs Edge*, a guidebook for young people starting their own business ventures. In Kushell's experience, talking with thousands of young entrepreneurs, women's businesses often tank because "although women generally give great customer service, they don't look at capital base, bookkeeping systems, taxes, or cash flow. This leads to money problems, which ruins their credit early. They don't look at the issue of money until their cash flow runs out." It's an MO Kushell knows about firsthand.

Like the women she talks to, Kushell never learned about money. Oddly, she comes from a family of entrepreneurs and was given great praise for starting businesses, which she did from the time she was 13. But her parents shared marketing tips instead of explaining the basic finances of their own businesses or hers. Her fiancé, whose family runs several Baskin-Robbins, was taught the books along with the business. The result of this gap in her education is that during the years when she could have made a pile of money running Young Entrepreneurs, she had none. She's finally turned it around by signing with a venture capital firm, which will shepherd her through the financial thickets of growing her business.

Unfortunately, even female entrepreneurs who have done their financial homework may find themselves up against gender discrimination. In Allen's study of female entrepreneurs in nontraditional fields she found that the leading supplier of automotive parts in Milwaukee had to run a gauntlet of unusual obstacles to stay in business. Her male competitors colluded against her, preventing her from purchasing key materials to make her products. They slashed her tires and threatened her. Going overseas for the materials instead turned out to be the silver lining in this dark cloud; the Japanese firm she dealt with not only had excellent materials, they eventually wanted to partner with her. Her products are still the highest quality at the lowest price, just as they were when she started out. Eventually, her male competitors learned to live with it.

For all the obvious woes, women do have some advantages in business. In addition to providing good customer service as a matter of course, Allen believes that women's management style produces a positive business culture and their tendencies to openness and nonhierarchical teamwork are, in fact, ahead of the curve. One female-owned business, a supplier for NASA, earned the trust and loyalty of the engineers working for her because they knew her door was always open.

Women are good at cooperation, Allen says, and teams are an excellent way to approach business—even ownership—now that enterprise has become so complex. Businesses with more than one owner may be able to specialize technical, marketing, and managerial responsibilities. With a clear partnership agreement that spells out obligations, team ownership doesn't have to be any more challenging in organizational terms than single ownership. It may actually be less so because of the emotional as well as professional support it provides. Think Ally McBeal and her partners.

Women Do Succeed in Business (But Not Without Really Trying)

As difficult as the obstacles are, women entrepreneurs have a success rate equal to men's, though their businesses don't grow as much or as fast. They're also breaking gender barriers by breaking into construction, engineering, and manufacturing. The top-growth industries for women, in fact, are construction, wholesale trade, transportation, and communication. While boomer women entrepreneurs and their predecessors mostly owned service businesses, the new generation is moving into finance, insurance, high tech, and all the other fields formerly closed to women.

How is it possible? Because women, tired of hitting glass ceilings, have decided to bypass them. Although the researchers keep expecting to find that women are starting businesses to accommodate their family obligations, they keep finding the opposite. Two professors of business, Dorothy P. Moore and E. Holly Buttner, did a study of 129 women entrepreneurs—mostly 40ish, married with children, with sales in the $250,000 to $500,000 range—and found that the most common reasons for starting a business were "in order to advance," "to be in charge," and "to work in an environment that reflected my values."

Another surprise is how women perceive the benefits of business ownership. They claim only a modest gain in work/life balance, working on average about 52 hours a week. That may seem like a big improvement on the New Economy's 60-hour week, but probably it isn't what they'd hoped. The real gain for women entrepreneurs is in control and advancement, which may reduce stress enough for a better work/life blend than they had in the corporate world.

While these women all earned more as business owners than they had before, they claimed that profits weren't as important to them as the gain in self-fulfillment, personal and professional growth. Jenai, the jewelry entrepreneur, for example, brings her cat and her favorite CDs to work. She knows all her employees and their children, which means a lot to all of them. While there are occasional long nights, they're not standard operating procedure. Nor does it have to be. Being competitive needn't mean outdistancing your competition through sheer endurance. It means staying in the game.

Fine, but how do women make their businesses happen in an atmosphere where financing is harder to come by, where venture capitalists—mostly men—often don't trust women or understand the businesses they want to start. What they lack in access to capital, they make up for in part with the terrific women's business network burgeoning as rapidly as women's businesses. These network resources range from the National Foundation for Women Business Owners to the National Women's Business Council, a governmental advisory board for women-owned businesses. Many local centers around the country, such as the Women's Business Development Center in Philadelphia, are now lending a few thousand dollars at a time, using money they've raised through private investors. There's also the Women's Economic Network, a private San Francisco group whose venture capitalists are committed to funding women's businesses. Other groups fund narrowly defined businesses, which women often have.

Yla Eason, a former business journalist, pioneered a business in dolls, board games, and toys reflecting African-American, Hispanic, and Asian-American culture. With seed money from the Business Enterprise Trust, a micro-lender for socially responsible business funded by TV producer Norman Lear, she began by making a black action figure. She started here because her small son thought he couldn't be a hero if he wasn't white, like the Power Rangers and X-men he played with.

Kay Koplowitz, who heads the National Women's Business Council, started Springboard 2000 to accelerate women's access to the equity markets. In the first six months of its launch in January 2000, it generated more than $160 million of investment capital and funding for women-owned businesses.

On the other end of the scale, Count-Me-In is calling on women to donate $5 or more to a fund that provides seed money to make $500 to $10,000 loans to help women begin their businesses. It's run by Nell Merlino, who explains that there are a lot of women out there without the resources to put together even $1,000 to start a project out of their kitchen. And for a lot of women, the goal is simply a small business that will pay the rent and feed their children: "Everyone isn't upper middle class and waiting for a quarter of a million to bring out a new line of handbags or start a dot-com." Forty-five percent of women working full time earn less than $25,000 a year, as compared to only 27 percent of full-time male workers earning that little. For them, Merlino argues, making $50,000 and being their own boss is a significant advance. "We have to start where women are, and micro-business is where many women are."

Merlino also believes that in some sectors of the new economy, small is better. These micro-businesses are the "very stuff that makes each community unique, the cake bakers, clothing makers, accountants, and transportation service owners." Count-Me-In's first loans are going to just these kinds of community businesses that get overlooked in today's big-splash economy because they don't follow a male model of aiming to make millions. But, of course, she reminds us, that model has destroyed a lot of men.

In her view, the dramatic rise in female entrepreneurs serves as a catalyst for changing business. Mainstream American business needs talent and since there just aren't enough men to supply it, they'll have to attract women who now have somewhere else to go.

Rosalind Resnick, Self-Financing

At 35, Rosalind, the single mother of two little girls, co-founded NetCreations from the spare bedroom in her south Florida home. It was the Internet's first "opt-in" (by invitation only, in contrast to spam) e-mail marketing company. Now, with over 60 employees and offices in Manhattan's fashionable Soho, NetCreations has gone public and is pulling in $20.7 million in revenues. Wall Street is predicting $67 million by the end of 2000. How did this single mother with a master's degree in medieval history end up as one of the top three female CEOs in Silicon Alley? Strategic planning.

As Rosalind admits, she wasn't interested in business. She dreamed of starting as a journalist at a small-town newspaper and building up to a big-city one. "But it was the recession, there were no jobs, so I fell into the nether world of trade papers." Turning this specialized experience with technical reporting to her advantage, she eventually landed a job at the *Miami Herald* as a business reporter. But divorce and child custody encouraged her to think of "at home" jobs, full-time being too hard on her family life. So she became a freelance writer and did far better than average, earning $100,000 a year. But it was grueling, she said, taking care of kids, waking at 5:00 A.M. to write, and working long after the kids were in bed. Essentially, she gave up sleep, particularly when she was writing her 400-page *Internet Business Guide* in 1994.

It was time to regroup. "I knew that instead of selling my time, which is what a freelance writer does, I had to create one thing and sell it over and over. But with two kids, I didn't want to take any financial risks. I saw my opportunity in the Internet. Her then-boyfriend (and current business partner) was a Web designer, so they teamed up. Rosalind's journalism connections got the customers, while her boyfriend provided the design services. It cost them nothing in working capital, though her boyfriend did quit his job. Essentially, they supported the new business with her ongoing earnings as a free-lance writer. Unfortunately, as Rosalind learned, Web design was a bit too much like freelance writing. They'd need more designers and sales people to grow the business.

That's when she started looking for something more "scaleable," that is; a business you can grow without changing the organizational structure or putting in more time. They tried an Internet dating service, then found a hole in the market for something far more lucrative: a business that connected products with potential customers who chose to learn more about them; in a word, opt-in marketing. Potential customers sign on for information on products and services related to their areas of interest, whether it's scuba diving or single-malt Scotch. Nine million prospects have opted in. They're making money while they sleep.

Well, not quite. Rosalind says she *should* be working less, but she's rarely home till 8:30 P.M. to be with her seven- and ten-year-old children. She travels a week a month, though she tries to schedule her days away into the half-weeks the children spend with their father. "I guess I'm a workaholic," she sighs.

But at least she has the option of working less. And she believes she's doing a good job professionally and personally. "My own mom was the total mother, from Girl Scouts to gorgeously cooked meals every night. Me, I yell, I'm tired, I work too much, but my kids say they respect that. They like that I don't talk down to them. To them, I'm the coolest mom. But I'm not trying to be the model mom. I'm just me."

Being Rosalind means outwitting biased lenders. It also means making another unusual move for a CEO: giving back. The Girl Scouts were not only a positive influence in Rosalind's life, they were a great leadership training ground. She started a troop in Miami's Little Havana, which was so popular it grew into 12 troops. When Rosalind's business took off, she gave the Girl Scouts $100,000 worth of shares and now volunteers by helping them with their high-tech infrastructure. Rosalind may work too much, but she hasn't forgotten about the rest of life.

Pamela Bergson, Friends, and Neighbors

Thirty-nine-year-old Pamela Bergson, founder of www.bid4vacations.com—the Internet's first vacation auction site—also initially self-financed with a combination of her savings and salary from full-time work. She couldn't even get a merchant account at the bank before she opened a CD account there as collateral. Like Rosalind, she, too, launched out of a home office, building her database at night while a local engineering company was building her site. All this with a marriage and two little children to care for.

Once launched, Pamela went the venture capital route, but with a twist. First she tried the big Silicon Valley companies, like Benchmark. But they would back her only if she moved to California, a move she was unwilling to make because she quite liked her life in Colorado. Finally, three local VCs supplied her with $2 million to expand. Not surprisingly, people invest more easily where they are. One of her VCs—a principal in the largest VC firm in Colorado—was actually a neighbor. He told her that he used to see her working in her home office at 4:00 A.M. on Saturday mornings when he was picking up his buddy to go fishing. He knew firsthand how hard she worked.

Now, a year after her launch, Pamela has 45 employees and 1 million users plus a million more unique visitors. No profit yet, but that hasn't stopped her from a successful second funding round, which brought in a fourth local investor. Her next round, she says, will be strategic. That is, she's hoping to sell enough of the company to exit in a couple of years. The pace is too hard to maintain. Generally she's not home until after her baby's asleep; sometimes not until 10:30 at night. Her dream is to cut back, limiting her work to consulting or helping other women get their companies off the ground.

In the meantime, Pamela's banded together with other local female entrepreneurs to discuss gender-specific issues, such as work/life balance and getting VC funding. Their slogan: "No Glass Slipper/No Glass Ceiling."

Harriet Hankin, Sweat Equity

Harriet Hankin, one of the owners of CGI Consulting Group, Inc., took another route entirely. A former human resources executive, she left the rigidity of corporate America to follow her father's advice and be her own boss. Her strategy was to use sweat equity to buy into an existing company in her field, one that does benefits consulting and outsourcing for medium-sized businesses. She earned her way in by giving up a piece of her annual bonuses, which were based on profitability, to buy stock.

After 15 years, Harriet has been able to meet her three goals: have a work/life balance, provide an excellent product, and create a work environment people would enjoy as much as she does. She works hard, she says, but she makes enough time to mother her child and four stepchildren. She also makes sure her employees have the same advantages, a courtesy that pays for itself. When Philadelphia had 13 ice-storm days in one year, she gathered the employees together and asked them to solve the problem of people getting to work. First they carpooled with the four-wheel-drive owners ferrying the others to and from work. Then they got the teenagers among staff children to take care of the little ones in a makeshift daycare center. The key, she believes, is mutual employer-employee respect.

Annette Catino, Sisterhood Is Powerful

Annette Catino, started QualCare, Inc., New Jersey's fifth largest preferred provider organization for health care (PPO), eight years ago with half a million dollars in seed money from the Sisters of the Sorrowful Mother. No kidding. The Sisters owned the hospital whose ambulatory care company Annette administered. It was a timely idea, and Annette had an 18-year history in health-care administration. Annette developed this interest in health care when she worked her way through college and business school as a pharmacist's assistant. She went on from there to working in many parts of the industry, finally ending up working for the Sisters of the Sorrowful Mother.

Health care, of course, is changing so rapidly most of us can't figure out how to fill out our insurance forms. In the early 1990s when New Jersey partially deregulated health care, Annette saw her opportunity. In other deregulated states, PPOs and HMOs filled the new gap between nothing and old-fashioned indemnity health insurance. New Jersey had neither, as the Sisters well knew. So, the physicians, matched the Sisters' half-million-dollar investment in signing on to QualCare themselves.

Annette launched both a PPO and an HMO with that modest $1-million budget, but realized that to grow beyond Morris County, the company would need more capital. So she approached other hospitals and physicians, all of whom she'd done business with in the past, and raised $17 million. While the PPO was turning out a 12 to 14 percent profit, the HMO was barely a break-even proposition. Annette dropped it. Now QualCare is valued by the market at $25 million, serves 400,000 people, represents 13,000 physicians and 80 hospitals. Her shareholders just gave her the go-ahead to raise more money through the venture capital market, which, as a profitable company, she's confident she can do.

Here's where great customer service comes in. I ask Annette the obvious question: What makes QualCare competitive with the nationals, like Blue Cross, who have tons more money and economies of scale in both marketing and fulfillment? "They don't have a passion for the business. I do," Annette explains. She's devoted her life to it.

Annette made a conscious choice not to have children. Working 60 to 80 hours a week, she just didn't see how she would have time for them. Plus, in her business, you need high visibility. She's politically active and travels a great deal to meet with the hospitals and physicians. She took up golf and learned to play competitively in order to network and be "one of the guys." Fortunately, she and her husband agree on their goals.

It's interesting to see how successful female entrepreneurs have so often found idiosyncratic funding solutions that bypass banks and major venture capitalists. It's exciting to imagine just how far women could go if they didn't have this extra hurdle.

The Family Business

Most of us have a sweet image of the family business as a mom-and-pop store with the baby sleeping behind the counter and the oldest at the cash register. Those small businesses, which don't generally grow, can indeed be ideal for family life. They may not make you rich, but they keep the family together in more ways than one. With a large-scale business, however, kids often watch their parents go by in a blur of business preoccupations.

The greatest challenge for the entrepreneurial couple is not to lose the family to the family business. Entrepreneurs, after all, are usually ambitious type-A personalities, plus they face today's grow-or-die pressure. And going into business at the same time as you go into a marriage, says psychologist Kathy Marshack, is like having twins. Marshack, who specializes in consulting with couples running family-owned businesses points out an alarming trend revealed by her research.

> In general these couples are rarely willing to leave for work late; very occasionally they may be late no more than fifteen minutes. However, they are willing to be late getting home one to four times a week by more than an hour each time. As well, these couples are willing to leave home for work more than thirty minutes early one to two times per week. On the other hand, they are willing to leave work early for home only once a month.

Why this happens is at the core of the work/life problem facing people today.

Work brings immediate payoffs, unlike relationships, which take time and togetherness. Also, work moves from crisis to crisis, drawing people in to the collective drama. Eventually, the business takes over, leaving no time for the children, no less for the couple. "As long as these tendencies prevail, entrepreneurial couples are giving themselves very little quality time to confront the inevitable conflicts in their personal relationships," writes Marshack. Her main admonition is never let the business run your life. Which is hard to do if you're a perfectionist or just compelled to do your best.

Let's look at one successful entrepreneurial couple who definitely fit the mold Marshack describes, but who have (and still are) learning from their mistakes.

Bonnie and Rob Gemmell

Bonnie and Rob, both in their 40s, take the long view—about marriage, about work, and about Silicon Valley. And they're entitled. Among the early settlers in this frontier land, they've seen all the changes and permutations. They came as young lovers in 1981 after Rob, a fine arts major, had called Steve Jobs so many times that he finally hired him as a junior industrial designer for Apple Computer. But Bonnie wasn't coming along just for the ride. She saw her opening when a distributor for the Apple II folded. Taking over, she became the first Apple-only distributor. Both of them were now official members of the tiny, crazy community of 20-year-olds building the New Economy and snorting platters of cocaine. It was a long way from Ohio.

To see her in her drapey black dress, Mary Janes, Day-Glo red-framed glasses, it's hard to imagine Bonnie on a farm in the heartland. But she assures me she was raised on a farm. Her broad, ruddy-cheeked face is the only hint of her Midwest past.

There's not a jot of farmhouse in her home. More designer-modern with a retro touch, like the multicolored '60s bar stools at a marble counter. Playful, with a chalkboard wall at the entrance sketched with holiday pumpkins, witches, goblins, and daily schedules. Rob's handsome abstract paintings hang over leather couches. The dog's bed is faux leopard skin. Ohio was never like this.

On the other hand, Bonnie got her entrepreneurial training there. For one thing, her grandfather always told her, the wave of the future is computers. Every day, when he took Bonnie with him to deposit his company's money in the bank, he'd tell her that in the future, they'd never have to see the guy in the bank. It would all be mechanical. As the only child on the farm, she was "the son" whom her father took with him to lay flooring and mend fences, an exposure to work girls rarely get. Dad even called her George, and everyone encouraged her businesses—setting up a vegetable stand by the road, grading pickles, merchandising whatever her family made. "I was one of the boys," Bonnie said, "Nothing could stand in my way."

Nothing did. She made her first $2 million while she was still in her 20s. She sold the distribution business, had Max and Sarah, their two kids, then started another business. This time she and Rob teamed up to produce one of the first upscale catalogues: "The Functional Design Catalogue," featuring beautifully made American products, like the Zippo lighter. "After Lillian Vernon came us!" Bonnie gloats. They were selling out the product line before they could produce the next catalogue.

Bonnie knew about distribution, Rob knew about design. Again, they were both ahead of the curve. So they did another—Home Book—and went from zero to a million in sales the first year. "We were 'can you believe this?'" Then another, which she sold when it wasn't working. Meanwhile, through most of their businesses, Rob was still working with Apple, which financed the businesses at first. And they were raising kids.

"What was life like?" I asked.

"I don't remember," she shot back. "Isn't that sad?"

They were definitely in the fast track; they blew through home in a blur. Bonnie's mother or her friend, Barbara, was there to be "mom" a lot of the time. Otherwise, she and Rob would drop the kids off at 7:30 A.M. and pick them up at 6:00 P.M.

"Why couldn't you control it? You were the bosses," I asked. The answer is just what it always is, just like Rosalind. They became workaholics.

"Fear of delegation, mostly. We couldn't be happy with someone else's imperfect work." Bonnie confesses that she's a perfectionist, Rob more so. "Rob is very driven," she tells me. "He didn't feel the guilt." But Bonnie felt like their life was spiraling out of control "We were go, go, go, go."

Even on weekends she'd work in the store that went with the catalogue because they couldn't get people to work for $10 an hour. She'd take her daughter with her, Rob would take their son.

Of course, they could have hired people to do the work, just not people who would do it as well as they would. So there she was: a millionaire working for $10 an hour.

As if things weren't speedy enough, she was about to become Cher's merchandising director back when Cher was flirting with bringing out a line of products. But then Bonnie's daughter, who was about five years old at the time, wrote her a note: "Mommy No Work No More." She had drawn a picture of a woman with a curved back. As if by voodoo, Bonnie's back went out, big time. For months. She hasn't worked since.

What's that like?

By now it's 7:30 P.M. and Rob's come home. He's as elegant as his paintings, with a slender, sculpted face and buzz-cut silvery hair. His navy blue shirt and slacks hang perfectly on him. He's soft spoken: "Bonnie has been so generous to support the kids and me like this," he says.

Not working, however, is as hard on Bonnie as working had been. From over by the fridge, Bonnie yells, "I'm stifling here."

"When my business gets off, I'm getting out of daily operations and it will be Bonnie's turn," Rob consoles.

The difference between Rob and a lot of other men is that he means it. He and Bonnie are a real team. You can see it in their mutual admiration, in the way they banter, confer, and laugh together, each boasting about the other's talents. Plus, Rob learned too that the fast lane isn't where they want to be.

"I could work all the time," Rob says. "I get sucked into it."

"He wouldn't even eat," Bonnie adds.

"I like to build things. Bonnie and I were never oriented toward money. We always did what we liked. I was an artist, then I went into design. But still, there's always more to build. You have to just stop."

And he did. For six months, Rob took off. The family traveled, Rob read and went mountain biking every day. With this new design start-up, Rob told them he would only work 40 hours a week—which means 50, he slips in. "But it's OK," Rob says. "I won't let my employees work 80 hours a week.

People don't work their best at 80 hours. They burn out. They get resentful if there's no pot of gold at the end of two years."

"I never ask people to work weekends. I encourage them to go home at night. If they're overworking, we ask them if they need more support. You have to institutionalize the fun or it won't happen."

The benefits of sanity are clear to Rob. They're in the service business, he explains, and people have to have good relationships with clients. If you slow things down, they deal with people better and work gets done faster. If you want to keep people long term, you have to give them time.

"I'm not asking for A+ any more. I'm looking for the A–," Rob continues. "Clients are demanding. Their hair is on fire all the time. They want it yesterday. And we're competing against a lot of younger Web-design firms. But we're experienced and can get to the solution faster. We're confident enough to avoid the craziest clients. We're able to articulate why they wouldn't want us to do the project in a week. Great ideas don't happen in front of a computer. You need alone time, self-indulgent time."

So he's *semi*-driven now, chastened by experience and coaxed away from work by the lure of his family. Several times during our interview, he gets up to go into see the children. He delights in their illumination solutions when the electricity goes out suddenly. When is enough enough? I wonder. "You really want to be doing another start-up?"

Rob smiles. "Half the time I feel great about it. A quarter of the time I'm neutral. A quarter of the time I ask myself why am I doing this?"

Bonnie dropped out, if only temporarily, because she couldn't slow down work enough to mother as much as she wanted. Well, almost dropped out: She always has a hand in new projects and trades stocks daily, making a bundle of money. Now Bonnie and Rob are headed in opposite directions. Bonnie's ready to pounce on her new Internet start-up idea, a site where women can learn about investment strategies. They seem perfectly in sync, primed to grow as a couple, to continue their entrepreneurial ventures, to reflect, to enjoy.

I ask them how they each knew the other would be a true partner, an equal in business and family?

"Oh, Rob expected Barbie initially," Bonnie remarks. "But once I proved to him I could make money, I wasn't dependent, he almost dared me to become a millionaire. He loved it that I could. I knew he would. I just knew from the way he loved his grandparents, parents, and siblings. How he respected his mother."

Rob says, "Bonnie is the real entrepreneur in the family." His choice goes back to his mother. "She was pigeonholed back then. But she was a rebel, an independent thinker who raised five kids but was an iconoclast. Something inside me sensed where I wanted to go in life, I couldn't get there alone. I wanted someone who would question me. Bonnie and I are each other's reality check. We're intellectual equals." At this point, Rob looks straight at Bonnie and says, "For better or worse, you're it."

And that's after close to 20 years.

The Bottom Line

Now, more than ever, starting a business is a smart choice for women. Not only is there more money available, better financial training, role models, mentors, and women's networks, but there are a lot of markets young women know best. As with all the entrepreneurs we've met, they must be initiators who follow their passions and strategize carefully, building on their skills, goals, and opportunities. They must know their fields well enough to choose well. They must have the inner control to modify their hours. Some of our entrepreneurs, like Dr. Tamara Sachs, factored family time into their business goals. Others, like Harriet Hankin, use their control to tailor hours to family needs. Rosalind and Pamela work their family life around their terribly long hours, while Annette chose not to have kids. Still others, like Rob and Bonnie, want both and have been consciously trying to move toward balance.

As the author of *The Millionaire Next Door* explains, you're more likely to become affluent if you're self-employed, though most business owners aren't close to being wealthy. Generally, those who get rich have been immensely frugal. They've consciously avoided the affluent lifestyle. And more often than not they made it in workaday businesses like prefab housing, wallboard manufacturing, and pest control—businesses that women are unlikely to have any experience in and are therefore unlikely to start.

The good news, however, is how well women entrepreneurs are doing in spite of the handicaps. All told, entrepreneurship is definitely a move beyond the glass slipper and the glass ceiling.

Work and Family: If You're Thinking of Kids (and Most of You Are)

Assume that the ambitious (and nurturing) young woman described throughout this book has found the nurturing (and ambitious) young man who shares her dreams. If those dreams are of work and family, the two of them face the greatest challenge most couples ever confront—sustaining their love after becoming parents. A child changes everything: your feelings, your finances, your relationship to one another, to your friends, to your work, to your parents, to your dog (who will resent the intrusion), to your third-grade teacher (whom you may not have thought of in years), to your neighbors (whom you may not have noticed before), and to your community (ditto). It's a challenge this generation is both more and less equipped to handle than the last two.

The most obvious difficulty for Gen XX'ers as parents is the absurdly expanded workday, which leaves barely enough time for dinner, no less dinner and playing with the baby, calling the pediatrician, bathing and feeding the baby, exchanging the defective crib, singing lullabies to the baby, returning your best friend from college's call of last month, and sending a thank-you note to your boss for the silver sippy cup. And parenting gets more time-consuming the older kids get. One mother of teens explains this phenomenon with three words: "drinking, driving, and drugs." However, the time bind can be managed if couples are psychologically prepared. And here's the real challenge. Not only does this new generation have few models of work-family balance, they have few models of lasting marriages.

More young adults today are the product of divorced parents than any previous generation, which almost certainly means they're at greater statistical risk of divorce themselves. To say the least. In her memoir, *Prozac Nation,* Elizabeth Wurtzel describes her inability to cope with life or relationships in terms of this uncommonly common familial background:

> It's not like I was beaten regularly, it's not like I was raised by wolves, it's not like I'm an exceptional case: I am just one of a whole generation of children of divorce whose parents didn't handle their personal affairs very well, and who grew up damaged.

Admittedly, Wurtzel's "damage" is far more extreme than average, but there does seem to be a generational fault line underneath an even greater commitment to the ideal of lasting marriage than the boomers had. The problem, as divorce researcher Judith Wallerstein puts it, is that "they don't have a clue how to make their relationships work."

I would add, *especially after they have a child.* Dinks (dual-income no kids) have far less stress on their relationships if they're both agreed on not having children. After all, they simply continue doing what they do: both working, sharing the few home chores, deciding together on leisure activities, and going off alone when they each feel like it and their jobs permit. Maybe they're just not kid people or maybe they can't imagine how they would parent and continue living the lives they enjoy. As one such disinclined male put it: "All of my friends [with kids] had lives that were so hectic they couldn't talk uninterrupted. They no longer had the time, money, or energy to do all the things we used to do."

Unfortunately, sometimes one partner feels this way and the other never knew it. The wife of the above-quoted man, who found herself in such a position, writes:

> 'How,' friends asked incredulously, 'could you get married and not have talked about having children?' It was easy. I was certain that he knew what I needed. He was confident that I knew what he wanted.

Clearly, this is an impasse that can be avoided if you make your dreams for the future explicit. Even if neither of you is sure what you want, you can at least agree on whether children are a possibility. Scary as that may feel, it's better than finding out later.

Dinks are a good place to begin a discussion on becoming parents because having kids is truly a choice today: No one thinks you're a freak if you don't have them, although parents may put the pressure on for a while. What's more, most partners who decide on parenthood started out as Dinks and probably shared some of the perceptions of Mr. Dink above. Generally, however, they think, "not us, we'll do better." And they will, if they've discussed how their parenting life will be. If not, one of them may find herself with a baby and a partner who, as it turns out, didn't know she expected him to take care of the baby in addition to admiring it.

Same-sex couples rarely have this problem because they don't have the homemaker/provider roles foisted upon them and generally they both parent and continue working. As one gay father put it, "Babywise, we each do what we're good at." Unmarried parents, at least those who have planned to become parents, have usually given a great deal of thought to their choice because they know they have to support themselves and parent at the same time. Ironically, heterosexual couples are more likely than same-sex couples or singles to become parents without having planned how to stay financially viable, do real parenting, and continue relating to one another in a civilized if not amorous fashion. It's easier to get lost in fantasies when a partner is there to cover a multitude of pesky details. However rudimentary the discussion, couples need to articulate their ideas about work and family as early and as candidly as they can.

Listen to one couple as they reveal their thoughts on the subject for the first time: Renato Ghio, 28, does computer graphics for his living. But what he loves is playing guitar in a hard rock band. "Ideally," he explains, "I'd like to raise my own kids. All my brothers and their wives work, and they manage. I also want a 50/50 relationship but music doesn't allow for being around. So I'll give it five years. Then if I can't call my own shots in music, I'll move on to other things. Like my own computer graphics business."

His girlfriend, Alicia Damia, worked at a newspaper for two years and hated it, mostly because she had to work such long hours. Now she's studying for a second B.A. at the University of Connecticut, this time in psychology so she can have more control over her work. Her father is her model. In business for himself in a small town, he was able to practice law, come home for lunch every day, and be home in time to help make supper. "He loved family life. That's the way I want to live."Although she adores her own homemaker mom, she doesn't want her life: "I could never let my husband support me. I'd be too guilty."

Renato and Alicia haven't worked out the details, but they are in sync and aware of the planning involved in being working parents. Both have fall-back plans, and some experience in what they do. And both are willing to sacrifice to make time for a family. Including, on Renato's part, giving up music if he doesn't "make it big." And if he does, he has a parenting standard he holds himself to. The two also have some models of work/life balance to help them shape their own family life.

While these partners have a good chance of blending kids and work, Alicia tells me that most of her college girlfriends have simply written off children. As we've seen, when you're in your early twenties just setting out, it may seem impossible to work, play, and also parent. So you eliminate the idea of children, which is so remote it hardly seems real anyway. But since that idea has a way of creeping up on you, it makes sense to figure out how to accommodate children *if* you do have any.

While a lot of people really don't want children, most apparently do. Some just take it on faith that children are worth having. Others have a surprisingly clear idea of the incomparable joy of bonding with a new baby which, though often not apparent from the outside in, fills the very air you breathe with love and a melting tenderness for just about everyone—since everyone, you suddenly realize, was once just as brand-new and perfect and innocent and trusting as that most remarkable of creatures, your infant. But few aspiring parents realize how a baby also sets the clock of your life on "urgent" and ticks you breathlessly through your now sleepless days and nights. This can take a toll on love. So if you and your beloved are thinking about children, get a close-up idea of life *en famille*, particularly of a family whose life you admire. Failing that, read on carefully.

What It's Like to Become a Parent: The Micro-View

If everything's gone well, the glow from that first few weeks with a newborn stands out in memory forever as an almost divine time where you taste the nectar of complete belonging—to one another and this child and even this world. Not only does everyone suddenly soften and smile at the sight of the new family, offer compliments, warmth, and genuine delight the likes of which you may never have encountered before, but with a baby in your arms, you're suddenly *like* everyone: multiplying, tending babies, assuming the most common kind of adult status to rear the young, claiming a new kind of stake in the future. As Prince Charles put it after watching Diana give birth, "It's such a very grown-up thing to do." Not that the glow of parental love, the new adult feelings, or the sensuous pleasures of baby flesh necessarily sustain the parents' love, as the prince along with half of the American married population well knows. Half of all marriages end in divorce, and a very large percentage of those end when the children are young.

If this depiction seems like a quick descent into hell, parenthood can be. After the ecstatic initial weeks of celebration and awe, the crowds thin, the flow of gorgeously wrapped baby clothes cease, the happy father often returns to work, his two-week "vacation" being over, and you're left—loopy from sleeplessness, the house in shambles, your body barely functioning, and the baby, now fully awake and of this world screaming at the top of his or her Olympian lungs. Maybe your mom is there, which is often a mixed blessing, throwing the two of you into a proximity you haven't experienced since your adolescence. When the father of the child (your too-often-absent husband) comes home at night, you suddenly find yourself living in a complicated commune of four.

In her novel, *Motherhood Made a Man Out of Me*, Karen Karbo describes how "dinner now was us standing in the middle of the kitchen, eating whatever straight from the refrigerator: cheese, peanut butter on celery, Nestle chocolate-chip cookie dough straight from its yellow tube." Racking her tired brain for a name she was trying to remember, she realizes that she could ask him "except I was irritated with Lyle, was always irritated with Lyle these days, and would punish him by not asking him when I got home."

At best, the transformation is breathtakingly dramatic; at worst, tempers flare for no discernible reason. He may have called six times to see how you and the baby and your mother were, but he wasn't there, moving through the strange aqueous atmosphere of languid baby rhythms—an hour or more to feed, an hour to soothe—punctuated by the fierce needs of the newly born at any time of the day or night.

While dad's clock is back on diurnal time, yours continues in hours differentiated only by whether the baby is asleep. Sleep comes to signify night, at any time. Like life under the sea, day and outside, the business of work, of going and coming, seem far away, Although five months later, the baby will usually sleep through the night, the feeling lingers. Listen to Harriet Lerner, in her book *The Mother Dance*:

> During that first year of Matthew's life, I moved in the world like a sleepwalker. Sometimes I blamed this on Matthew's atypically slow development and on Steve's [her husband's] denial of it, but

> these factors were only a fragment of the broader picture. At a subconscious level, I worried about what was happening to me and where it all would lead, now that I was a mother. I felt as if an invisible force field had pushed Steve back into his previously normal life, while I was being pushed in the opposite direction. The force field was everywhere—in the structure and policies of our work system, in the unspoken attitudes of colleagues, in the cultural traditions over generations, in the roles and rules of the families we came from, in the outposts in our heads, and in the very air we breathed.

That passage describes parental life for dual-income professionals, both psychologists, twenty-five years ago. But it's not terribly different today. As determined as Lerner and her husband were to remain equal partners and as conscious of that commitment as two psychologists at the height of the feminist movement could be, they "did just great—until the first baby arrived."

Dad's point of view is concisely summed up in a letter to the advice columnist in *Dads* magazine. Although it's a composite of several letters, it's typical enough to be in the premier issue:

> I'm a 33-year-old new dad with a 1-year-old. I'm finding that my wife, who stays at home, now, has suddenly sprouted a whole new group of friends—women who are in her playgroup with their infants. But she increasingly has little or no interest in my friends, who are mostly from work. It's getting to the point where she is telling me that she has to simplify her (and our) lives, and I need to outgrow those old friends. I resent that, but of course my marriage and child are the most important things to me.

This new dad now lives a daily life that is so different from his wife's, the divide between them keeps expanding just when the baby might have brought them closer. Even more troubling, neither understands why it's happening.

In our post-feminist era, and here comes the second disadvantage of this generation, women aren't necessarily conscious of having been or wanting to remain the equal partners they were at the outset of their relationships. Jennifer Kushell, the forceful leader of Young Entrepreneurs Association, talked to me about how she and her fiancé fantasize about a house on a lake where they can be with the kids they plan to have. But that's a fantasy about having enough money so they can both take time off. They don't have a fantasy about how they'll parent and work if they still need to earn money. They've not talked about who will work and how much.

Young women now take equal partnership for granted, meaning they can lose it more easily than their mothers did. Nor do they have the voice of their generation cheering them along, offering advice and guidelines. Most couples today are on their own when they make this profound transition, which makes it that much harder.

Simply put, at times motherhood can feel like a natural disaster. Not only are you dealing with a "crying, pooping larvae," as Greg so baldly put it, or by year one, with "an entropy machine," as my husband liked to say. But an avalanche of expectations come crashing down, expectations you didn't even know you believed in, ones the culture gets suddenly vocal about.

"What do you mean you're going back to work in two months? You're putting your baby in daycare! You're not breast-feeding! You're making [sic] James stay home once a week to take care of the baby?"

This could be your mother, your best friend, the pediatrician, the elevator operator, the grocery clerk, or the author of an article in *Gurgle* magazine. It's still the culture's view that good mothers devote their every waking moment to their child, sacrificing anything else she may have been, wanted, or needed. The attitude is out there; it will find you. You have to be prepared, or else other people's attitudes will dominate or confuse your own.

New mothers are often tigers, ready to slash at any danger to baby. But they also feel more vulnerable than ever before, suddenly in charge of the survival of a tiny infant who, as

Anne Lamott put it, doesn't come with an owner's manual. Few people without children know how frightening parenting can be, the panic new parents feel when a child has a fever or won't stop crying or doesn't develop according to the book. Or confusing. Forget Disney. Rent the video of Nancy Savoca's *The 24 Hour Woman*, the aforementioned film about two hard-working Gen XX'ers becoming parents. Take a good look, a deep breath, and get ready for reality.

Sometimes new parenthood goes swimmingly, but, as Lerner notes:

> When you add the stresses of interrupted sleep, unruly postpartum hormones, the endless demands of babies, the mother's predictable loss of libido, and all the feelings that get stirred up from one's own past, it's amazing that all marriages don't fly apart by the time of the baby's first birthday. Surely it's no surprise that intimacy in the couple's relationship is typically the first thing to go.

If the father of the child isn't "in it" along with the mother, if he's off at work for ten hours a day, then he may fill that former intimacy with greater immersion in work, which is a far simpler emotional endeavor than marriage and parenthood. Especially if he isn't around enough to become as much of a baby expert as his wife.

Sometimes the mother feels like the lucky one to be alone with the baby. But if the couple isn't prepared psychologically (armed is more like it) that won't prevent them from diverging as he strides along in his work while she creates a different kind of life, one with different rhythms, pleasures, and often with different friends.

As mutually satisfying—even interesting—as this arrangement may feel for a while, in the long run, parents may drift apart so much that they lose empathy for the others' problems and desires. They may see life from their now distinct points of view as in, "Why doesn't she understand how hard I'm working to support her and the baby now or how much more scared I am of not doing well at work? She's just baby-crazed."

Or (her view) "Why doesn't he get how much harder it is to take care of a baby all day than go to work? All he can think about is work."

And they'll both be as right as they are righteous; their fury at the other's lack of understanding growing stronger every time they fight about money (since expenses are mounting), housework (since he now expects her to do it all), in-laws (who now demand more frequent visits), and sex (which they can barely remember).

If dad is "in it" with mom, it's easier, but hardly tension-free. Maria Hinojosa, urban affairs correspondent for CNN, wrote a book about it after her son, Raul Ariel, was born. Her husband, Germán, a painter, was as involved as she, which was hard for a Mexican-American with "mamacita" expectations of herself:

> Oh, the joys of co-parenting. Before, women ran the house and that was that. Now everything had to be debated and agreed on in conjunction and a mother's intuition had to be constantly explained to fathers. It was hard enough just digging deep enough to find out what my mother's intuition was. I knew it had to be there. Somewhere. But now I had to give reasons for everything I did to my baby's father. Ay. More work.

Just like her more traditional counterparts, she and Germán also had to fight for their intimacy:

> By the end of the evening we were so exhausted, we weren't up for long, intimate discussions about things. We talked about work and schedules and about Raul Ariel. Our conversations during the day revolved around my calling and doing military checkup of what was going on in my household. Did he sleep? How long? What did he have for lunch? Did he play with any friends? How long was he at the park? "One day it would be nice if you asked about how I was doing," Germán said to me one afternoon when I was calling from the car on our way to do a shoot. "I do care about you, honey. I love you," I said and then paused. "Anyway can you have Patty make the chicken for Raul Ariel's dinner. I'll see

you later." The space between Germán and me was getting thicker and icier as every day went by.

It took them several major arguments, negotiations, and a lot of mutual understanding before they found each other again. But they did, and with as much passion as existed before, even after a second child. The challenge is how to find one another again after you change, because a child will change you in ways you cannot anticipate. And continue to change you, need you, and create family crises.

It's not just babies who make parenting feel like a full-time job. Remember the partner in Galia Swetschinski's law office who quit to take care of her teenage children? "The consuming nature of parenting shifts," says Ellen Sklars Shapiro, mother of a 9- and 11-year-old. "It doesn't lessen." As she describes parenting older children, "it's no longer about basic plumbing and loving. There's much more emotional and social processing, there's homework, school issues, and all those after-school activities." Donna Bohling, mother of a 12-, 19-, and 22-year-old offers one image that captures those increasing demands: "Walking the floor with a crying baby at night is hard. Walking the floor waiting for your teenager to come home is agony."

Fortunately, and here's the good news, this generation is better equipped than previous generations to provide adequate parenting time while both parents also flourish at work.

Real Options: Parenting Life in the Macro

Although couples today are often on their own making the leap into parenthood, they're not nearly as constrained by economics or custom as previous generations. Mom *or* dad can stay home; both can work part time, both can work full time, grandma can live with them, the baby can go to daycare, or come to work with dad (easier if he's the boss) and no one is going to call the Child Welfare Hotline. And as we'll see in the portraits that follow, couples are taking advantage of their options, making the rules as they go along.

That is, many are. Many more certainly would if they just knew how and were able to figure out a way around long and rigid work schedules. First, however, they need to understand a few hidden, and not so hidden, costs.

Kids are expensive. According to the Department of Agriculture, it costs $160,000 to raise one to the age of 17. A third of that goes to housing, 10 percent to childcare, 8 percent to educational costs, 7 percent to health care. And don't forget the bunk beds, bikes, boom boxes, braces, SAT courses, car insurance, and other essentials of child rearing. Then there's that horrifying post-18 college tuition money: Let's add another, oh, $100,000 or so. When couples have babies, money disappears. Even faster for single parents, who spend as much on children, but use a lot more of their income to do it.

The immense advantage in parenting today stems from women's new earning power. Not only can they pay for child costs more easily, but they can stay closer to the people they were before they had children. So a woman's potential to earn brings that immense advantage not only for the woman but for the couple. It means they can figure out how to parent based on their own desires, not on roles assigned according to his far greater earning power, her parents, the movies, society, or just plain guilt.

No matter how much boomers would have liked to parent equally, employers didn't allow it. Remember how Middlebury College dismissed my predecessor because she had a child. In most marriages back then, women weren't the sole earners and if both partners worked, women rarely earned as much as men. Now, they have access to good jobs at good pay.

Even if a woman chooses to drop out of work to raise her kids, she knows she has a choice. The process is, or should be, a negotiation, so both partners accept what they're doing as a couple. And just as important, agree to change their deal if it doesn't work.

Earning so much more than previous generations, contemporary women are generally less tempted to forego their work to take up "professional mothering." They also have more money to buy quality childcare and the leverage at work to negotiate for the flexibility they need as parents. If women do cut back at work, they are more likely to have the skills to rejoin the labor force at the appropriate level. Unlike life among the boomers, both partners today are more likely to respect her earning power and the importance of her work. No matter how much we hate to believe that money affects love, the dollars and cents in contemporary relationships add up to more parity between partners, making marriage more democratic than it was when ideology alone drove the desire for equality.

Why, then, do so many couples who start out as dual-career partners become traditional parents? Why has the parenting picture not changed even though women now have the economic power to change it? Why do mothers play superwoman, doing everything at home and work, or drop out of work to do his share of the parenting as well as her own?

In her book *Unbending Gender,* legal scholar Joan Williams analyzes Deborah Fallows' "choice" to drop her linguistics career to stay home with her children, as described in Fallows' book, *A Mother's Work.* First, Fallows switched to part-time work, but that didn't help: "I missed meetings; I bowed out of last-minute crises; I wouldn't travel; I couldn't stay late. In short, I was not the kind of employee who could be counted on in a crunch."

Now, much of the reason why Fallows was so unavailable for work was that her husband, James Fallows, a well-known Washington journalist, was so immersed in *his* work: "Jim did what he could, pitching in when he was home. But the simple fact was that he wasn't able to be home very much. The tone was set by the workaholics . . . who made it seem wimpish to leave work before the dead of night."

Eventually, Fallows made some sacrifice by trading his White House correspondent job to become the editor of *U.S. World and News Report.* But Deborah Fallows gave up her career, moving the family to where Fallows would assume his lesser (though hardly inconsequential) position.

Variations on this story are repeated millions of times each year among couples in which she is as well trained as he and worked with ambition and pleasure until the baby was born, which is happening later and later in women's lives, after they've had substantial work experience. The truth is that what often passes for a mother's "choice" to stay home with her child are the unexamined assumptions and expectations that lead women to respect male ambition more than their own. Sometimes they tell themselves they just aren't as ambitious. But let's say a wife is only half as ambitious as her husband. Why isn't she acting on her lesser ambition and sacrificing proportionately—if they're going to be really fair.

A woman will generally ask more sacrifice of herself than of her husband, both because "that's the way it is" and because she (not he) fears being a bad mother by pursuing her own goals or using childcare. In Fallows' case, she didn't believe in childcare, although her experiences with it were very positive and her children liked it. Instead of profiting from her experience or researching the very positive reports about childcare, she passively accepted the view that mother is better than any alternative. And by the way, yet another huge study of the childcare question was published in March 1999 in the *Journal of Developmental Psychology:* Elizabeth Harvey, a University of Massachusetts psychologist studied the mental health of 6,000 children and determined that those in childcare do not suffer any ill effects. Few women calculate the extent to which fear and guilt affect their mothering choices.

Now, to be brutally honest building a career can be hard, especially if you haven't chosen life-friendly work. Creating an identity in the world, after all, is the greatest existential challenge. Isn't that why everyone has fantasies of moving to Tahiti, where they can live a completely natural life among natives, whom they assume don't worry about identity? Might that not be why professional motherhood can seem so alluring to some formerly well-employed women? Poof! You're a mother, therefore you are. No questions, identity problems, struggle to perform, to be acknowledged, to fail and try again, to find the right niche. The Tahiti fantasy is still an acceptable one for all women, though not for many men. And some women succumb, no doubt aided by applause from family.

Mothering—parenting—is an immensely profound and, yes, even sacred experience. In ultimate human terms, it's more important than, say, chairing the Securities Exchange Commission. But it's not a job. Nor, usually, is it a full identity, not in today's world. Childcare is a full-time job, at which some people excel. They get the benefits of work while also helping children grow. Nurturing your own children is quite different, as different as the relationship with your husband versus your male colleagues. You may ask yourself, why is it I can have a perfectly reasonable discussion with Andy down the hall about next year's office budget, but my husband and I can't plan a vacation budget without a fight? Work identities, work relationships, and work are just different from personal life.

We deliberately raise children to have work identities, to find out what they like to *do* in the world. And most of us have work identities in the first phase of adulthood, identities we've cultivated and trained for. So to give them up or trade them in for a purely private identity can be dangerous. We may lose an important part of ourselves, not to speak of the pleasures of colleagues, a paycheck, and approval for work well done. That doesn't mean we should work so much that there's no time left for private pleasures. Or that there aren't people who are truly domestic creatures, flowering in their private roles (hobbyists, putterers, and volunteer types). But most people need both.

Right now, couples hover between the old, constrained this-is-how-parenting-must-be and the new free-form family life where both partners make conscious choices and accept the need for sacrifices in order to raise children. Some do very well; others straddle both the old and the new, conflicted but managing. The couples who do best with free-form family life are usually those in which women ask their men to make family-friendly career choices and changes comparable to their own.

OK, not so simple. If it were, women would just do it. Instead, many women still fear pressuring the men too much, asking too much of them, going against tradition. They fear losing them. The irony is, as countless psychologists concur, treating men as equals keeps them as intimates. Sacrificing for his ambition is ultimately alienating to him because she has to suppress an important part of her self to do it, the self he initially connected to. Hence, the phenomenon of husband leaving wife of 20 years to marry a go-getter from the office.

Going traditional *is* easier at first: Both partners know what's expected. No one has to dig beyond their most culturally reinforced responses or risk angering anyone. Holding out for a real negotiated partnership usually means more strain up front, but more gain later on.

Psychologist Leah Fisher, director of the Center for Work and Family in Berkeley, California, explains that new parents feel they have no choice but for the wife to scale back while the husband tries to earn more. But that's not true. There are no *easy* choices. He may not be able to climb the professional ladder quickly while the baby is small or a parent is ill. But if he can accept that delay, he can cut back just as she can. The couple, she says, must look at their values, goals, and priorities to make the hard choices. Also, as Fisher explains, more and more professional decisions belong to the marriage, not to the individual. One partner can't make a unilateral decision to move when the other's job, the kids' schools, the support of the extended family nearby have to be considered.

Just a few decades ago, developmental psychologist Eric Ericson made famous his notion that a woman kept her life unformed in order to mold to the man's life. How unfortunate that women, who have worked so hard to "form" their lives, still feel compelled to act as if they must "mold" to their men's. Fisher believes that it doesn't matter who earns more. Partners today are equals and must negotiate so that both can be fulfilled. The negotiation's the tricky part because it's predicated on women's finding and raising their voices, then both partners living with the consequences of real change.

Example. In fixing up our new home during an especially busy work time for both my husband and myself, we split the decorating tasks that would normally have been mine. This took some courage on my part to insist that he take the time to shop and to accept his choices in curtains and chairs. It was hard for both of us, but we met our deadlines and are happy with our new home, curtains and all.

I told this story to a reporter from the *Boston Globe* who was interviewing me about shared parenting. She said, "You let him do *what*?" She was both hysterical and horrified at the idea of relinquishing decorating control to a man. Of course, he did it his own way, refusing to work with the convenient Princess and the Pea curtain store, settling for a lesser-known but more gender-neutral source. Also, our home tends more toward Pier One than I usually like and our selections didn't always harmonize, but who cares when we're sitting in wicker rocking chairs (his purchase) on our porch, our daughter in his lap, watching the sun go down. Lest this seem too easy, it's because decoration isn't all that fraught. Segue to another more complicated situation where negotiation rarely works as well.

Amy Lowe, the head of a New York City literary agency, negotiated what seemed like a great deal with her husband, then a senior editor at one of the larger publishing companies. They agreed that two high-powered publishing jobs were making their parenting life too hard, both of them working a million hours, both bringing work home. So he quit to become the designated at-home parent while working as a free-lance editor and writing a weekly news column about publishing. The problem, according to Amy, is that although "he does a lot, it's nothing compared to mothering."

As she describes it, he's organized about work, which he does from 4:00 or 5:00 A.M. until 7:00, when the children get up, then rushes madly through breakfast while also making their lunches, clearing the table, finding boots, homework, then flies out the door with them to school.

Amy leaves home before they get up because she can't stand his morning routine: the rush, the hair left uncombed, the trip permission slip forgotten. On weekends and in the evening, she does what he neglects. "Otherwise," she says, "who's buying new shoes for starting first grade? Who's talking to the teacher to discuss a problem? Who's making play dates? Who's doing the laundry?"

"Can't laundry be on his 'to do,' list?" I ask.

"It is," she protests. "I've even given him folding lessons, but he'll throw a load in the washer where it sits all day or he'll leave it in the dryer so it's all wrinkled by the time I get home from work."

Later, I ask my husband to explain her husband's behavior. Without a moment's reflection, he says, "He doesn't want to do it. I understand perfectly."

My husband understands because, like Amy's husband, parenting brought with it infinitely more domestic work than he ever imagined himself doing and certainly more than he saw his own father doing. Like a lot of male parents who've gallantly accepted their responsibilities, they still struggle with the role. Women, on the other hand, are trained from toddlerhood to play house. Given this grand transition we've undertaken, we're not doing badly.

When Men Become Dads

More parity in earnings goes a long way toward helping couples maintain their intimacy and equality. So does the changing male character. Despite the workaholic economy, a lot of young men today are determined to eschew materialism for a richer personal life. The younger they are, the more determined: 81 percent of female high school seniors and 72 percent of males said marriage and family life were "extremely important," an enormous jump from just a decade ago according to the University of Michigan's School for Social Research. The Radcliffe Public Policy Institute found that 70 percent of men aged 20 to 29 were willing to give up pay to spend more time with their children; 63 percent said they'd spend an extra hour with their families if they had it. Our culture is filled with "dads" right now. Being a dad is cool. Dads are trying harder.

That may be why I've been seeing a lot of books with titles like: *Zen and the Art of Fatherhood* and *The New Father Book:*

What Every Man Needs to Know to Be a Good Dad. Two new magazines just came on the market in time for Father's Day 2000: the aforementioned *Dads,* with Cal Ripken Jr. on the cover, and *Dad's Magazine,* sporting a picture of Tiger Woods and his father in a tight embrace. *Dads'* editor, Eric Garland, the former senior editor of *Money* magazine, says his publication seeks to help men find balance in their lives. Timely, I think, Garland's shift from balancing the checkbook to balancing life.

You wouldn't have seen these books when your parents were becoming parents because no one expected much of fathers. As witness, only 12 percent of men reported a work-life conflict in 1977, while 84 percent did in 1994—both because they were working less and because dads didn't have a lot of parenting to do.

Even worse back then, low expectations meant fathers were dismissed as irrelevant bumblers—by the courts, the workplace, the psychologists, the hospitals, the pediatricians, La Leche League, the parent handbooks, and the schools. Too often, they still are. In 1999, to take one of a thousand possible examples, a Maryland state trooper who was refused paternity leave to care for his new infant daughter and her older sister while his wife was in the hospital with postpartum complications was finally awarded $375,000 in damages. But look what he had to go through because his boss didn't believe men could be primary caretakers.

Fortunately, attitudes are changing fast and these new fathering books are one of the culture's ways of helping men catch up. Women need to help, too, by respecting and *expecting* men's hands-on, 50/50 (that's attitude, not a time count) fathering.

Psychologist Francine M. Deutsch makes this argument in her book, *Halving It All,* but notes how women frequently excuse men from child-rearing by telling themselves that men don't have as strong a need to nurture, that they're more ambitious, or that they (women) are better parents. Men, who understandably succumb to the cultural pressure to define themselves by their work, and who are also sometimes afraid of parenting, not only tacitly agree with their wives' view of them as poor parenting material, but they reinforce it, as Deutsch explains, by

- passive resistance (I don't see the mess. I don't hear the baby cry)
- strategic incompetence (I can't get the baby to stop crying)
- inferior standards (so the diaper's backward, big deal)
- use of praise (Jenny, I really admire your patience with the kids)

The gender pressures to conform to nurturing mom and high-earning dad are always there. Deutsch concluded that parents who remained equal refused to submit to those pressures; the women felt entitled to men's childcare, fought for it when necessary, and in some cases, wouldn't agree to have children otherwise.

Sometimes men become involved dads just because their wives insist. As one dad in Deutsch's study said, "I couldn't get away with [not parenting] with Janet. She would hand me the baby and head out the door. I guess I'm kind of amazed that women let their husbands get away with it." Me, too. But they do. Which may ultimately harm men as much as it harms children.

When men give into the system, relinquishing their fathering desires, they often feel such shame, they shut themselves off or even leave the marriage because they cannot bear the pain. If divorced, they may cut off contact with the children instead of being a partial parent. One women who, as an adult, tracked down her long-absent father, asked why he had fled from his children. "Don't you understand how ashamed I am? Don't you understand that I feel like a failure," he told her. Even when he was dying, he couldn't face his children. His new wife asked them to just stay away.

How many stories do we know about absent fathers? About fathers who just weren't there? Susan Faludi's *Stiffed*, her moving examination of men's anger and alienation in today's America, turns up tales of distant fathers, "spectral" fathers, and violent, broken father-son connections; of unfathered men who flock to organizations like the Promise Keepers or who hang out stoned after high school, aimless and jobless.

In one study of dads lost to work, entitled, "Why Executives Lose Their Balance," author Joan Kofodimus quotes a bewildered wife saying, "Eventually I no longer relied on him to be around. But when he came home he'd feel excluded. He was angry at me and the kids because he felt we excluded him." This dad didn't start out saying to himself, I just won't be around. He, too, had standards for himself as a father. But he just couldn't make the compromises or bear learning how to be a parent. So, little by little, he withdrew.

Kofodimus points out that many high-achieving men pursue mastery at work but are also masters at avoiding intimacy, which is what child rearing and family life are all about. Many are uncomfortable with the expression of emotions and the vulnerability and dependency involved in intimacy. Work focuses attention outside oneself into "safe" areas such as goals like the last meeting or the next project. Idleness brings an uncomfortable confrontation with the inner self. But avoiding intimacy, this kind of man can preserve his ideal self-image rather than accepting emotions, which, by definition, include one's dark side, the feelings of loneliness, guilt, regret. But lonely at the top, he will feel them nonetheless.

What may be sadder than men's withdrawal from intimate parenting is the way women exclude them from it. Research by Ross Parke, a psychologist of fathering, shows that the mother's attitude toward her partner's fathering is a better predictor of his involvement than his own desires. Her attitude actually overrides his own, either boosting or destroying his confidence as a father. Most men had less exposure to babies than women and may need more help in handling them—but not from Mom, who more often than not controls his fathering. A lot of hospitals now offer dad training. As one study done by researchers Jane Dickie and

Sharon Gerber concluded, dads with just eight classes to their credit, "touched, held, looked at their infants more and were more responsive" than dad's with no training. With some confidence building, they can reassure their child's mother that they are perfectly competent.

A news article charmingly entitled, "Boot Camp for Dads: Cuddle That Baby, Maggot," documented the success of a three-hour seminar given by veteran dads (who bring their babies) for soon-to-be dads. Not only do the now-dads show the new-dads how to diaper, soothe, and burp, but they share feelings and anticipate problems. They tell the "recruits" to spend four consecutive hours alone with their infants. "It'll be horrible but you'll learn a lot." This program spread to 30 hospitals and boasts 2,000 graduates. Only two gazillion more to go.

What's amazing is that even without training, exposure, or explicit encouragement, most men do bond powerfully with their newborns. Ross Parke and his colleagues observed fathers who had not been to birthing classes or to the delivery room (yes, many still decline) and found that just like their more gung-ho counterparts, "dads were just as interested as moms in their babies." They also showed the same biological responses as moms did (heart and respiratory rate increase) when their infant was distressed.

The bottom line is that even when men want to be involved fathers, there's an awful lot of pressure not to be, not least of all from their wives who often undermine their fathering by just taking over, acting like *the* expert, or even criticizing their parenting. In almost every one of these new books about fathering, male authors say the key is for men to have time alone with their babies. As long as mom is around, her tendencies toward maternal control will overwhelm his paternal instinct. If moms want their husbands to be parenting partners, they'll have to respect their fathering style and refrain from criticizing their efforts, no matter how awkward.

Awkward, reluctant, or untrained as dads may be, don't imagine that paternal instinct isn't there. It may get stifled or suppressed, but it's always there according to Kyle Pruett, the foremost expert on the subject of fatherhood.

Pruett, a psychiatrist at Yale and director of the major longitudinal study of men as (accidental) primary caregivers, recently wrote his second book on the subject of men's paternal instinct. In *Fatherneed*, he argues that whether men acknowledge it or not, they are as strongly drawn to their babies as mothers are and, lactation aside, are as equally necessary to their babies' healthy development.

Pruett's point of departure is a review of developmental research proving that "children are born with a drive to find and connect to their fathers, and their fathers have the internal capacity, the *instinct*, to respond." They nurture differently, and in doing so, provide an invaluable alternative model of love for children. They play with kids more and with fewer toys or entertainment. They encourage more exploration and independence, teach frustration tolerance and task mastery, and discipline less with shame and disappointment than with real-life consequences.

So what does fathering look like? Well, in my home, my husband rolls on the floor with our daughter for, say, twenty minutes of tickling, roughhousing, and silliness while I'm more likely to play a card game with her. When she refused to put on her jacket in 45 degree weather, he took her to preschool without one, muttering as I gasped by the door, that children don't get colds from the weather and she won't make the same mistake again (which she didn't). Of course, these are generalizations. Some fathers are more conventionally maternal than moms, and vice versa.

Whatever a father's parenting style, Pruett emphasizes that fathering must be daily work—taking kids to school, bandaging cuts, knowing their friends, giving them baths—because daily tending *is* intimacy with children. Going to the circus is not. And children know the difference. By six weeks, infants will calm more easily to a father's voice, if well known, than a mother's. They anticipate the different maternal and paternal styles with different postures and biological responses. By a year, they have less separation anxiety if fathers are involved. Not only are they more exploratory and better at school, but they exhibit more control over their impulses.

When fathers are the primary caregivers, dads bond and nurture as adequately as mothers do. And when they are single fathers, they express the same concerns that single mothers do. According to Pruett, studies have actually quantified "fatherneed" by showing that children who feel close to their fathers are twice as likely as those who don't to enter college or find stable employment, one-fourth as likely to have a teen birth or spend time in jail, and half as likely to experience depression. Of course, many of these father-hungry children also suffer because of poverty and mothers so overworked they cannot parent well. Still, the numbers attest to how much fathers bring to children's lives.

And what do fathers get out of their involvement? Involved fathers are less likely to die young, to abuse drugs, to spend time in the hospital, and they are more likely to report a sense of well-being. In fact, men who do housework and childcare are not only healthier, they are less likely to be overwhelmed by their wives' emotions. Another plus: They're more likely to stay happily married. As psychologist Robert Frank says, "Two parents who are equally involved in the care of their children are closer as a couple. Not only do they have common interests (their children), they also develop better ways of communicating with each other about other topics."

On some level, men know this. They want a family life.

James Levine, coauthor of *Working Fathers* and director of the Fatherhood project at the Family and Work Institute in New York, says that the dirty little secret among men is how torn they are between work and family, how guilty they are for not spending more time with their children because they're so worried about making money. A recent study by the Family and Work Institute corroborated Levine's insight by showing that employed fathers experienced as much work/family conflict as employed mothers did. Psychologist and fathering expert Jerrold Lee Shapiro found very similar feelings in his study:

> Of the more than eight hundred fathers I interviewed, an overwhelming majority reported feeling guilty about their limited con-

> tact with their children. They truly "regretted" the loss of that time. Their wives agreed. Many believed the children often suffered from a "daddy deficit."

Most of the children he interviewed said they wanted more time with their fathers.

The difference between mothers' and fathers' guilt, says Levine, is that men don't talk about it and don't believe they have the option to cut back or to negotiate their work schedules. Instead of asking if they can come in an hour late on Wednesdays so they can volunteer at their child's school, they assume the answer is no. In today's labor market, however, the answer's often "sure, go ahead." As we've seen, bosses sometimes have no choice if they're going to keep good employees. And the more men who speak up, the easier it will be for the others. In fact, one reason the workplace has loosened up is because more and more men are demanding family time.

So where does this new approach begin? With the couple planning for a man's paternity. It includes him at every stage of pregnancy and preparation. To this end, Robert Frank advises replacing the traditional baby shower, which is for women to connect as mothers, with a parent party, asking men and women to bring their best advice for the soon-to-be parents. And while a male partner can only be a coach and helper with the birth itself, Frank advises mother never to treat fathers as "helpers" once the baby is born. That done, the next challenge—paternity leave—awaits every couple.

Paternity leave is the first great work-family hurdle, and one that can set the tone for how involved a father will be. Most men *want* to take off. A report to the Commission on Family and Medical Leave stated that 73 percent of men would take three months or more if they had *paid* paternity leave. And that was back in 1991. Presumably, more men would sign on now.

Still, most men don't take paternity leave even if they have the option. They use one or two weeks of their vacation instead. This is a real mistake since becoming a parent is surely among the most profound transformations a person will ever make, and becoming a hands-on, nurturing parent is a major challenge for men.

By taking parental leave, men can move into parenthood with their wives, riding its roller coaster of fright (how do people live without sleep?) and ecstatic delight (she smiled at me!). Both have the chance to bond deeply and develop their expertise.

Cost, of course, is a real concern, since men's leave is almost never a paid benefit. But parents don't have to take full parental leave at the same time. Depending on their negotiations with each other and their employers, mom might take the first two months. Then dad and mom might both work part time for the next two months, leaving Dad in charge for one or two days a week—which will catch him up fast in the expert department. Alternately, they could take leave sequentially, with dad taking two months off after mom's three.

This takes both a nest-egg and a willingness to tighten belts. For example, if she's a nurse earning $35,000 and he's a high school teacher making $37,000, saving $200 a month in bank CDs for three years produces $8,000—the equivalent of two months' after-tax income. In lifestyle terms that savings is roughly the difference between keeping a Honda Accord till it's worn out and leasing a Jeep Grand Cherokee every three years.

Couples earning more, a lawyer and a systems analyst, for example, whose combined income is $90,000, can save $600 a month for two years, giving them $15,000, or three months of after-tax income. Maybe they have to forego a vacation in Bali, but they can still loll about a nearby lake.

Having enough time with children is the greatest luxury you can buy. Strategic planning is called for, including cutting back on nonessentials like the dream house, the Ford Expedition, the designer nursery. Making time for mom and dad to fall in love with a baby comes at a cost. But becoming parents can be far more exciting than a trip to the South Pacific. It can strengthen a marriage, and the individuals in it, particularly if the partners do it together.

Taking paternity leave is a man's first opportunity to make his family needs a priority at work. Presumably his employer has had ample time to find him irreplaceable (or, at least, costly to replace) and will respect his needs. If not, it's best to know early on that you better change jobs. After all, what would mom do if maternity leave weren't permitted? Dad has just as much right to that bonding time as mom does, even if he isn't physically recuperating from childbirth.

At work, strategize, then offer the boss a clear plan with plenty of advance notice. Most people on parental leave will be able to do some work from home after the first few weeks, so factor in what you think you can handle. In a letter to the editor of the Sunday Business Section of the *New York Times,* one man explains why it's worth it.

> During my three-month paid leave, I have the joy of watching our daughter grow in a way that is only possible with a lot of time.
>
> I realize what a priceless gift paternity leave is. I wish that more fathers could experience the delight of taking care of a baby on their own, in an unhurried way that is difficult to do on weekends alone, or shoehorned around busy workdays.
>
> I have never appreciated the demands and rewards of childcare until I started doing it solo—and not just for two-hour stretches on a weekend while my wife was running errands. Taking care of our baby is making me a more competent parent who doesn't feel the need to take a back seat to my wife—something that happens by default in practically all families where the mother is the de facto primary caregiver, particularly when it comes to babies.

Paternity leave and male parenting are, as news headlines sometimes confirm, the province of all men, high and low. When the prime minister of England is called upon to take paternity leave, both by his wife and a vocal portion of the voting public, the issue has clearly become politically "legitimate." Although Tony Blair ultimately declined, his very pregnant attorney-wife, "went to court to win an argument [for paternity leave in union jobs] against his government that she has not fully won at home" even though, as she remarked, the prime minister of Finland, Paavo Lipponen, had recently stopped running his country to spend a week at home with *his* newborn. And, take note, in August following the May birth of his son, Tony and family took three weeks of vacation in Italy. Clearly, choosing not to take a week off at the birth was a personal choice, not a political obligation. Had he said, "I'll take my month's vacation now—to be with my wife—or I'll take a week now and only two later," he would have acceded to the new rules of fatherhood, perhaps more than he wanted to.

That said, the issue having been raised is a sign of progress. And there is progress. If the Finnish prime minister, even if he does govern a wealthy and stable country, can take a week off to be a father, the "new man" of the 2000s—that caring, feeling, fringe kind of guy—may finally have a chance to become Everyman. However, this will happen one household at a time, and more often than not, with some glitches, as the next real-life portrait illustrates.

Jordan and Sheri Levy: Before and After

At age 32, Sheri is pregnant and the mother of two-year-old Samantha. She and Jordan, 34, are very much the postmodern parents, working and parenting passionately, thoughtfully, and with a strong sense of equality. But parenting moved through their lives like a tornado, setting them down in a very new place. Now, like many of their contemporaries, they find themselves straddling two lifestyles.

To meet Jordan and Sheri is to feel the excitement of this new generation, their anything-is-possible spirit and their business savvy. With their well-scrubbed good looks and casual but confident loose-at-the-collar clothing, Jordan and Sheri could both be news anchors. Sheri's an animated blonde with a cheerleader personality, a striking complement to Jordan's dark hair and even temperament. They are also warm, connected people who address the answers to my questions as much to one another as to me, and enjoy the other's responses even as they amend and joke. So far, with a unique ingenuity, they've managed to stay both in the business and the family game by changing all the rules—a trick not everyone can pull off. But there's much to learn from their strategy.

Before Samantha, Jordan and Sheri were a typical professional couple. They'd met at Focus Media, an advertising firm with big entertainment clients where they were both up-and-coming, both immigrants from other careers—his, economics and hers, acting. The consummate professionals, they didn't date until she left for another job as the manager for video at MGM Home Entertainment. Then it was love, very much between equals, at second sight. Jordan wanted a real partner and loved it that Sheri was also a corporate type in the same field as he was. He explains, "I didn't want to be out and about on the town meeting new challenges and she's not." But also, Jordan was consciously avoiding what he calls the "disconnect" in his own family life, where his mother *was* the family and his father always gone, working.

In their discussions about children, Jordan and Sheri agreed they would have two and that she would continue to work. "I had definite career goals," Sheri reflected. Like Jordan, she had an absentee dad, loving and respectful, but "not a sit-down-and-have-a-conversation-dad." Only once did he accompany his wife on a family vacation.

When her parents divorced, her mother managed the family nursery and became president of the Horticultural Association, but she wasn't a passionate business woman. Sheri, on the other hand, was.

"We had a lot of conversations about guilt and money and motherhood. I thought I knew exactly who I was. Then, with a kid, suddenly I wanted to be a mommy." In fact, that's what happened to three of Sheri's colleagues at MGM Home Entertainment who'd been pregnant at the same time, two in positions above hers: "They would all have thrown over their careers on a dime," Sheri said. One did leave, explaining that she "simplified" her life—code for downscaling so that they could live on his salary. Another would have liked to do the same, but couldn't get out of her contract. A third just couldn't afford to.

So there they were, three out of four women, leaving their infants after three months and three weeks, expressing their milk at the office, feeling conflicted, weeping between business calls. And among them only Sheri had had the foresight to hire a nanny two months earlier, so that only she felt confident in her childcare. In addition, she has a mother-in-law who stays with the baby once a week and is there for emergencies, as well as a sister and brother-in-law who live close enough to frequently help out. She even has neighbors who swap "emergency" help with her. And still she wept.

Even though Sheri had informally worked from home, unasked, all through her maternity leave, her supervisors never recognized her efforts and wouldn't allow her (or the others) to formalize the arrangement. MGM Home Entertainment wouldn't even allow them to telecommute one day a week or to leave at 4 P.M. In the end, MGM Home Entertainment lost three of their four trained and loyal management staff. As Jordan commented, corporate America doesn't know how to handle parental leave. Moms spend two weeks crying, then ask for flextime so they can work two days from home, and their bosses say no. "It's an emotional factor," Sheri believes. "You have to have the courage to get through the first two weeks, then you calm down." Sheri also had relatives urging her to stay home with the baby.

But Sheri didn't quit. "Something inside of me wouldn't let me be an 'at-home' mom. I didn't want to put my husband in the position where he had total responsibility for supporting the family. I don't feel comfortable spending his money. I think it would lead to a strain in our relationship. Now, we're both contributing."

Not that being a mommy had no effect. Sheri began to evaluate what she was doing at work: In her words, she became more ethical. Money and prestige were no longer her goals; she wanted the films she was bringing out to make a difference. She had "a mission." She was also desperate to find some way better than telephone of reassuring herself that her infant was fine while she was at work. It was actually easier to be at work, Sheri confided. People thought I was miserable, but in fact I just wanted to feel secure about my daughter, then I'd be fine. That's when she realized she wanted a video program to see various places in her house, so with the click of a mouse she could check on Samantha.

Over the centuries moms have probably thought of a lot of devices to improve parenting. But given their lack of business savvy, money, and connections, few have been able to produce them. Times have changed. As Sheri explained, "The idea smacked me in the face. I could log on to a secure site to see my child. It wasn't being done. So I would do it."

With her marketing background, she put together a presentation and showed it to Moshe and Debbie, an attorney couple she'd met in her Lamaze class. They "got it" so fast that Moshe volunteered to quit his job to carry the plan forward. With Moshe as CEO, and Sheri as VP of Business Development, they went into business, funded with $1.2 million seed money by the second "angel" who saw their business plan.

With NearCom, a sea change took place in Sheri and Jordan's household. Parenting had changed not only Sheri's identity, but Jordan's as well—in the opposite direction. Jordan always knew he'd be an involved dad. And he is, Sheri readily adds. He wanted to go to "daddy and me" classes; he wanted structured experiences with his daughter. And like Sheri, he can't wait to see her in the evening. But when Samantha came along, Jordan was an account executive at Focus Media, having worked there eleven years. He earned five times what Sheri did and they needed his paycheck. In preparation for parenthood, they had bought a half-million dollar house and a new car.

After Samantha, part of Jordan "wanted a traditional wife-mother," not that he'd ever push Sheri to quit. But he soon got the point. He took two weeks' vacation when she was born, then would rush home early for a while to see her. Once he got comfortable, though, he stopped rushing. He'd work until 8, 9, or 10:00 P.M. again while Sheri, who used to work until 8:00 P.M. was home by 5:00 to relieve the nanny and her guilt.

"Sheri would tell me I was disconnected," Jordan admitted. But he felt even more professional drive than before. "I was unwilling to move backwards. I didn't see it as my obligation to cut back. I saw it as my obligation to move forward, getting ahead is part of my daddyhood."

But Focus Media closed. To Sheri, Moshe, and Debbie's delight, Jordan signed on with NearCom, which couldn't afford to hire someone of Jordan's expertise. "And still," Sheri giggles, "Jordan always leaves the house before I do, even to work at *my* company. *He* takes a week's business trip and just leaves. *I* took a week's business trip and brought my mother and Samantha along, because I couldn't be away from her that long."

Jordan did take a week off to take care of Samantha before starting at NearCom. It was a revelation, "What an enormous amount of work it is. Nonstop. At the office, you can drink a cup of coffee, talk to a friend. Not with Samantha. I couldn't do it. I could never be home with kids all the time. But every guy should have to spend a week with a kid. Guys come home and don't believe how stressful taking care of a kid is."

Jordan's respectful of full-time parenting, but what he's realized is that even if NearCom made a fortune, he'd never stop working. "Part of my feeling fulfilled is where I am in my career, what I've conquered, how high I can go." For Sheri, who's expecting her second child, NearCom's a different story entirely. She's discovered that she's committed to the company, but it's not her passion. If NearCom makes their fortune, she'd be a mommy full time. Though she admits that if she were home she'd "make her household her work." She'd do classes with her children, projects, volunteer work. Then she'd resurrect her true passion, acting, by creating a theater.

They might both achieve their now very different dreams. The fledgling NearCom incorporated in September 1999, and has 5 employees plus 20 to 30 freelance specialists on contract. As Sheri gets more pregnant, Jordan gets more involved in the business. They've gotten their patent, their Web site, the engineering firm to manufacture it, and they're negotiating to distribute through home security companies. Now, they're on their second round of financing, and doing well.

The Levy's might well end up as both an American entrepreneurial and family success story: two children, an involved dad, a smart, active stay-at-home mom with a large independent bank account and many feathers in her professional cap. In fact, meeting them, one has the distinct impression that they'll be an American success story no matter what happens with NearCom.

However, like a lot of their generation's stage-mates, they're looking at two very different images of themselves—before and after parenthood. While there's no friction between the two now, with babies and families so excitingly new, either Sheri or Jordan or both might one day wonder how two people so alike became so different, or why there's "a disconnect" in their family life.

If they don't like where parenthood transported them, they can regroup, reevaluate, reflect, and retrieve some of their preparenting selves. Their life design is good enough that they're both set to enhance whatever choices they make. If they remain a dual-income working couple, they have a terrific support network. Jordan's whole family lives 15 minutes from them, which wasn't part of their life design but has turned out "to be a godsend," as Sheri says. If she opts out, she'll be independent financially and with the money to create a theater, bringing a different kind of entertainment into their lives.

Parenting changes everyone, but sometimes we don't understand the change or realize that we thrive to the extent that the change preserves, or strengthens, our truest identities. That is the challenge for so many of today's couples who, like Sheri and Jordan, set out with postmodern identities and find the culture's oldest ones are lying in wait. Those who can adjust personally are the lucky few; the rest will just have to change the world.

New Rules, New Parents, New Choices

Today, no one raises an eyebrow at dads who stay home with their babies, prime ministers who contemplate paternity leave, mothers of three-year-olds who command space shuttles, or ballerinas who perform solo at Lincoln Center five months after giving birth—rare as they may be.

In this hodgepodge of postmodern lifestyles, couples who feel entitled to choices can make up their parenting lives as they go along to suit themselves, their goals, and values. Mothers whose work is important to them can create the kind of family life that supports their goals. More and more women are doing just that, including those in some very visible couples. Jamie Rubin (not the stock analyst we met earlier, but Madeline Albright's assistant secretary of state for Public Affairs) recently gave up his VIP position to follow his wife, Christiane Amanpour, to London. He'll spend the year caring for their new baby while Amanpour continues as a high-profile reporter for CNN. Nick Macphee, former VP of Operations at Microsoft, quit to become a stay-at-home dad when his son burst into tears one day and said, "You're never here."

Often high-powered women who are mothers don't feel sufficient peace of mind if their husbands aren't covering home base. That's why it's not unusual to hear that the husband of a high-level executive woman is doing the lion's share of parenting. Four of the top five women on Fortune's 2000 "50 Most Powerful Women in Business" list have husbands who don't work: Carly Fiorina, Debby Hopkins, Donna Dubinsky, and Ellen Hancock. Not a coincidence, really, because executive level work as it's designed by corporations today requires the near-total energies of someone emotionally and socially supported by another. Among such executive women househusbands are more common than usual. The husband of Schwab vice chairman Dawn Lepore left his job at Visa to be an at-home dad when she had their first child. The president of General Motor's Saturn Division, Cynthia Trudell, is married to a high school math teacher who has stopped working for stretches of time in order to care for the family. The husband of Katrina Heron, editor-in-chief of *Wired* Magazine, is in charge of their young twins.

Men have always had this kind of support when the roles were reversed, though perhaps they can no longer take it for granted. Women, however, have very rarely had it, and that is a major reason why they haven't achieved what men have. Think about all the male entertainers who thank their wives for traveling with them, bringing the children, and keeping the home fires burning. I heard country singer Garth Brooks on a talk show say he'd never have been able to have such success if his wife hadn't kept him grounded by bringing the family on his tours. Now, at least, more women can exploit their special talents without giving up the grounding of a stable home life.

The good news for men is that free-form family life gives them the option to father more fully. For one thing, their wives can take on some of the financial burden in order to free them to do the kind of parenting they would like. They can count on a lot more cultural approval for fathering than they once could. And, as fathering expert James Levine explains to every corporation that invites him to speak, when men limit work time to make time for family, it's good for children *and* business. He cites the studies showing that when men aren't stressed, worried, or guilty about their personal lives, they work more efficiently and are more loyal to their companies.

As companies get the message, so do the men who work there. At a lecture on "Ten Things Every Working Parent Needs to Know" that Levine and I did jointly at Agilent Technologies, a couple of hundred people took time from their workday to learn how to create a better work/life balance. And at least half were men. Not only do many corporations today provide supports for working parents, many parents—including men throughout the ranks—feel they can take advantage of them.

Fatherhood no longer has to mean working 12-hour days and seeing the kids on weekends, between naps and lawn care. For some, it's a full-time secondary or primary job. As far back as 1993, 1.3 million employed fathers took care of their kids under age five while their wives worked—the swing-shift style of family life. About 5 percent of fathers are the primary caregivers; 2 million of them are at-home dads. There's an annual At-Home Dad's convention, Dad-to-Dad, a support group with chapters all over the country, a Web site (www.slowlane.com) as well as an award-winning documentary, *Homedaddy*, by Kent Ayyildiz, an at-home filmmaker dad, and a charming TV sitcom, "Daddio," written by stand-up comic, Matt Berry, about his life as a stay-at-home dad. New dad sites crop up daily (www.newdads.com; www.fatherslove.com) as does expertise from psychologists like Robert Frank (involvedfather@aol.com) who was himself an at-home dad.

With these networks, at-home dads no longer need feel isolated, even when they're abroad for their wives' work. In Europe, a Brussels-based organization called STUDS (Spouses Trailing Under Duress Successfully) is in place to help dads and other husbands adjust. Asia doesn't have anything of the kind. Casey Spencer, at home with his five-year-old daughter while his wife is director of finance and business for Universal Studios in Osaka, Japan, tells me that he found another at-home dad through the net. Though the other at-home dad is a Canadian rather than a native, the two are making quite an impression. In Japan, the category is still unheard of, and hands-on fathering is still so taboo that a simple government "fathering campaign" billboard depicting a man holding a child was perceived as too pressuring.

At the Japanese school Casey's daughter, Kelani, attended, he became an instant celebrity. The other primary parents, all mothers, created a title for him, Kelanichanpapa, invited him for lunch, then bombarded him with their questions, all pointed at how they might get their husbands involved with the children. Unfortunately, as in most mom's groups, Casey tells me, the women ended up complaining bitterly about their absent husbands who never "help" with the children. By comparison, Casey is a hero.

Casey doesn't see himself as heroic. He and his wife did what made most sense for them. Having agreed that one parent should be at home with their child, "economics" chose him because he earned so much less. And he was totally willing, having missed a lot of his two older children's childhood because of divorce. He also adored professional fathering, especially once he accepted his new status and reassured himself that he'd get back to his photography work when Kelani went to school, which he has. When he was still in the States, he found dad chat rooms and started a play group for at-home dads; in Osaka, he became actively involved in his church, made a place for himself as the school photographer, and even learned to cook and keep house, which he'd never done before. Now that Kelani is in school full time, he's feeling the separation: "I was so attached to her and these years were a time we had together." For Casey and his wife, this parenting arrangement was simple; it worked for them.

Their current plan reverses the parenting roles. In a year, when they return to the states, Casey will work while his wife "takes a rest," even though that means living a very much scaled-down life. The plan is fine with Casey, although he thinks his wife is too restless to take to homemaking. But if it doesn't work for her she'll just go back to work, either as a consultant or in another less-pressured position. By then, they agree, Kelani won't need a parent at home full time.

Women are now arranging their parenting lives in unprecedented ways to suit themselves and their families. Even when that means arduous physical exercise five weeks after a baby is born in order to prepare for a ballet performance. Stacey

Calvert, age 36, a soloist ballerina, and Margaret Tracey, age 32, both danced with the New York City Ballet at Lincoln Center for the first four months of their pregnancies, then continued one-and-a-half-hour classes for another three. Returning to dance so quickly was a pleasure for both.

Renee Fleming, opera diva and mother of two little girls, went back to work two weeks after her second daughter's birth, and has worked ever since. The children travel with her whenever they're not in school; otherwise they stay with their dad, from whom she's divorced. Now that the girls are both in school, instead of taking leading roles that would keep her away from them too much, Fleming does more recitals, which are shorter and easier to prepare for than operas. Union rules limit rehearsals to six hours. So, she's actually home a lot.

Is she guilty? No way. "My mother was a voice teacher and I have very strong memories of really, truly feeling proud of her because she worked. I'm a model for them of a woman with work she loves."

In the words of her husband, Eileen Marie Collins is "the only NASA shuttle commander with baby bottles on her office desk." As mother of a toddler, she still goes off proudly on missions, taking the same risks a male commander takes. Nor did NASA hesitate to assign the mother of a small child such a sought-after job. It works for the government and it works for the Collins family.

Janeith Glenn-Davis, lieutenant on the Oakland, California, Police Force, took her eight-hour exams just two weeks after giving birth to her son. Her husband, already an officer, rented a room in the hotel where the test was given so she could pump her breast milk during her breaks. Now the couple, both on the Oakland Police Force, work different shifts, each caring for their son when at home. "It has made me a stronger parent," says Janeith's husband.

Balancing Schemes That Work

In today's frantic work world, there are no easy ways to balance work and family. But if both partners are willing to make some hard choices, family life need not be stifling to either parent or bad for their children. However, the first thing to remember when considering parenting choices is that the 24/7 economy prefers unencumbered workers to real people with real lives. Recall the "drag coefficient," that perverse Silicon Valley term to describe how much someone's personal life might reduce his round-the-clock work availability.

The first step in creating a work/life balance is finding or creating work that allows for other aspects of human life. This may mean nothing more than quietly resetting the boundaries at your present job, or nothing less than getting a new job, starting your own business, or even changing careers before having a child. It usually means that if your husband is a heart surgeon or a war correspondent or a rock star, he'll probably rarely be home. There are women who accept that fact. But children don't. A dad who's officially there but hardly ever home can be more painful than one who is just plain gone.

Nothing predicts failure in family life more certainly than one or both parents' working around the clock. Sociologists Phyllis Moen and Yan Yu, at Cornell's Sloan Center for the Study of Working Families, found that couples "most apt to experience work/life success are those where both spouses are working 39 to 45 hours a week. When one spouse (typically the husband) puts in over 45 hours a week, both husbands and wives are less likely to report work/life success."

Children often feel rejected by parents who work all the time. If one parent does, then it feels as if that parent (usually the dad) is missing in action. The partner's resentments (along with the kids') can eventually erode their love and compromise the family. Look at what happened to the urologist Betsy Kavaler, who left her husband in charge of their toddler when she went across the country to pursue a fellowship. Had they not had a child, he could have immersed himself in work while she was away, visiting her as often as he liked. With a child, he felt "stuck," overwhelmed, and cheated of his work just like women in the same position can feel. If you want to have kids, figure out how both of you might sequentially, together, or in tandem make time for the family. Other people can and hopefully will support family life, but mostly parents create it.

When it seems impossible to simply relax the job in order to make more time for parenting, one or both parents may decide to try "sequencing." Sequencing is when one parent at a time, like Casey in Osaka, Denise Thomas of Off Road Capital, or Susan Rietano Davey of Flexible Resources, stops working full time to be the at-home parent for a while. In effect, they're sequencing periods of work and parenting, either by parenting and then going full swing into a career after the kids are in school, or by working up to a sufficiently high level to assure an easy return after dropping out during the children's early life.

For all three parents, this plan worked because it suited their individual personalities and circumstances. Before she had children, Susan Rietano Davey had been a very successful sales executive earning as much money as her husband, who owns his own financial planning company. They talked about who should stay home since both wanted a bunch of kids (they now have four) and one parent at home most of the time. Susan rejected the idea of working for her husband because she didn't want to be a "junior" partner to him, which might compromise their relationship. "Also, in my heart I knew I wanted to stay home more than he did."

So she quit. But because Susan also knew she needed to work, she helped create Flexible Resources, where she puts in a 20-hour workweek. In her well-heeled suburb, where many women do become professional mothers, Susan has to walk a fine line, never discussing business with the homemaker moms at her children's school who resent "working mothers." But, she says, "I'm always the happiest mom there, the least complaining, because I can get away from parenting enough to cherish it when I'm there."

Her advice to parents who decide to sequence: Keep working at something. "As a manager, I'd never hire anyone who hadn't worked in five years." Practically speaking, it's hard to just drop out. With technology, work changes constantly. New product life-cycles have shrunk to a half of what they were in the '80s. In order to keep current, stay in the game, either by working part time, like Susan, or by volunteering your work services like Denise Thomas and Casey Spencer. It may be worth joining a sequencing organization like Mothers and More (which used to be Formerly Employed Mothers at the Leading Edge—FEMALE).

For the lucky ones who work at corporations like Eli Lilly and IBM, which guarantee jobs after a three-year leave, sequencing is easy. For those without such work flexibility, sequencing might not work as well as it has for Casey, Susan, and Denise. Attorney Risa Gerson, whom we met in the chapter on lawyers, tried it for seven years. Working part time from home, she felt disconnected from colleagues. Also, all of her spare time was spent mothering. If any childcare issue came up, she had to deal with it. "Now that I'm full time, my husband [a *Newsweek* journalist] takes over at home in an emergency." The problem with being the primary at-home parent, says Gerson, is that "nothing else you have to do feels as important as childcare, so you just don't do the other things as much or as well as you want."

If, like Risa, you want to do other things, working part time from home may compromise the rest of life and create resentment between partners. If, like Casey or Susan, you're fine with it, then the arrangement will feel right. You have to know yourself and also agree to change lifestyles if the experiment fails. And don't forget that both partners can sequence at different times, first one, then the other cutting back for a while, so that neither is out of the loop.

Coparenting is when both parents try to balance work and family by adjusting their work to accommodate family needs. Unfortunately the form this usually takes is both parents work and she *also* does the kids (with whatever "help" he chooses to give). But when mothers end up working full time and also doing everything at home, "free and easy happiness never emerged," concluded Francine Deutsch from her study on couples who parent in these different modes. The answer to balance isn't for women to learn how to cook dinner in under three minutes. What you have then is a frazzled, burnt-out woman who is less emotionally available for her husband and children. In Deutsch's same study, these working mothers whose husbands did little at home reported less happiness than traditional at-home mothers whose husbands did help.

The superwoman problem is stated eloquently by Joan Morgan, the 30-year-old author of *When Chickenheads Come Home to Roost*, who says good-bye to the superwoman MO:

> This is not to be confused with being strong, Black, and a woman. I'm still alla that. . . . What I kicked to the curb was the years of social conditioning that told me it was my destiny to live my life as a Blacksuperwoman. That by the sole virtues of my race and gender I was supposed to be the consummate professional, handle any life crisis, be the dependable rock for every soul who needed me, and yes, the classic—require–less from my lovers than they did from me because after all, I was a STRONGBLACKWOMAN and they were just ENDANGEREDBLACKMEN. Retirement was ultimately an act of salvation. Being an SBW was killing me slowly.

Morgan speaks for all women who are trying to do it all, though black women do even more and with collectively fewer resources, often having to shore up families in dangerous neighborhoods and always having to fight racism.

Coparenting requires two parents to take responsibility for making the household run. That may mean dividing the tasks, assigning each parent a certain number of on-call days, or just spelling each other according to fairness and need. But generally, coparenting doesn't just happen. It has to be worked out, enforced, and negotiated because it goes against the cultural grain and our own internal parenting programs.

If you choose coparenting, however, women have to give up maternal control, allowing fathers to clothe and feed children in their own fashion, which turns out to be tougher to do than most women anticipate. Either women have impossibly high standards (because their good-motherhood reputations depend on them) or in their heart of hearts they believe mother knows best. For their part, men, who may never have felt incompetent at anything, have to live through what Kyle Pruett calls the "clumsy" fathering stage until they are comfortable taking full care of a child. If parents succeed at both these challenges, then they have each other as real allies in parenting, which is (trust me) the hardest work anyone ever does. Each parent also gets the needed relief from the ceaseless demands of children. And dads feel perfectly competent when mom isn't there.

As mothers have taken their place at work, fathers must take their place at home. Otherwise the ambition, training, and equality of this generation's women will fly out the window. Another generation of children will grieve for their "ghost fathers" who vanish into work. Sometime individuals can simply work fewer hours more intensely and make more time for their families—without flextime or special arrangements. If you are a valued employee and believe in yourself, by just doing a great job when you're there, often there are no questions asked when you're not. My husband, who had written for the *New York Times* for over a decade when our daughter was born, quietly defied the rigid rule about working in the newsroom by writing from home three days a week. Since he was not a jot less productive and could always be reached by phone, people just got used to his new work mode. Eventually, they formalized an agreement that he would, indeed, appear at the office twice a week.

But until the work world is generally more yielding, a lot of dual-income coparents will probably have to request flextime or telecommuting, give up top posts or turn down promotions. They may both have to work part time for a while or both become consultants, at least while the children are small. Whatever it takes, they'll have the reassurance of two jobs and two paychecks. And they'll have each other's understanding of whatever career limits they experience, though they may not experience any.

Finding Time, Making Time, Buying Time

Even men and women who work full time on the fast track find ways to maintain a work/life balance. One *Wall Street*

Journal article examined the growth of sabbaticals among executives by companies afraid to refuse them: "Rather than lose talent in this tight labor market, a surprising number of employers are approving these breaks: Nearly half of Fortune's 100 Best Companies to Work for in America, in fact, now provide sabbaticals or similar leave programs—up 18 percent from just a year ago."

Fast Company magazine often inquires how top execs find time to live. Vinod Khosla, a partner in the biggest venture capital firm, Kleiner Perkins, Caufield, and Byers, and a founder of Sun Microsystems, has a wonderfully male approach to balance: "I track how many times I get home to have dinner with my family. My assistant reports the number per month and that way I can maintain a goal of 25 per month. I have four kids between the ages of 7 and 11. Spending time with them is what keeps me going. Work is just a hobby." He spends 50 hours a week at work, but says, he could easily work 100. He just refuses to. At home, he turns off his cell phone, the pager was abandoned long ago.

Maggie Wilderotter, CEO of Wink Communications, Inc., an interactive television company, says, "I have three golden rules: Weekends are for my family. I take four weeks of vacation a year. And I try to maintain a healthy lifestyle by sleeping enough, eating well, and exercising often."

Stacey Snider, the 38-year-old Universal Pictures Chairman, has two children, one of whom comes for lunch at mommy's office once a week. Weekends are for her family, and she makes a point to leave the office by 6:45, late by parenting standards but early by Hollywood mogul standards.

Charter Communications CEO Jerald Kent, 43, blocks out time on his calendar to coach his kids' soccer, hockey, and basketball teams. At a meeting with software billionaire Paul Allen, who was purchasing a controlling share in Charter, Kent left at 7:00 P.M., telling Mr. Allen's lawyer that he'd promised his kids to see *The Parent Trap* with them. He returned a few hours later.

Once the right attitudes toward balance are in place, parents still have to buy time in order to have it. If there's money enough, they can outsource the more tedious upkeep work in order to have stress-free time with their children and spouses. Often they have goods and services delivered. From pet groomers to car mechanics and even physicians, the service industry comes to you—for a price. And people are buying. According to the *Wall Street Journal*, these services are up by 25 percent in the last five years. Online groceries have increased business 50 percent in less than two years. Their take: "Exhausted from hectic work schedules, long commutes, and family demands, people are increasingly reluctant to go out again, for any reason, once they get home." In cities, people can hire dog walkers and "kangaroo vans" to take the kids to their afterschool lessons.

Along the same lines, a recent ad in the *Industry Standard* read: "What are you doing to save time?" The image was of a baby bathing in one side of a double sink, the dirty dishes piled up in the other. Quixi, the ad claims, goes beyond providing *a* service: "Our live helpers will shop online for you, give you movie times, directions, or connect you to the people you need to reach."

So now we have service and *meta*service. Which is fine if you can afford it, but even better if you're not so exhausted from work that you don't have time to do the things you enjoyed doing, like walking your own dog or going to the farmer's market or taking your child to school.

And let's be real here. The executives, divas, ballerinas, commanders, and lieutenants who have managed balance are top-notch in their fields; not only can they can write their own tickets at work, they can pay for a superb support system. The rest of us, especially those starting out, have to plan carefully and be willing to make sacrifices in order to ensure the kind of time these balance-warriors maintain. Or else, exhausted, we still have to spend every spare second doing the errands that make our lives work. One engineer told me he was a Boy Scout leader, and while he always made time for his sons, he saw parents who just couldn't. In fact, he and the other leaders jokingly renamed the Boy Scouts of America, the Baby-Sitters of America because of all the "drive-by parents" who push their kids out of the car at the meeting hour and drive off, without showing their faces.

Sometimes it takes a little heartbreak to prompt parents to change their priorities. In a letter to the editors of *Fast Company,* Trip Pilgrim, of Nashville, Tennessee, shares his epiphany:

> I am a senior manager at a start-up, working the usual scary hours and experiencing the requisite levels of stress. A couple of days before I read this column [on fathering], my seven-year-old daughter sent me an e-mail expressing concern that I had spent too much of my time helping her sell Girl Scout cookies. I hope we can all figure out a way to make sure that our children know that they come first.

In *Ask the Children,* the biggest study done on how children are faring now that their parents mostly work, a study in which the children themselves were asked to assess their lives, the Families and Work Institute found that most children said they didn't mind their parents working; they just minded how stressed they were when they were home. Kids need to know that when we're there, we're really there, and that they do come first. The better balance we have as individuals, the more our children get what they need, and we do too.

Family Lifesavers

So far, we've been talking about family life in terms of parents' responsibilities and choices. But when work demands so much and communities can be so anonymous, parenting requires a lot of personal family support. Parents just can't do it alone. Nor should they. It's too stressful and can be dangerous for children, who need a safety net of reliable adults for emergencies and daily life. Parents usually do better at parenting if there are other people to discuss the sorts of challenges that never show up in the how-to parenting books—like dealing with a grade school teacher whose approach is all wrong for your child, like helping a miserably clumsy kid in a jock environment, like consoling a teenager whose best friend moved away.

The "it takes a village" approach is not only good for kids, it's great for parents. But one nanny or one grandmother does not a village make. Parents need one of each and more who will be involved to some extent. Not to mention broader community services. All of which is a lot of work to find, cultivate, set up, maintain, but is totally worth it in the long run. Not only does a group of caring grown-ups provide alternative models of love, but their caring lessens the isolation that characterizes parenting now that extended family is often far away and groups (religious or otherwise) are less central in people's lives than they used to be.

Parents who move to new places are often shocked by the sudden loss of support systems they hardly knew they had. My husband and I experienced exactly that when we moved with our seven-year-old from New York City to a small California town. In Manhattan, we had three baby-sitters my daughter had known since she was tiny, and their families; we lived in a building with about a dozen children in her age range, all of whom she saw practically every day in the late afternoon when the doorman (whom she'd also known since birth) presided over their playing in the lobby. Any of their parents could be called upon to help out in an emergency, and several would just spell us when we needed time out (and vice versa). Since we'd hosted a Monday afternoon play group for these kids, we knew one another intimately. Our kids were comfortable in each other's homes, even to sleep over. We also had two sets of childless friends who acted as godparents, visiting often, coming for birthday parties and that sort of thing.

The list continues with family members an easy drive or short plane trip away, with pediatricians and specialists we knew well, the ice-skating teacher my daughter adored, the lifeguard at the pool we went to every Sunday. These people were our daughter's world and our family life. Not that we thought of it that way. It just seemed like a cozy, safe place to raise our daughter.

Arriving in California, we had only one link, the family with same-age kids whom we had visited here before. In the first months, our daughter was so daunted by a new school, new home, new landscape, new doctors, new everything that she wouldn't even stay alone with a baby-sitter. She made friends, but they had to come to our house to play because she wouldn't step foot in theirs. At least not without one of us present. Sleepovers, which she used to love, were out of the question. We had no parenting relief, except when grandparents came to visit, which was rare now that we were far away. For months, we maintained an almost stifling togetherness.

Now, two years later, we once again have a comfortable parenting community with just enough people to make a village. Our daughter has a best friend who often comes with us on our vacations; she spends weekends with her cousins, sleeps over with friends in Los Angeles, two hours away, goes on class camping trips with her teachers, and when mom and dad are both traveling at the same time, she's glad to stay home with her tutor, a woman who raised five children and whose parenting wisdom helps us all.

This didn't just happen; we worked at it. Hard. At our daughter's school, I became a class-parent representative to the PTA; my husband got on the finance committee. We hosted a multitude of kid visits and kid parties. Through trial and error, we found baby-sitters (who only came in the daytime at first, until she got used to them), tutors, and doctors. We made the hour-long trip back and forth to a cousin's house so we could become an extended family for each other's same-age children.

Parents have to *create* a community peopled with enough adults who can serve as an extension of the family or simply provide an alternative environment for a child to experience. Someone else might take a child camping if you're not the camping types, might bring out the artist in a child, become a model or a mentor. Of course, with smaller children, the adventures and experiences might be more modest, but no less important. All these "significant others" offer suggestions and feedback, or at least know what you're talking about when you discuss your child.

New parents can make their parenting life more fun and much easier by cultivating a parenting community, or at least developing a strategy for how they'll create one. There are three main avenues to travel: same-stage parents, extended family and friends, neighbors and neighborhood. How? By networking.

Most successful people know how to network and know how those connections can lead to jobs, solutions to work problems, and new opportunities. It's the same with parenting, even though it may seem like a totally private experience at first. Sherry Levy realized that she didn't treat the other parents she met in her daughter's dance or gym classes the way she treated women in business, talking with them about what they do, who they know, and so on. She also realized that she should. The earlier that new parents network, the better network they'll have when they need it most, after those first astonishing weeks.

Same-stage parents have children the same age as your own. What's so engaging about them is they know exactly what your day is like, what you're going through, and they're struggling with many of the same issues, from teething to homework. Also, as one friend pointed out, other parents of infants are the only ones up at 5:30 A.M. She and her husband spent one morning each weekend having *very* early breakfasts with friends who had an infant the same age as their son. Not only did they get some social time, but their friends, whom they hadn't known that well before, understood the constant interruptions in conversation (to feed, soothe, diaper, wipe the mess from the floor), their bizarre sleep-deprived mentality. Eventually their boys became best friends. Whenever a parenting problem arose, they consulted each other first, since the four knew each other's boy so well.

Becoming parents is one of those rare opportunities to make good friends fast. You're thrown together in a way people rarely are otherwise: unhinged from the daily routine, open to a new experience, and experiencing life intensely. You're eager to share their experiences, offer advice, and just keep each other company. Remember Sherry and Jordan Levy who became business partners with another couple they met two years earlier in their Lamaze class! Certainly, you don't bond with every couple who happens to be a new parent. But if there's bonding potential, parenting infants and toddlers can be the glue. There is so much to talk about, and learn. Amy Lowe, the publisher of a small New York City press, found women in her postpartum exercise class who helped her figure out to wean her baby to a bottle before returning to work, told her about the local children's consignment shop, and gave her the inside scoop on local pediatricians. If you become friends with same-stage parents, you'll have the chance to get to know their child through all the growing stages.

Great. Where do you find them? Well, at childbirth classes, to start, or at the adoption agency. If you're open to making friends of same-stage parents, you might as well try to get to know someone before the dam breaks. Once it does, there's the postpartum classes, the pediatrician's office, and the park. Later, there are play groups (you might start one), the baby swim classes, your church or temple, and all the other places where children and parents converge.

Look close to home. Proximity plays a powerful role in family life. Even neighbors with older kids can become an extension of family. Older children usually love new babies and will often visit to play with them, cooing and distracting the baby far more than a grown-up can. Meanwhile, you'll get to know those kids who might one day baby-sit for your own. If there's some chemistry, the kids will soon be running in and out of each other's homes.

Neighbors without kids can also be part of family life. My friend Penny, who has no children of her own, travels to Costco to stock her cupboard with the kind of pretzels the neighbor's child likes because she is completely charmed by the little girl who just appears at her door to play with the cats.

Kids make people social, both as parents and, unless they don't like kids, as neighbors, friends, shopkeepers, and bus drivers. Whenever my daughter and I took the subway in

New York City, either a grown-up or some other child would engage her. Often, with my immense gratitude. On a plane, when she wouldn't stop crying (babies' ears often hurt), an older man played peekaboo with her for 20 minutes straight. My friend Angela was on a plane with her crying baby when her seatmate just lifted the baby to her enormous bosom, whispering as the baby immediately calmed that it works every time.

Donna Bohling, mother of three older children, points out that at the later parenting stages, you don't choose a child's friends—and sometimes don't like a child's choices—so it can be a serious diplomatic undertaking to get to know them and their families. But once you do, you can have important allies in helping your teens. James Levine, coauthor of *Working Fathers*, describes how the parents of his daughter's close friendship group met once a month for supper just to talk over what their kids were doing. Knowing their parents talked frequently, the kids obeyed the curfews and rules both because they all had the same ones and because they couldn't use their friends as an excuse.

Parents need help; they need people. Of course, extended family has been the traditional source of that help, and still is great if the members are close by. Grandparents, aunts, uncles, and cousins enrich family life enormously.

Grandparents especially. Parents feel safe when kids are with grandparents, and children usually love their adoration and acceptance. Child psychiatrist, Dr. Arthur Kornhaber, has written several books on the importance of grandparenting, both to the older and younger generations. He maintains a Web site (www.grandparenting.org) and speaks nationally to promote the grandparent connection. Often, he says, a grandparent or older person will be able to reach a distressed child more readily than a parent because of the respect and trust children often naturally feel for elders.

Living close to parents may be worth considering, even when it means a move. As Sherry Levy said, she would never have moved somewhere in order to be close to Jerry's family, but, it turned out, being only 15 minutes away was a godsend once their daughter was born. Dr. Beth Davis Phillpotts and her husband pay her mother to take care of their daughter, just as Carol Ann and Greg do. Beth's mother saw this as a great sabbatical from teaching high school, which she'd done for many years and will do again when Zoe is older.

So many successful families I've interviewed tell me that their lives couldn't run smoothly without grandparents nearby. Grandparents will often consider an urban retirement plan instead of, say, a Sun Belt move, because the sense of purpose in caring for their grandchildren outweighs the pleasures of easy living.

Short of a move, helping grandparents who live far away by defraying transportation costs and visiting often is wonderful for children. It also may give parents the opportunity to take a day or even some nights away during visits. Maintaining grandparent contact through phone calls, videos, cards, or even audiotapes of Grandpa reading a nighttime story can strengthen a long-distance relationship. But if the distance makes a close relationship difficult, consider a grandparent surrogate.

Peculiar as that concept may be, it often feels as natural as family, particularly if the adopted senior is a neighbor who comes over to lend a hand. My daughter assumed that our neighbor, the 80-year-old Mabel, *was* family, and never hesitated to visit her even after she went into a nursing home. Proximity, as I've mentioned, is a powerful force; she just knew Mabel so well and in such a daily way.

If no neighbors are handy, the local senior citizen group or any elder organization, including a retired teachers organization, might provide names of elders interested in baby-sitting. Then you hire them, if only to lend a hand during a busy day, but with the real purpose of getting an older person involved in the life of your family. They bring their wisdom and experience to the table—not to mention the time to make a real connection. They might be available in emergencies when no one else is; when, for example, two sleeping babies need someone to stay with them while the only available parent takes an older child to the emergency room for a broken finger.

Grandparents, aunts, uncles, and cousins all provide a child with a sense of belonging and enduring connection. Somehow, children realize they'll know these people all of their lives. Everyone benefits from the enhanced sense of belonging.

Childcare: Separating Reality from Myth

The very word has become almost as freighted as "choice." It seems that for every parent who uses commercial childcare, there's another who pointedly says, "I don't want a stranger raising my child." Where did this image come from? Most parents don't want to "dump" their children while they race from exciting jobs to fancy dinners or the club scene. They want to see their kids; they're dying to be with them. For this majority, the caregiver, whether a baby-sitter, a childcare center teacher, or a live-in nanny will be *helping them to raise their children.* Sure, children will love the caregiver, but will always know who their parents are. The key is being an engaged parent and setting high standards for assistance.

The same way that networking skills support parenting life, so do consumer skills. Nowadays people are used to comparing the quality and price of everything from vacation packages to long-distance telephone service. They shop in advance, anticipating the competition for the best stuff. Oddly enough, though, shopping smarts can vanish when it comes to childcare.

Not so odd, really. For starters, parents can be ambivalent about using childcare. Or they're just too emotional to go about purchasing it in a businesslike fashion. But that is precisely what finding good childcare requires. Even when there's a licensed agency involved, too few parents inquire about what that license assures them. With childcare, judging is really up to you. But there are some excellent indicators to rely on.

First, a brief overview for the parents who aren't sure whether they want a live-in nanny, a baby-sitter who comes daily, a childcare center, or family daycare: all four have plusses and minuses, as well as quality-control challenges.

A live-in nanny or daily baby-sitter can be a blessing for parents who can afford one and, in the case of the nanny, who have the space. After all, you know there's someone there all the time who can take over if you're late or sick or a work emergency comes up. Plus, the children get to stay in their own surroundings and get one-on-one nurturing, which is so important to a child's full development. In such intimate living, you'll get to know your caregiver very well and vice versa, so that when the chemistry is there, you really have another family member. Often, too, frazzled parents feel nurtured by the caregiver, who may be a soothing presence, like "a wife" who takes care of all the little details of life and frees them to enjoy their child.

The down side of the nanny/baby-sitter choice is the dependency. If parents delegate too much responsibility to this one person, she becomes so crucial to the family that her departure can cause a crisis. How many stories have we all heard of the adored nanny who left after six months? Most nannies have children and families of their own; unforeseen problems can emerge. Cultural differences are sometimes so pronounced that a baby-sitter will quit instead of trying to explain a grievance.

A businesslike approach helps prevent this sort of parenting disaster. With thorough interviewing, references, and a trial period, you're likely to find a reliable person. By being a good manager, you'll probably be able to keep her. That means setting clear expectations, offering incentives for staying, inquiring how the job is going and what she may need to do it better, and how her own life is, just as you'd ask any employee. Nannies' biggest complaint is how unprofessionally they're often treated. As obvious as it sounds, the better the nanny/baby-sitter is treated, the better she can nurture your child.

Which brings up the second down side to nannies and baby-sitters: a parent's (usually a mother's) jealousy. Because they work in the home one-on-one with your child, it's easy for mothers to feel "replaced." After all, now there are two women who nurture the baby. And babies *must* be attached to their caregiver or they will feel far too alone when parents leave. That child-nanny love is absolutely necessary—a sign that your child is being properly nurtured—and must be respected, even when perfectly understandable feelings of competition emerge.

What to do with those feelings? Make your own parenting central in your child's life. When you come home, take over. Let the nanny leave or retreat, even when you'd love nothing better than to flop down on your bed and read your mail for a bit. Perform the child's cherished feeding, bathing, and going-to-bed rituals. As long as you're the last person the baby sees before he or she goes to sleep and the first in the morning, if the child knows you'll come when they cry in the night, that child is totally yours.

Having said all that, four personalities are involved here: a baby, two parents, and one (or more) caregiver. There are bound to be crossed wires and unforeseen problems, so prepare for them. Have a plan for when she's ill. Is there someone else (grandparents come in handy here) who can come on a moment's notice. Do you have a plan in place should she have to leave suddenly? Like your mother's aunt and uncle, once removed, who can come for two weeks while you search for a replacement? Just raising these crucial nightmare questions may be sufficient evidence of the plusses of childcare centers.

Childcare centers and family daycare can offer a stimulating environment for children and reliability for parents. Both have their advantages when parents choose them carefully. For one thing, they're always there—no worry about someone quitting or getting sick. If a caregiver is sick, there's a substitute. For another, the other children and caregivers provide fun for kids and a fail-safe for parents, who know the caregivers are watched and supervised.

Both centers and home daycare should be licensed, though licensing usually requires only minimal civility, such as a sanitary environment, and, depending on the state, one caregiver to four toddler ratio (Connecticut) or 1 to 12 ratio (South Carolina). You want to know the caregiver-child ratio; that is, how many children will one caregiver be responsible for and, in the large centers, the caregiver turnover. In the best centers, the child will have one caregiver whom s/he knows is "hers." Sharing her attention with three other babies or toddlers can be like having siblings. But sharing her attention with too many other children may result in neglect.

Family daycare often feels more cozy because it's in the home of a woman or couple who lives nearby. Perhaps there are only six or nine children in all. Even in family care, however, it's better if the provider is licensed by the state, which then inspects for that minimal civility parents usually hope for. Better still, the provider is part of a family daycare cooperative, a support organization that not only supervises the individual provider, but supports her with advice, literature on child development, and play equipment.

The proof for either of these alternatives is in the feeling of joy the parent experiences in the place, the sense that the kids are having fun. Make a few surprise visits to see what it's like when visitors aren't normally there. Whichever you choose, consider it an extension of your family, a group who knows your child over the years and wants to know you're involved with what they're doing.

So what should a good center look like? I leave you with a picture of Betsy DeWolf's center called Work and Play in East Windsor, Connecticut, one of these enchanted places where dedicated women offer high-quality, accredited care and adore the kids. I came at nap time to see the littlest ones snug on cots with the stuffed animals they brought for the teddy bear picnic. Teachers were kneeling and whispering to some; other children were listening to a story on tape; others were sleeping. Out back, bigger kids climbed on the play structure in a wooded yard, while their teachers were setting up paints for them on the picnic tables. What goes on here is a level of educational care that few individual parents are up to, plus a level of socialization only possible when kids are part of a group.

Then there's the money factor. As with everything, there are bargains, but mostly you get what you pay for. If you want caregivers to be happy in their work, you need to pay them for it. Do so, knowing it's the most worthwhile parenting purchase you'll ever make. Where childcare is concerned, pay the most you comfortably can; everyone benefits.

There's one more area of support for parents—the neighborhood. Sometimes the best parenting help is free. Whether it's the local library's story hour or the recreation department's baby gymnastics classes, communities often put a lot of money into helping families. They provide entertainment for kids as well as networking opportunities for parents and caregivers. Nannies and baby-sitters can often feel as isolated as parents at home on rainy days or in winter cold. Why not tell them about these activities where they'll surely be able to meet other caregivers? Most important, participating will help connect your family to the community so you can feel more a part of where you live.

Of course, no matter how close your extended family and friends, how great your childcare, how rich your parenting community, you're still the parent. So whatever else you're doing, you may have to drop it sometime in order to be there. Which may be a great thing all around, as we'll see in the next portraits of two executive moms who created the flexibility to make their lives work.

Barbara Marcus, Jean Feiwel: Making Your Work Work for Your Family

Barbara Marcus was the vice president of the book division of Scholastic, barely making the work and family ends of her life meet. Now she has risen higher, to president of Scholastic's Children's Book Division. But during a six-month sabbatical, she also figured out a better blend than she had before.

When I first interviewed her, Barbara was still VP of the book division. She sat in just the sort of office you'd expect—one with a gorgeous view of Manhattan's rooftops and bridges. In an aqua suit, her streaked blonde hair blunt-cut at the neck, Barbara's own glamour complemented the surroundings. We didn't have long to talk because she was taking off for California to meet with filmmakers who were adapting some Scholastic books. Screenplays filled one of the three brimming briefcases she was taking along. Dream job? Mmmmm.

At that time, her usual day at the office started at 8:30. She was home by 6:30 to eat dinner with her husband, Michael, and two children, then put them to bed. Between 10 P.M. and 12:30 A.M., she did her mail, talked on the phone, and finished work. Sometimes, she admitted, it was really more like from 10:00 P.M. to 2:00 A.M. By Thursday, she was always beat. After eight years at this pace, she was about to take a six-month sabbatical, which the company granted to such a productive executive.

Ideally, Barbara told me, she would work 9 to 5 three days a week, but she couldn't get her job done in those hours. "A lot of people report to me, from truck drivers to senior vice presidents. About 600 white-collar and 1,000 blue-collar people," she explained.

Is that the whole problem? No, as she confessed, part of the problem is Barbara herself. Neither she nor the company created boundaries. "I think I could work more efficiently and delegate more, but I haven't been able to make myself do that. The job you could do in less time would be project- or content-related instead of management." Which is true to some extent, as her associate, senior vice president Jean Feiwel, concurs.

Jean's part of Scholastic's work *is* "content driven." That is, she's responsible for ideas such as *The Babysitter's Club* book series and franchises as varied as Scholastic's computer games and dolls. "I can do that alone," she says, "I don't have to wait for other people's part of the work. But I'm a self-regulated, creative person, so I do that very well."

Her day is long, but not as long as Barbara's. "It's a joke at the office," Jean says. "If someone is jumping out the window, I'm still out the door at 5. *I can just stop*. First of all, I learned that if I don't, I burn out. Better to work fewer hours productively. Second, if I didn't stop, I could work 24 hours a day. Stopping is arbitrary. If I didn't get up and go, I'd be expected to stay. But I manage because I'm successful. No one challenges my work methods."

"Content-driven" means that, unlike Barbara's work, Jean's doesn't involve hours on the telephone, which, from Jean's perspective, creates the time bind with all the inevitable chitchatting. She's also a type-A personality, but only to a point. "I love my work," she tells me, "but my work is not who I am. It's just part of who I am. My private life is me as well." One of Jean's strategies has been to separate work from life with an hour-and-a-half commute each way. The train ride means reading time, quiet time. Then when she's home, she's completely there, far from the maddening crowd. She gets up at 5:00 A.M. to exercise, has breakfast with her daughter, and is on the train by 7:00 A.M. Her only regret is having no time for a social life. On the other hand, at night, when she walks into her home, she can just hang with her family.

Barbara believes that Jean is just as productive as she is, but more efficient. So while it's true that Jean's job doesn't depend on a lot of other people (nor do a lot of other people depend on her), she's also able to set limits, something Barbara couldn't do easily. However, it's important to note that both women are married to men who work from home, love family life, and offer emotional support to their executive wives. That is, they both have families that supported their work, but only Jean had work that worked well for family life.

Barbara asked for a sabbatical both because she felt burnt out and because her older daughter had had a hard year and needed some extra help from her mom. Barbara structured her sabbatical well. In order to keep in touch with a job she'd be returning to and help everyone do their jobs in her absence, she came in once a week. Mostly, she says, she just listened to them, but her presence was much appreciated. She also did lunches to stay connected and remained available by phone to help solve problems.

The rest of the time Barbara enjoyed "civilian" life. She spent a great deal of time with her daughter, got totally involved with her school and homework. She set up a support system for her next academic year, finding good people to help and generally "getting a handle" on her daughter's challenges, none of which she had been able to do while working full time. She went to the gym often, took two courses, one in history, the other in French, went on a three-week family trip to Australia, and a shorter Italian vacation with her husband.

At home, Barbara was careful not to interfere with Michael's routine. He had always run their domestic life and she didn't change that at all. She also realized that while she enjoyed her at-home sabbatical thoroughly, she wouldn't want to do it permanently (though she thought she would). "I've seen the other side," she explained, "and work is just a lot of fun for me." But those six months were invaluable for getting a handle on her challenges, too. Barbara returned to work "much less agitated, with a bigger vision of what life is, and a sense that problems weren't so pressing."

With her new perspective, Barbara redefined her work. First, while she accepted her promotion, it was on the condition that she would not be doing *more* work; she would just do it better. Every day she takes her daughter to school, getting to the office at 9:00. Instead of going to the gym at night, as she did before, she goes twice a week from 9:00 to 10:30. "Everyone knows my rules now. They make lunch dates instead of breakfast meetings." Although her evenings are the same, she takes more vacations and more vacation days.

As a manager, Barbara plans on encouraging sabbaticals for others, and earlier on than she took one. That's how useful she found it. Having taken one, she can help others to do it. "I think it's an excellent policy," she says, "and I just have to take the chance that they'll come back." Of course, she works for a very informal, nonhierarchical company where the CEO jumps up from an important year-end meeting and says, "It's 5:00, I've got to go. I have to get Ben to the doctor." It was always that way. Barbara just couldn't take advantage of her options like she does now. That's attitude for you.

Not only has Barbara learned to set limits, she's also learned to delegate. "I'm operating at a different level," she says. "More administrative. I don't try to do it all. I hired a products' person and I let her be in charge. Period. Although I had to give up some parts of the work that I love, I have a more workable life. I miss the other stuff, but it's a choice."

As these two executives illustrate, there's often a lot more choice available at work than people use. And more choice in family styles as well.

No Woman Is an Island

Hopefully, the story of one or another woman so far has hit home, maybe even inspiring a reader to design her work life more thoughtfully or demand more fairness in a relationship than she might have otherwise. But it's the ideas behind these stories that give them their bite. It's their political implications that can serve as ballast, a life raft in the deceptively calm dollar-green waters of today's America. They are what will change things for women.

The basic idea is simple: Women of this generation, who for the most part want both work and motherhood, have the power to remake our culture so that they can do both well. But women can't do it alone. They can initiate the process, just by being true to their dreams, forthright with their partners, and savvy about work. But to blend life and work, they'll need to make alliances with one another and with men.

As we've seen, the I-can-do-it-alone superwoman is no model. There's only so far women can go by toughing it out as individuals, giving their all at work, tanked on double espressos, then planning the meals, buying the children's clothes, supervising homework, keeping social life (not to speak of intimate life) alive. It's just too much. Too often they snap, deciding to switch from a career to a job-job or to simplify life by quitting work. Others go in the opposite direction, pretending the children can do fine with a kiss good-bye and a daily phone conversation.

Women who want to work, have a rich marriage, and kids need partners in parenthood—men who also race home to relieve the baby-sitter, who shop and cook, who know the pediatrician and their children's friends. Women who want to work and have kids have to be aware that's what they'll need from a partner, and the men have to be aware too. Fair is fair, of course. Men who do this deserve wives who will pull their own weight financially.

Adam (and Mrs. Smith) Revisited

We're all familiar with Adam Smith's "invisible hand" of the market, which keeps the awesome machinery of an economy going without planning by bureaucrats or businessmen. But this eighteenth-century Scottish economist never worried his old gray head about the other invisible hand—the left one, no doubt—that maintains the equilibrium between home and workplace by lifting new parents out of their former lives and setting them down in roles that keep men free for work and motivate them to do it devotedly.

When markets work well, we want to maintain the present equilibrium; when they don't, the invisible hand must orchestrate the elements differently. Right now, our economy is booming, but at the price of jeopardizing women's hard-won equality, not to mention men's souls and children's welfare.

Economist Shirley P. Burggraf, who also notes Adam Smith's lack of attention to unpaid female labor, hypothesizes a wife for Smith who would correct this egregious oversight:

> Like any woman who has actually done it, Eve Smith would surely inform Mr. Smith that family caretaking is a lot of work and not something to be taken lightly. . . . [She] would surely try to figure out a way to make the market system serve the family in some of the ways that it serves the rest of the economy.

Conceding that this won't be easy, she reminds Mr. Smith that "changing the social arrangements by which half the human race allocates its labor can hardly be a small project in any economy." And change it must.

The stress level in most people's lives is over the top. Mothers still give up their dreams of achievement at work, underutilize their talents, and relinquish their independent financial security (often with disastrous results in the case of divorce or a husband's job loss). By the same token, many women who soar at work feel obliged to give up their dreams of motherhood. And despite their best intentions, too many men give everything they have at the office, turning into their own ghost-fathers.

Think about this: The market could find the same equilibrium if both invisible hands moved in concert. To be blunt—if not a smidgen idealistic, I admit—the market could, for example, divide one high-powered job between two workers rather than have one exhausted breadwinner putting in 12-hour plus days with a resentful wife and an early coronary to look forward to. It makes sense, no?

Now that women are educated, trained, and know the satisfactions of work (as opposed to overwork), they aren't going back to the kitchen. They aren't as quick as they once were to give it up for motherhood. Despite the trend stories telling us that women are quitting their high-powered jobs to stay home with kids, and despite the small studies they sometimes cite, the Census Bureau tells us that 73 percent of mothers with children one year and older are employed, most of them full time, and those numbers are increasing. End of story.

Significantly, twice as many women with college degrees as without them return to work within a year of having a child. That is, the more educated women are, the more likely they are to stay employed and women everywhere—but especially in America—are getting more and more education. Just as significantly, in places where men do little parenting, like Italy and Japan, the birthrate is dropping at an alarming rate. It's dropping throughout the developed world. The women who believe they can't have it all are now often choosing a paycheck. The free market doesn't care, but the countries do, particularly when they find themselves with more old people than young.

The invisible right hand will just have to factor in what the left hand is doing. That means the free market will have to attract women who want to work and also raise families. But women who want both to work and have children will also need to resist the invisible left hand of *traditional* motherhood. Instead of getting swept up in their partners' rhythms—the rhythms of the market that keep him at work for long hours—they can engage their partners to make family happen with them, even when it means slowing the pace and sacrificing a certain level of ambition. They'll also have to patch together a family support system with every aunt, uncle, grandparent, and caregiver they can find, with neighbors and parenting groups and local libraries and recreation centers. That's a tall order, particularly when you're closing deals or putting out fires at work all day. But it will pay working parents back tenfold with both a rich family life and a workplace that adjusts to people's needs.

Right now, it's mostly women who press for parental leave, flextime, sabbaticals, part-time options, on-site childcare, after-school programs, and decent work hours, leaving men stranded in their workaholism. Just as problematic, if it's only women taking advantage of "work life" and "family-friendly" options, women can't possibly rise as high as men or use their creative powers as fully because success in the market will always demand full availability for work. Women will not run things because running things will exclude "mommy-track" types and most women are mommies.

So what, you might ask, if we have a two-tier system where women work half-time in subordinate positions and men run business and politics with their 12-hour days. There are some *serious* ramifications, for women today and for our sons and daughters.

First, the part-time paradox. If you're working 30 hours a week and he's working 60, which of you will likely do the domestic chores? Which of you will become ever more preoccupied with work? Which will have family cares in mind?

Second, as an employer, who would *you* hire? A woman, who will probably take costly leaves, demand childcare, flextime, and eventually work part time, all of which is either expensive or inconvenient? Or a man, who makes no special demands and is plainly prepared to work until he drops?

Without enforced affirmative action, what will motivate businesses to hire and promote women? Presumably, businesses that have come to rely on women, like accounting and nursing, will continue accommodating them. But that means women's work ghettos will remain a permanent fixture of our labor force. And what will motivate elite graduate schools to fill half their scarce slots with women if women are contemplating attenuated careers? In 1970, only 3 percent of law students were women; only 8 percent of medical school students were women. What would keep us from reverting to these dismal statistics? If women demand to work half as much as men, they'll rightly train half as many women, maybe fewer. Because that's the way the invisible hand works. That's the free market.

I'm hardly the first to have noticed that in free markets, women's caretaking undermines their equality: If you rock the cradle, you don't rule the world. Remember nannygate, when Zoe Baird and Kimba Woods were eliminated as candidates for U.S. attorney general because undocumented aliens took care of their children? While no male officeholder's childcare arrangements have ever been examined, the fact that these distinguished women employed undocumented aliens (not in itself a crime according to the law) was regarded as too controversial for the Clinton White House.

No one mentioned the obvious: that parents often *have* to resort to undocumented immigrants for reliable childcare because America has so little infrastructure to do the job. In this system, high-powered working fathers have wives and high-powered working mothers have housekeepers, many of whom are, indeed, undocumented aliens. President Clinton simply took the safe but politically correct course by appointing a childless woman. As I've said repeatedly, gender discrimination today isn't so much about women versus men—though let's not forget it's still there—as it is about mothers versus others.

Of course, a lot of people argue that mothers shouldn't have any special privileges at work or anywhere else. As one reader wrote to the editor of the *New York Times*: "This is not discrimination against mothers but a recognition that people make choices and there are consequences." Ah, but isn't it a bit unfair that it's women who have to make this choice, even though men are also parents and the society as a whole needs the next generation to pay for the retirement of the current one? Besides, there is the matter of numbers. If the vast majority of workers require "special" treatment, why do we insist on defining it as "special"?

In *The Baby Boon: How Family Friendly America Cheats the Childless*, Elinor Burkett argues that with the child tax credit, subsidized childcare, and now a cry for paid parental leave, parents are given unfair advantages. But, within reason, society has a strong interest in both reproducing itself and assuring that the young have a good start in life. If parents had to bear all the costs, we wouldn't have public education or, therefore, an educated public. In any event, the sorts of changes needed to make the country in general and the workplace parent friendly aren't all that expensive for either government or businesses, as we'll see. And to be fair, they should benefit everyone.

If everyone who wanted sane work hours, flextime, and paid sabbaticals could have them, wouldn't everyone be less resentful than the author of the letter to the editor or the author of the book? What if everyone could take a 10/4 week or leave at 5:30 every evening? Sure, there would always be those who choose to work 60-hour weeks, but the 60-hour week wouldn't be required or expected for most employees. It wouldn't be the norm.

What if workplaces offered a cafeteria plan that gives employees a predetermined amount in benefits of their choosing? Some might want spousal health coverage, others could choose parental leave, and still others might take the sabbatical to do relief work in Bosnia. For those who take fewer options, a bonus. Life's never perfectly fair. One childless employee may end up using a lot of workmen's compensation because he fell out of his new ergonomically correct desk chair while the employee with three kids gets to use the on-site childcare.

There are those who think workplace adjustments, tax credits, and social assistance don't go far enough to help families. In *The Feminine Economy and Economic Man*, Shirley P. Burggraf suggests replacing the Social Security System with "parental dividends" paid proportionally from grown children's salaries directly to their parents. Her system would tie generations together economically and give parents incentives for investing in their children—in the age-old manner. Nonparents could simply save for their own old age.

The parental dividend may be too radical a change for the moment, but it does underscore our desperate situation. We need a new accounting; the old one is killing us. When women work and do all the caretaking (pant, pant), or hire undocumented aliens to run the household while they work 12-hour days, or reluctantly quit work in order to take care of their kids—that is, when women accept the status quo—society won't change. Mothers will rarely get into public office or the Fortune 500 or the winning "genome" science team. But when men and women together press the workplace to respect personal life, real change will happen for everyone.

Professor Lotte Bailyn at MIT's Sloan School of Management has proposed that as a matter of sound economics, it pays businesses to offer humane policies for everyone in order to reduce stress, fatigue, absenteeism, turnover, and build morale. Creating successful experimental units at Xerox, Corning, and Fleet Financial Services, Bailyn showed how companies could switch to flextime, telecommuting, and so on, and either sustain or increase their productivity.

Bailyn offered an alternative for some kinds of workplaces. But feminists have been calling for this kind of overall change since the dark ages. Sociologist Mirra Komarovsky,

Barnard College's first director of women's studies pointed to the need for "modified work patterns for both sexes" as well as cooperative ties among child-rearing families, and high-quality childcare for all economic classes.

Supreme Court Justice Ruth Bader Ginsburg once wrote (back in those dark ages) that true equality requires affirmative action "to eliminate institutional practices that limit or discourage female participation." She herself offers flextime to her (male) clerk so he can be with his family when he needs to be. The invisible hands must work in concert, or at least shake.

Feminism: Friend, Foe, or Who Cares Anymore?

I have to stop here a moment to defuse that now charged and twisted term "feminist." A lot of young women I've interviewed tell me they're not feminists. When I ask them what a feminist is they say: Women who hate men, women who don't want children, women who are political zealots. Merriam Webster would like to say a word:

"Feminism: (1) the theory of the political, economic, and social equality of the sexes; (2) organized activity on behalf of women's rights and interests."

Anyone say anything about boiling men's private parts? In fact, isn't it a bit pathetic that we have to advance a *theory* that women and men are equal? And do women's rights and interests need a special agenda?

It's worth noting that the National Organization of Women's agenda, as expressed in its original Bill of Rights, included childcare, so it's not like they were dissing mothers. Note, too, that the three main demands of the 1970 Women's March on Washington were: childcare, equal pay for equal work, and legal abortion. Radical? Not where I come from.

On some level, women, even very young women today who don't think of themselves as political, do have a political agenda, and it is feminist, as defined above. In a January 2000, poll done by EDK Associates, a public opinion research firm in New York City, the most important issues raised by women were:

1. inequities in pay
2. workplace discrimination
3. resources to fight breast cancer
4. reliable childcare
5. violence against women
6. paid medical leave for new parents
7. shoring up social security
8. health coverage

In a more recent poll called "Women's Voices 2000," two of the major concerns stated were the time-crunch and equal pay for equal work.

Jennifer Baumgardner and Amy Richards, authors of *ManifestA*, call this the "I'm not a feminist, but . . ." phenomenon, which as they note, limits women's effectiveness: "The only problem is that, while on a personal level feminism is everywhere, like flouride, on a political level the movement is more like nitrogen: ubiquitous and inert."

The majority of women today do seem to be feminists. They just don't want to be bothered with politics, and they don't want to be like those women who protested, marched on Washington, and got nasty about men. As one woman put it, we just want to do what we want, including stay home if that's what we want. But, ironically, "doing what you want" takes some doing, in the political sense. Doing nothing means kissing your choices away.

Take "choice" itself, which a lot of young women take for granted, even though, on June 28, 2000, the Supreme Court narrowly upheld a lower court's decision to invalidate Nebraska's ban on certain abortion procedures. Along with banning third trimester abortions, a ruling in favor of Nebraska would have allowed states to limit other abortion procedures—including those in which the mother's health was endangered.

In effect, the Supreme Court held that every abortion regulation must contain a health exception, allowing for a doctor's judgment about the effect on a mother's health—but only by a 5 to 4 margin. Three justices have gone on record as wanting to overturn *Roe versus Wade*. Does everyone get that? President George W. Bush will appoint three Supreme Court justices. If they are conservatives, women could lose their "choice" in a nod.

Of course, this does unsettle some young women. One summer intern at Connecticut National Abortion and Reproductive Rights Action League (NARAL), University of Connecticut student, Kate Farrar, writes to her contemporaries:

> As a young woman I have more choices than I truly know what to do with. I have the right to an equal education, to any career, to watch professional women sports, and even the option to wear pants every day of the week. I have the rights to my own body, and this is the most powerful choice. It is easy for all of us to take our reproductive rights for granted. But the fight is never over as long as you have the other side still fighting back.

Unfortunately, she's the exception, someone who chose to intern at a feminist political organization.

What about equal pay for equal work, which a lot of young women today take for granted. Under 1991 civil rights legislation, women are entitled to financial compensation when they win sex discrimination suits under federal law. But individually they can't be awarded more than $300,000, although there's no equivalent cap in race or ethnic discrimination cases. That cap makes it more difficult to find lawyers to take sex discrimination cases, which typically take eight years to settle. My own case, by the way, which I could not have afforded if my lawyer had been billing by the hour, took about five years.

Men wrote and voted for legislation that patently discriminated against women seeking equal rights. Women in Congress noticed the fine print, but didn't have the clout to change it. Most of the rest of us (and I include myself here) weren't even aware of the exception.

So what happens to choice and equal pay when our daughters come of age? Will they pay the price of our apathy? We'll all pay. Maybe not tomorrow, but the day after.

"Outside of Voting, We're Just Not Political"

It's not just young women. Only half the adult population even voted in the last two elections. But a lot of young women who do vote aren't that well informed. While there are some pro-women zines, like *Bust* and *Jane*, and Web sites like "Ask Amy," "Pop and Politics," "Chickclicks," and "estronet," their messages don't seem to inform enough of the choices young women are making. Little is happening on the national level, although there are some notable exceptions that may indicate a turning of the tide.

The 5,000-member Third Wave Foundation (www.thirdwavefoundation.org) offers scholarships to women with an interest in social justice and funds groups like Portland, Oregon's, Sisters in Action, which supports leadership for young women. Another group, Active Element (www.activelement.org), funds youth groups such as the 21st Century Youth Leadership Movement in Selma, Alabama, which helped elect the first African-American mayor in this mostly African-American city. To encourage young people's political involvement, Active Element is also creating a directory of local action groups called, the Future 500. Hopefully, the name is predictive.

For the moment, though, young activists are a rare breed. Twenty-six-year-old Gita Drury, one of the five founders of Active Element, became politically active during an internship that took her into women's prisons and opened her eyes, as she says, to the problems in this country. Before that, like a lot of young people, she "sensed the inequities and problems in the country, but didn't have a broad picture or any idea how to plug into what was happening." Twenty-six-year-old Julie Shah from the Third Wave Foundation came to activism from politically aware parents, but worries that young people today "live in a bubble, not looking outside their own lives."

They don't have visible enough spokespeople, agendas, lobbyists, political journals, and newsletters to help them articulate their issues. Outside of the occasional campus protest against Nike's overseas sweatshops or the 1992 demonstration for reproductive freedom on the Washington Mall, this new generation rarely demonstrates or organizes political action groups.

Of course, there was the antiglobalization demonstration at the World Trade Organization meeting in Seattle. Whether you agree with their position or not, at least they got a lot of people to think about things from another point of view. But the leader of that group, Naomi Klein, is not an American. She's from Canada, where the economy is not booming and where average income is well below ours. Unfortunately, a strong economy can breed political apathy.

Dave Eggers, author of that Gen X bestseller, *A Heartbreaking Work of Staggering Genius*, makes this point in describing the bunch of writers and editors of an influential San Francisco magazine:

> It's not that we don't want to support [do-gooders and progressive nonprofit organizations] because we do. . . . It's just that, given little to no contact with economic insecurity of any kind, we have a hard time finding the fire in the belly for such things. We want to join them in complaining about the burdens of student loans . . . we want to complain about jobs, but we don't really want jobs ourselves. . . . And Social Security? Well, personally at the least, I cannot in my wildest fantasies see myself making it past fifty or fifty-five, so find the issue moot. All we really want is for no one to have a boring life, to be impressive, so we can be impressed.

The woman who quotes this passage in an article about Dave Eggers for *hipMama*, an online magazine, writes with understanding about the very people who might "want to breathe fire and make the world over in their image—to lead a kind of brilliant, unco-optable rebellion—but who find themselves stumped because they have nothing much to protest."

And it's not just bohemian types at radical art magazines. Remember Heather Neely saying, "We have no dialogue." Or Dr. Betsy Kavaler commenting ruefully that "most of us are very shallow because we've never had to think about anything but ourselves and our comforts." Without dialogue and political reflection, life can be very lonely. Self-centered people don't make for communities and networks. It can be disconcertingly isolating when you are the only one who would like to change things. Think of the way Betsy, who wants to change women's medicine, is viewed as a weird "Joan of Arc" type among her acquaintances.

Dr. Beth Davis Phillpotts and her husband Garfield are educated, aware "buppies," as they grinningly call themselves (black yuppies). Although Beth's uncle was a Black Panther who ended up in exile in Cuba and Garfield's parents are immigrants from Jamaica, for them it's different: "There's no political drama in our lives. We never lived through a war or a depression or a civil rights upheaval. All of that happened before our time. Life is pretty good for us."

They point out how hip hop, a ghetto phenomenon that's taken over music and youth culture, may have started in the spirit of resistance but now has one theme: I'm getting mine. That's today's culture, they explain. "We're not group-think; we're 'get mine.'"

The bottom line may be that these are good times economically for the very people who might have been political leaders; they're not confronting life and death issues, like boys being drafted or young men, like Beth's uncle, getting shot by the police right in front of their homes. Women hit glass ceilings, but they don't get doors slammed in their faces anymore.

Yet, when I ask Beth and Garfield how they would improve society if they had a magic wand, they have a definite wish-list: quality public education and daycare, a paid month vacation for everyone, safer neighborhoods, *more time* so that people aren't so stressed that their frustrations turn into violence, child abuse, and addiction.

Well, Betsy, Heather, Beth, Garfield, Dave Eggers, and all of you who would like things better but aren't motivated enough to get on the bus, you don't even have to. With very small changes, awareness, voting, and a little bit of pressure, people can have it all. Everyone can.

Renovating Culture

Start with business, since business is responsible for the time bind that's turning up the stress. Business is now booming. But in order for an individual to be a part of the boom requires long hours, no drag coefficients, and, for all intents and purposes, a wife or facsimile at home. Most women are still in low-paying, female ghetto jobs. Caregiving—the essence of "woman's work," is still nearly valueless—with the average wages of childcare workers stuck at $12,000 a year. Note, too, that in states without communal property, full-time caregiving does not even have the legal status of a man's salary. A divorced woman doesn't have a claim on half of what her husband has saved from his salary since the time she stopped working to raise their children, nor can she demand a part of his future earnings, except for child support.

That equation will change as more men and women change, but change is hard. The truth is, we pay lip service to families and nurturing while we actually value work—both as individuals and as a culture. Not only does this reflect traditional male values, but, as one astute psychologist put it: "Work is a major source of satisfaction for adults. There are immediate payoffs with work, unlike relationships. . . . Most Americans admit that their families are more important to them than their work, but they derive more personal satisfaction from work."

Work analyst Joanne Ciulla observes, too, that "once time pressure is added to [household] tasks we begin to experience home life much the same way that we experience work for pay." That is, home life is pressured and performance oriented as well, but without the immediate payoffs work offers.

Men stay in the workplace, getting more involved; women take themselves out of the game but retain workplace values and therefore don't challenge men's overwhelming commitment to work. Women's unconscious thinking goes, we *have* to nurture, men don't. Or, someone's got to nurture and women are better at it. However, we're getting the job done. Too many elderly are languishing in crummy institutions and too many kids are in inadequate childcare. Women are no longer willing to do caretaking for free or for appallingly low salaries, nor should caretaking be solely a woman's job. For sanity's sake, we all have to value nurturing—caring for the old and the young and the sick and disabled—and we all have to nurture to some extent, particularly if we have children. We also all have to work (or have independent sources of income) if we're to have true equality. Yet we don't have to work as much.

The increasing demands for work/life balance are gradually bending business; the popularity of these demands is slowly bending politicians; the very idea of balance and family support will eventually bend the culture. It's starting to happen in all three spheres:

Re: Business. The Bureau of Labor Statistics reports that in 1997, 28 percent of workers had flexible schedules; 32 percent in 2000, and a continued increase is expected.

Re: Politicians. In his last year as president, Bill Clinton pledged to make working parents a "protected class." Although he lacked the clout to do much, he's a bellwether of change. Pennsylvania, New Jersey, Michigan, and five other states have banned job bias directed at parents. Furthermore, under new U.S. Labor Department regulations, states are permitted to provide unemployment checks "on a voluntary or experimental basis" for parental leave.

Re: Culture. Ten New York City labor unions along with two dozen religious and women's organizations began lobbying New York State lawmakers to spend $200 million on childcare and give six months of paid maternity leave—as they do in Europe.

How much change is possible? A lot. How fast? Very fast. When America went into World War II, the government provided $52 million between 1941 and 1943 (equivalent to $600 million today) to create daycare centers so that Rosie the Riveter could keep America's factories running.

Recently, in order to combat high unemployment, France legislated a 35-hour workweek (and surprise inspections to ensure there's not a minute more without overtime pay). A lot of the French protested, wanting the higher income from longer hours. A lot of businesses are postponing the changeover to just before the 2002 deadline. But many of the businesses that have already cut to 35 hours find no loss of productivity. In one example, cited in the *New York Times*, a jam factory with 18 employees upped productivity by 30 percent when it added 2 workers, divided the staff into 2 teams working different shifts, and kept the factory open 12 hours a day instead of 8. While service industries will have a harder time, on the whole analysts expect that change—in itself—will rouse stagnant businesses to be more flexible and productive.

Ciulla points out that it's not always true that the more time employees spend at work the more they produce. "The ability to go home when the job is done," she writes, "is a powerful motivator because it gives people a sense of control over their time and work. Perhaps what is most unsatisfying about modern work is that people are frequently paid not for what they produce, but for their time." She herself enumerates many examples of how the promise of leisure motivated people to work faster—including one famous one from 1930, when the Kellogg Company switched from an eight-hour to a six-hour day in order to hire more workers and thus reduce unemployment during the Depression. To their surprise, however, they found that productivity increased so much they didn't have to hire more workers.

What if we had a six-hour day or a 35-hour work week, flexible schedules, part-time options, paid parental leave, and universal quality childcare? Even if we were almost productive there would realistically be some cost. Who would pay the bill for these civilities? Everyone thinks that this sort of thing constitutes the "welfare state" approach that ruined Europe. However, while the impulse of politicians to give everything to everybody—think of the right to full retirement at age 55—might have bankrupted France, for example, France didn't *have* to guarantee such extravagant benefits. Quality childcare and paid parental leave *on their own* didn't bankrupt Europe. Nor do their typical month-long vacations destroy business in, say, booming Holland or Italy.

The real question is who should pay. Government or business? That's the controversy raised, for example, in using unemployment benefits to pay for parental leave, which Vermont, Washington, Maryland, and Massachusetts are now experimenting with. The U.S. Chamber of Commerce and other business groups are suing to repeal the executive-order regulations, charging that unemployment insurance is for those people who lose jobs. But the real issue is that employers are charged a tax geared to the unemployment they cause through layoffs and they don't want to pay more. In fact, if they anticipate that tax hike, they might be understandably reluctant to hire those people who are most likely to take advantage of those benefits—that is, women of childbearing age.

Business can foot some of the bill for work/life supports, offering sabbaticals and parental leave and real vacations, for example, or setting employees up in home offices. These policies ultimately pay for themselves in reducing turnover and absenteeism. But as a matter of good economics and good politics, business probably shouldn't be asked to pay the entire bill, nor would it be good for anyone, women included, if it did so to its detriment. Business can offer a lot more of these supports than they are, and a lot more businesses can offer them. As Elisabeth Lasch-Quinn, Syracuse University historian, comments in *The New Republic,* "Surely there must be a little give in a system that pays corporate executives an ever-increasing and astronomical $250 or so for every $1 that workers earn." (That is, Yahoo's Tim Koogle: $1.7 billion; America Online's Steve Case: $1.1 billion. Which means that Koogle's income is $4.7 million a day compared with the median household income of $40,000 a year!) Yes, there should be some give.

But government must be our real ally. Or, more precisely, our representative, the voice of the people, particularly of the majority of workers, who are working parents. We can, if we want, legislate money for parental leave. Washington can kick in money to state unemployment insurance in order to cover parental leave costs. This way, government eliminates incentives to avoid hiring prospective parents while still exploiting an efficient existing administrative structure. The government, you may not know, already kicks in money to state unemployment insurance benefits funds when unemployment reaches high levels. In the same way, Washington could appropriate money for preschool, after-school, and childcare. We can choose to spend our money to help children along with those who parent them.

The World Is Governed by Those Who Show Up

Even if you don't have or want kids, consider the issue of childcare because it's such a concrete example of the problem we face in this transitional period. State childcare support programs are happening, but at a snail's pace. First of all, there is a crisis in childcare. In 1995, "Cost, Quality and Child Outcomes in Child Care Centers," a federally funded four-state study of American childcare, concluded that the majority of it is poor quality. The study also pointed out that the cost is so high—up to 25 percent of the annual income of lower-income parents—that parents are frequently forced to buy cheaper, unlicensed, and unsupervised care, that is, pay the lady down the road who sets a bunch of kids in front of her television all day. Nine out of ten children who qualify for subsidized care are on waiting lists. Even parents who can afford quality care often can't find it. That's because average salaries in childcare are so low that teachers don't stay long and centers can't hire enough of them to properly look after the numbers of children they have.

This is a crisis. We are not nurturing the children of this country sufficiently. Dr. T. Berry Brazelton, the leading authority on childcare and author of, most recently, *The Irreducible Needs of Children*, believes that children were better off 30 years ago, before the stresses on young parents logarithmically increased and before they were forced into using poor childcare because they can't pay for or find good care.

States have responded to the crisis, but they can't or won't pay the bill. Georgia used its lottery money to create free, universal pre-K programs for four-year-olds and after-school programs for kids who qualify. It's a start, but doesn't help parents of the under-four set or the parents of kids who don't qualify for after-school programs.

Mississippi "has taken meals on wheels to new heights," boasts June Boykin, director of the Forum on Children and Families. With help from local businesses, they keep two Winnebegos on the road to reach Mississippi's rural childcare centers. One, with a childcare expert at the wheel and a load of loaner materials; the other packing a teacher and library to train staff people right in their own parking lots.

Now, really. Is that what we're reduced to? Using lottery money for childcare and sending out two Winnebegos where an entire state support center is needed. This from the richest nation on earth, while preschoolers in France are guaranteed quality childcare (including *sole meuniere* for lunch) for a government subsidized $5 to $12 a day.

Yes, America can be proud of the occasional high-quality center run by saintly women with other sources of income. And we do have good chains, like Children's World and Kindercare, which deliver decent services at prices affordable by parents with good jobs. And yes, there is Bright Horizons, a company that runs state-of-the-art centers for corporations eager to keep skilled workers. But that's a drop in the bucket.

Why am I telling you this? Because children are the future. Because a lot of parents are in despair about how to care for their children while they work. You might one day be among them. Because women's equality ultimately depends on it. And because a lot of children are being neglected in lousy childcare. No one wants that. Not even the most politically apathetic bohemian magazine editor.

We could, as a body politic, eliminate the problem in a heartbeat by legislating funding. For example, the $200 million budget for federally funded after-school programs in 1998 was five times that of 1997. It could be ten times that in 2001 if people demanded that their senators and representatives vote for it. But that requires voting, sending a letter, maybe, signing an e-mail petition, reading the paper, joining an advocacy group. Not a lot. Just being there, politically. Being aware.

It's too easy to dismiss politicians as peas in a pod. No matter how alike they look, voting records do matter. And if we could limit campaign spending, we might elect some candidates with the freedom and inclination to work on issues that matter to ordinary people. We could also elect more women to Congress. Today, just one member of Congress in eight is female. How representative is that? Women, it's worth noting, do vote differently. A higher percentage of women in Congress vote for choice, childcare, education funding, and gun control. With just a bit of effort, this generation of women could do so much. Start with balance in your own life, create networks of supportive friends, mentors, and nurturing men. The rest will follow.

That, of course, is my vision. But my vision is limited by my feminist, '60s, civil rights, professional, middle-class, white, and maternal perspective. What truly inspires me is what I don't know, and what the young women of today do. Their experiences, wisdom, and ingenuity could take this culture somewhere I can't even imagine. Women like Carol Ann Kalish, Kemba Extavour, Trini Quinn, Kimber McKenzie, Sarah Vickers Willis, Sarah Pearson, Dr. Betsy Kavaler, Dr. Beth Davis Phillpotts, Dr. Tamara Sachs, Galia Swetschinski, Risa Gerson, Hillary Billings, Jennifer Kushell, Sherry Levy, and Bonnie Gemmell will all alter our culture and change the workplace, affecting the lives of other American men and women for years to come. The more they understand their options, their worth, and the consequences of their own life choices, the more women can do for themselves and each other. They'll need to take time to reflect, to check in at the end of the day—with themselves and their partners—to be sure they're living their values. When they are, they are the real masters and mistresses of the universe. Not necessarily by making huge sums of money. But by raising the quality of life for everyone and increasing the "spiritual currency" of our culture.

The younger the women, the earlier they are starting to conquer their culture in a way I and my contemporaries couldn't have fathomed. Joline Godfrey, CEO of Independent Means, who works with "digital girls"—teens who learn from her programs how to handle money and start their own businesses—writes:

> These girls who understand intimately their place in the economic web of the nation—and the globe—are going to have a voice in the policies and practices we see emerge in the next decade or two. For every one Donna Dubinsky and Carly Fiorina we celebrate today, we will have a hundred powerful female entrepreneurs inventing, producing, and shaping our world. How men and women share resources, negotiate roles, and uncover new relationships in such a world will be the story of our very near future. Buckle your seat belt, it's going to be a bumpy—but oh so exciting—ride.

With an inheritance of new reproductive and social possibilities, women have roared into education, pioneered new territory, and (literally) shot into outer space. They've created a dizzying multiplicity of lifestyles and family arrangements. And they're moving into the future with unprecedented information, access to power, and a belief that the culture belongs to them. My money's on all the young women of today—and their daughters. From my final front-porch rocking chair, I know I'll be yelling, "Go girl," marveling at how women have reinvented the world I once knew.

Notes

"In Dreams Begin Responsibilities"

10 *Poet Delmore Schwartz's mysterious phrase*: Delmore Schwartz, "In Dreams Begin Responsibilities," title of a short story published in 1948, reprinted in a paperback of the same title, New York: New Directions Books, 1978.

11 *They are the first to create predominantly dual-income marriages:* Gene Koretz, "Economic Trends: Wives with Fat Paychecks," *Business Week*, Sept. 7, 1998, p. 22.

11 *More than half of whom own their own homes*: Julie V. Iovine, "Castle First, Prince Later: Marketing to Ms.," *The New York Times*, Oct. 21, 1999, pp. B1, 3.

11 *Single women not only dominate the home renovation market*: according to a Young and Rubicam study cited in Tamala M. Edwards, "Flying Solo," *Time*, Aug. 28, 2000, p. 48.

11 *"the Stepford economy"*: Jon Caroll, Escape Column: "The Stepford Economy," *Business 2.0*, Nov. 1999, p. 336.

14 *"nearly all of the women I spoke with"*: Peggy Orenstein, *Flux: Women on Sex, Work, Love, Kids, and Life in a Half Changed World*, New York: Random House, 2000, p. 105.

14 *I probably use less of what I learned at the Harvard Business School*: Ken Auletta, Annals of Communications: "In the Company of Women," *The New Yorker*, Apr. 20, 1998, pp. 75–76.

16 *While childless women earn wages close to men's*: Jane Waldfogel, "Understanding the 'Family Gap' in Pay for Women with Children," *Journal of Economic Perspectives*, Vol. 12, No. 1, Winter, 1998, pp.143, 153.

16 *Women fear that combining work and family*: Elaine Wethington, coresearcher, 1992 Cornell University Study quoted in Alison Bell, "Making Work Work," *American Baby*, Feb. 1998, p. 53.

Generation XX: No More Business as Usual

21 *Nearly doubling of women in the labor force*: Howard Hayghe, U.S. Department of Labor, Bureau of Labor Statistics.

21 *Though close to 46 million women work fulltime*: Ibid.

21 *The 51 million women and men born between 1960 and 1980: 120 Years of American Education*, table 28, National Center For Educational Statistics—in 1961, females earned 38.5% of the B.A. degrees, 43% in 1970, 50% in 1994 (50% of M.A.'s as well); projected for 2000, 56.3%.

22 *8 million women attend college and graduate school*: Ibid. Note, however, that the higher the status school, the lower female attendance: Daniel Sadker, "Gender Games," *Washington Post*, Op. Ed. Column, July 30, 2000, p. A37.

22 *The majority major in business*: Jerry Jacobs, Department of Sociology, University of Pennsylvania, from an ongoing unpublished study, phone interview, December 1999.

22 *Forecasters predict that by the year 2007, they will have achieved parity or majority*: "Addressing the Prospect of a Matrilinear Millennium: A Forum," *Harpers Magazine*, June 1999, p. 33.

22 *A quarter-million women received master's degrees last year*: Tanya Schevitz, "40% of U.S. Doctoral Degrees Earned by Women in '96–97," *The San Francisco Chronicle*, Nov. 3, 1999, p. 2.

22 *Right now, more women than men are starting their own businesses*: "Key Facts," National Foundation for Women Business Owners, www.NFWBO.org.

23 *Some of them, such as Patricia Dunn, chairman of Barclay's Global Investors:* Patricia Sellers, "These Women Rule," *Fortune*, Oct. 25, 1999, pp. 94–95.

23 *In 1999, for example, more than 40% of the legislators in Washington State:* Sam Howe Verhovek, "Record for Women in Washington Legislature," *The New York Times*, Feb. 4, 1999, p. A14.

23 *That same year three women all held top posts in the launch*: William J. Broad, "Three Women Wait Anxiously for Their Spacecraft to Reach Mars," *The New York Times*, Apr. 18, 1999, p. A10.

23 *Meanwhile, 42-year-old Col. Eileen M. Collins*: William J. Broad, "Blasting Off on a Mission for Cosmic Science," *The New York Times*, July 13, 1999, p. D3.

23 *Even one-third of the scientists and staff working in Antarctica*: Cornelia Dean, "After a Struggle, Women Win a Place on the Ice," *The New York Times*, Nov. 10, 1998, p. D1.

23 *A quarter of the Pittsburgh police force*: Michael Janofsky, "Pittsburgh Is Showcase for Women in Policing," *The New York Times*, June 21,1998, p. A14.

23 *Avon Products, Inc.:* In November, 1999, Avon, Inc. appointed 41-year-old Andrea Jung CEO. Jung is the mother of an 11-year-old.

24 *"Future Homemakers of America"*: Michelle Healy, Lifeline Column, *USA Today*, July 9, 1999, p. D1.

24 *In a classic suburban parenting magazine*: Pam Ratliff, "Motherhood: A Proud Profession," *Ventura County Parent*, May 1999, p. 16.

24 *"The biggest challenge for our generation"*: Meredith Bagby, *Rational Exuberance: The Influence of Generation X on the New American Economy*, New York: Dutton, 1998, p. 7.

24 *"Unlike the boomers, few of us"*: Ibid., p. 12.

25 *A 1999 PricewaterhouseCoopers survey*: quoted in Sue Shellenbarger, Work and Family Column: "What Job Candidates Really Want to Know: Will I Have a Life?" *The Wall Street Journal*, Nov. 17, 1999, p. B1.

25 *Teens report that they don't get enough time with their parents*: Sue Shellenbarger, Work and Family Column: "Would Your Teen Give You High Marks on Career-Handling?" *The Wall Street Journal*, May 20, 1998, p. B1.

25 *"In the eyes of Gen X, their parents devoted their lives"*: Ron Zemke, Claire Raines, Bob Filipczak, *Generations at Work: Managing the Clash of Veterans, Boomers, Xers, and Nexters in Your Workplace* , New York: AMACOM Books, 2000, p. 99.

25 *"Sanity, Balance, Butterfat"*: "It's Your Choice," survey conducted by Roper-Starch Worldwide Survey, *Fast Company*, Jan/Feb., 2000, p. 202.

26 *"Initiate discussions with managers"*: Debra F. Schleinholtz, ed., "Cracking the Glass Ceiling: Strategies for Success," a study done for the Glass Ceiling Commission of the U.S. Department of Labor by Catalyst, New York City, 1994, p. 12.

27 *More than 3,000 high schools*: Sue Shellenbarger, Work and Family Column, "Students Get Lessons in How to Manage a Well-Balanced Life," *The Wall Street Journal*, Feb. 24, 1999, p. B1.

27 *Women are the majority of the electorate today*: Gail Collins, "A Social Glacier Roars," *The New York Times Magazine*, May 16, 1999, p. 78.

27 *According to surveys, women's priority issues are all about supporting families:* Sam Howe Verhovek, "Record for Women in Washington Legislature," *The New York Times*, Feb. 4, 1999, p. A14.

30 *Meg Whitman, CEO of eBay*: Patricia Sellers, "These Women Rule," *Fortune*, Oct. 25, 1999, p. 122.

31 *The Cornell University Careers Institute:* Penny Edgell Becker and Phyllis Moen, "Scaling Back: Dual-Earner Couples' Work-Family Strategies," *Journal of Marriage and the Family*, No. 61, Nov. 1999, p. 1001. Also, phone interview with Penny Becker, Sept. 30, 2000.

31 *Harvard Economist Claudia Goldin:* Claudia Goldin, "Career and Family: College Women Look to the Past," *Gender and Family Issues in the Workplace,* ed. Francine D. Blau and Ronald G. Ehrenberg, New York City: Russell Sage Foundation, 1997, pp. 20–58.

33 *"Too much introspection":* Gail Sheehy, *Passages: Predictable Crises of Adult Life,* New York: Bantam, 1977, p. 126.

35 *In "Children of the Gender Revolution":* Kathleen Gerson, "Children of the Gender Revolution: Some Theoretical Questions and Findings From the Field," eds. Arlene and Jerome Skolnick, *Family in Transition,* 11th edition, Needham Heights, Mass.: Allyn and Bacon, 2000.

Reality Bites

41 *"With Labor Day Comes More Labor, Less Play,":* Jodi Wilgoren, *The Los Angeles Times,* Sept. 7, 1998, p. A1.

41 *37 fewer hours, to be exact:* Louis Harris Poll, 1991, cited in Robert Frank, *Luxury Fever: Why Money Fails To Satisfy in an Era of Excess,* New York: The Free Press, 1999, p. 50.

41 *While the 40-hour week still exists on paper:* Jerry Jacobs and Kathleen Gerson, "Who Are the Overworked Americans?" *Review of Social Economy,* Vol. LVI, No. 4, Winter, 1998, pp. 443–459. In a phone interview, Sept. 2000, Professor Jacobs explains the discrepancy between the BLS figure of 39 hours a week (released in August 2000 by senior economist Randy E. Ilg) and the Families and Work Institute figure (quoted in their 1997 "National Study of the Changing Workforce") of 47.1 hours a week by pointing out that the Bureau of Labor Statistics factors in part-time hours, which have risen significantly with the rise of women in the workplace. As for studies showing that we have more free time, Jacobs reminds us that most is accounted for by household technology and smaller families, not by less work.

42 *Back in 1992, the average was just 43.8:* 1997 "National Study of the Changing Workforce," Families and Work Institute, a nonprofit research group in New York City.

42 *82 percent of 5000 executives:* "Work Week," *The Wall Street Journal,* July 6, 1999, p. A1.

42 *In the global scheme of things, our average vacation time is a pitiful 13 days:* Stephen Mihm, "Traveling: A Box Score," *The New York Times,* July 12, 2000, p. D5.

42 *What's more, a recent AT&T survey:* of 35 corporate representatives from the International Tenant Representative Alliance, cited in "Work Week," *The Wall Street Journal,* June 8, 1998, p. A1.

42 *Almost half the workers in a study done by Rutgers University and the University of Connecticut*: "Work-Week," *The Wall Street Journal*, Sept. 21, 1999, p. A1.

43 *Consider 29-year-old Joe Minton*: Jonathan Kaufman, "An Aspiring Game Mogul Finds a Boss's Life 'Weird'," *The Wall Street Journal*, June 18, 1998, p. B1.

43 *The average part-timer is paid 60 percent*: Polly Callaghan and Heidi Hartman, *Contingent Work: A Chart Book on Part Time and Temporary Employment*, Washington, D.C.: Economic Policy Institute, 1991.

43 *68% of the part-time workers*: Reed Abelson, "Part-Time Work for Some Adds Up to a Full-Time Job," *The New York Times*, Nov. 2, 1998, pp. A1, A16.

43 *Most working parents say time pressure*: "Family Matters: A National Survey of Women and Men Conducted for the National Partnership for Women and Families by Lake Sosin Snell Perry and Associates, Feb. 1998. See www.nationalpartnership.org.

43 *On the books, two-thirds of American companies offer flextime*: "1998 "Business Work-Life Study," Families and Work Institute, p. 8.

43 *According to a study of over a thousand managers*: Gene Koretz, "Economic Trends," "Hazardous to Your Carreer: The Risk of Taking Unpaid Leaves," *Business Week*, Jan. 17, 2000, p. 26.

43 *When the Ford Foundation studied of a group of engineers*: Leslie A. Perlow, *Finding Time: How Corporations, Individuals, and Families Can Benefit from New Work Practices*, Ithaca, New York: Cornell University Press, 1997, p. 104.

44 *According to another study, this one in the* Academy of Management Journal: Gene Goretz, "Economic Trends" "Hazardous to Your Career: The Risk of Taking Unpaid Leaves," *Business Week*, Jan. 17, 2000, p. 26.

44 *Deloitte Consulting in Pittsburgh:* James Lardner, "World Class Workaholics," *U.S. News and World Report*, Dec. 20, 1999, p. 52.

44 *While absenteeism has eased*: "Work Week," *The Wall Street Journal*, Sept. 21, 1999, p. A1.

44 *The National Institute for Occupational Safety*: (Reuters) Science Times, *The New York Times*, July 6, 1999, p. D.6.

44 *The World Bank, with 5,000 employees regularly criss-crossing the globe:* Joe Sharkey, Business Travel Column: "The World Bank Gauges the Toll Travel Takes on Employees and Looks for Ways to Soften the Effect," *The New York Times*, May 10, 2000, p. C6.

44 *A Gallup poll found that four of ten Americans*: cited in Robert Frank, *Luxury Fever*, p. 50.

45 *The meetings go late*: Stanley Bing, Bing! While You Were Out . . . Column: "Sleep Faster," *Fortune*, Nov. 22, 1999, p. 95.

45 *"Thirty-five years ago":* David Cay Johnston, "Vice Chairman of Fidelity to Retire Next Week," *The New York Times*, Jan. 26, 2000. p. C1.

45 *"World-Class Workaholics,":* James Lardner, *U.S.News & World Report*, Dec. 20, 1999, p. 53.

45 *The Families and Work Institute study found that 63 percent*: reported in Jodi Wilgoren, "With Labor Day Comes More Labor, Less Play," *The Los Angeles Times*, Sept. 7, 1998, pp. A1, A 12.

45 *Harvard University's Juliet Schor*: Ibid.

46 *Today's generation is graduating college with an average debt of $10,000*: Rational Exuberance, p. 195 (see note for p. 28).

46 *Those who get through medical school:* Ask Annie Column, *Fortune*, Oct. 25, 1999, p. 374.

46 *For example, the actual starting salaries for economics and finance graduates:* National Association of Colleges and Employers, "Work Week," *The Wall Street Journal*, Nov. 23, 1999, p. A1.

46 *The average lawyer earns*: Lists of salaries from The Bureau of Labor Statistics.

47 *In the wake of the Asian financial crisis*: Elizabeth Bumiller, "Free Fall in the Financial District," *The New York Times Magazine*, Nov. 15, 1998, pp. 74–75.

48 *"We learned from Wilma Flintstone"*: Meredith Bagby, *Rational Exhuberance*, p. 196.

48 *She notes that two-thirds of Gen X'ers:* Ibid., p. 204.

48 *"I am the internet generation"*: *The New York Times*, Feb. 9, 2000. p. B2.

48 *Juliet Schor argues*: *The Overspent American: Upscaling, Downshifting, and the New Consumer*, New York: Basic Books, 1998, p. 74.

48 *Meghan Daum:* "My Misspent Youth," *The New Yorker*, Oct. 18 & 25, 1999, p. 162.

49 *As Cornell economist Robert Frank argues*: *Luxury Fever*, New York: *The Free Press*, 1999, p. 53.

51 *A professor at the Graduate School of Management at the University of California at Irvine*: Judy B. Rosener, *America's Competitive Secret: Women Managers*, Oxford: Oxford University Press (Oxford Paperbacks), 1995, p. 34.

51 *Catalyst, the leading non-profit research organization*: quoted in Laura Ricci, *Views from Women's Eye's: Managing the New Majority*, Austin, Tex.: R3 Press, 1997, p. 65.

51 *Dorothy P. Moore and E. Holly Buttner, two professors of management*: *Female Entrepreneurs: Moving Beyond the Glass Ceiling*, Thousand Oaks, Calif.: Sage Publications, 1997, p. 47.

51 *"I had the overwhelming"*: Ibid., p. 8.

52 *"Ms. Fiorina's appointment"*: "Cracks in the Glass Ceiling," *The New York Times*, July 21, 1999, p. A22.

52 *Only 11 percent of corporate officers*: all figures from "Catalyst Facts: Women in Business," 1999.

52 *Less than one-half of 1 percent of the highest paid managers and corporate officers are women*: J. Fiermen, "Why Women Still Don't Hit the Top," *Fortune*, July 30, 1990, pp. 40–66.

52 *Even women nurses*: these two studies are cited in Judy B. Rosener, *America's Competitive Secret: Women Managers*, p. 59.

52 *In a Report to the president*: "A Question of Equity," report to the President and Congress by the United States Merit Systems Protection Board, Oct. 1992, ix. Ibid., p. 54.

52 *After a five-year investigation, MIT found,*: Carey Goldberg, "MIT Acknowledges Bias Against Female Professors," *New York Times*, Mar. 23, 1999, p.A1.

52 *Another study,* Who Succeeds in Science? G. Sonnert and G. Holton, *Who Succeeds in Science? The Gender Dimension,* New Brunswick, N.J.: Rutgers University Press, 1996.

53 *Dr. C. Megan Urry*: Natalie Angier, "For Women in Astronomy, a Glass Ceiling in the Sky," *The New York Times*, Feb. 15, 2000, p. D5. All quotes are from this article.

53 *One result of gender discrimination*: Joseph Kahn, "Morgan Stanley Is Target of Sex Bias Inquiry," *The New York Times*, July 29, 1999, p. C.1.

54 *Ann Hopkins*: Tamar Lewin, "Partnership Awarded to Woman in Sex Bias Case," The New York Times, May 16, 1990, pp. A1, A12.

54 *More recently, on June 5, 2000, the EEOC determined that Morgan Stanley discriminated:* Patrick McGeehan, "Morgan Stanley Cited for Discrimination Against Women," *The New York Times*, June 6, 2000, p. C1.

55 *After examining a large number of sex discrimination cases, Deborah L. Rhode*: Deborah L. Rhode, "Perspectives on Professional Women," *Stanford Law Review*, No. 40, 1988, pp. 1163–1207.

55 *"As one of the first women to run for statewide office in a maternity dress"*: Ellen Goodman, "It's No Wonder Women Enter Politics a Decade Later Than Men," *The Hartford Courant*, Jan.11, 2000, p. 33.

55 *Six months later, the Massachusetts State Ethics Commission*: Carey Goldberg, "Ethics Ruling Faults Massachusetts's Official," *The New York Times*, Aug. 24, 2000, p. A14.

00 *One Los Angeles Times piece*: Dana Calvo, "Female Anchors on Local TV Paid 28 percent Less," The Los Angeles Times, June 1, 2000, p. A1.

56 *Women, she concluded, are generally viewed as less qualified*: Virginia Valian, *Why So Slow: The Advancement of Women*, Cambridge, Mass.: The MIT Press, 1998, p. 8.
56 *"An analysis showed"*: Ibid., pp. 234–235.
56 *"A woman does not walk into the room"*: Ibid., p. 5.
56 *In a test where women and men were trained to take leadership roles*: Ibid., pp. 130–131.
57 *What should be understood, Valian argues*: Ibid., p. 160.
57 *As of 1994 women comprised 35 percent of the associates*: Ibid., pp. 201–202.
57 *M.B.A.'s fare no better*: Ibid., pp. 203–204.

Rethinking Modern Romance

60 *"the head of a public relations firm"*: *The New York Times*, June 20, 1999, p. A1.
60 *most girls report having unpleasant first sexual experiences*: Karen Bouris, *The First Time: What Parents and Teenage Girls Should Know about Losing Your Virginity*, Emmeryville, Calif.: Canari Press, 1994, pp. 3–4. A National Opinion Research Center poll determined that one-quarter of women's first sexual intercourse was forced, cited in Marcia Douglass and Lisa Douglass, *Are We Having Fun Yet: The Intelligent Women's Guide to Sex*, New York: Hyperion, 1997, p. 3.
61 *Just today, I caught a VH1 segment*: July 14, 2000, Carmen Electra guest host.
62 *Fox Family Channels*: Lisa Bannon, "Why Girls and Boys Get Different Toys," *The Wall Street Journal*, Feb. 14, 2000, p. B1.
63 *Psychologically primed as well, according to marriage and family therapist Carol Zulman:* interview, March 1999.
63 *"American men, for the most part"*: Susan J. Wells, "What Happens if Harriet makes More than Ozzie," *The New York Times*, Aug. 1, 1999, p. B.10.
65 *Lorna Wendt, one such "dumped" corporate wife*: Betsy Morris, "It's Her Job Too," *Fortune* (cover story), Feb. 2, 1988, pp. 65–78.
65 *"The world travels in couples"*: Ethel Person, phone interview, May 2000.
65 *Married women who work for pay*: M. C. Lennon and S. Rosenfeld, "Relative Fairness and the Division of Housework: The Importance of Options," *American Journal of Sociology* No. 100, 1994, pp. 506–31; and Arlie Hochschild, *The Second Shift*, New York: Viking Penguin, 1989.
68 *Passive resistance, strategic incompetence*: Francine M. Deutsch, *Halving It All: How Equally Shared Parenting Works*, Cambridge, Mass.: Harvard University Press, 1999, p. 74.

68 *"Honey, where do you keep the ice cubes?"* Marcia Byalick and Linda Saslow, *The Three-Career Couple,* Princeton, New Jersey: Peterson's, 1993, p. 70.

72 *"datey dates"*: Melissa Banks, *The Girls Guide to Hunting and Fishing,* New York: Bantam Books, 1999, p. 271.

72 *"to be a truthball"*: Ibid., p. 274.

79 *Studies in Scotland and Japan*: Natalie Angier, "Nothing Becomes a Man More than a Woman's Face," *The New York Times,* Sept. 1, 1998, p. B9.79

79 *"desire to be closer to other human beings"*: Nicholas Lemann, "The Battle Over Boys," *The New Yorker,* July 10, 2000, p. 80.

80 *"You and your partner"*: Stephen C. Miller, "Moved by Love, and Work," The New York Times, Money and Business, Jan 23. 2000, p. 2.

Designing a Life

85 *"The overnight success":* Amy Wu, My Money, My Life Column: "Twentysomethings' Lament," *The New York Times,* Sept. 31, 1999, p. B15.

86 *"spiritual currency"*: interview with Dr. Arthur Kornhaber, May 2000.

86 *Two economists, David Blancheflower of Dartmouth and Andrew Oswald of the University of Warwick, have quantified*: cited in Judith Stone, "Trust Us," *Mirabella,* April 2000, p. 118.

87 *In her book, The Working Life: The Promise and Betrayal of Modern Work:* Joan B. Ciulla, New York City: Times Books, 2000. The discussion of classic wisdom is on p. 6, of David Riesman, p. 110.

87 *Pat Raskins, psychologist and director of Columbia School of Education*: phone interview, Feb. 2000.

88 *"So many people walk around with a meaningless life"*: Mitch Albom, *Tuesdays with Morrie,* New York: Doubleday, 1997, p. 43.

88 *"Ummm, just stop moaning"*: Ephos diva, "Chickclick Boards," posted Mar. 1, 2000, http://estroclick.chickclick.com/ubb/forum26/html/000236:html.

90 *"That work seemed much more satisfying"*: Sandra Dallas, "From Desk to Disaster Area and Loving It," *Business Week,* Nov. 8, 1999, p. 14 E2.

90 Follow the advice of Dr. Ben Carlson: Lucy McCauly, "Don't Burn Out, *Fast Company,* May 2000, p. 106.

94 *Connecticut state-funding initiative*: Connecticut School Readiness initiative helps fund the start-up, building renovation, and kicks in $7,000 per child. Hartford's "Over the Rainbow" childcare center reopened as "The Right Place" in 1997.

95 *The Big Five are so desperate*: Greg Winter, "In the Boom, Desperately Seeking Bean Counters," *The New York Times,* June 28, 2000, p. C11.

95 *The New York Times interviewed one woman*: Steven Greenhouse, "All College Graduates, Please Apply," *The New York Times*, June 4, 2000, p. A 12.

95 *A national report from the American Association of University Women*: Knight Ridder News Service, "High Tech Culture Failing to Draw Girls," *The Honolulu Advertiser*, Apr 11, 2000, p. A1.

95 *Apparently, women are uncomfortable enough at the computer that in mixed classes: Sixty Minutes* segment: "Women on the Web," March 19, 2000, Leslie Stahl, correspondent.

95 *In 1999, women were chief executives of 6 percent of Internet companies*: Leslie Kaufman, "The Dot.Com World Opens New Opportunities for Women to Lead," *The New York Times*, Mar. 9, 2000, pp. C1, C4.

100 *"Welcome to recruiting in the New Age":* Sue Shellenbarger, Work and Family Column: "What Job Candidates Really Want to Know: Will I Have a Life?" *The Wall Street Journal*, Nov. 17, 1999, p. B.1

100 *The vice chairman who made Ann Mulcahy the president and CEO of Xerox:* Patricia Sellers, "The 50 Most Powerful Women in Business," *Fortune*, Oct. 16, 2000, p. 154.

101 *"I don't believe people succeed on their own"*: "Secrets of Success," *Working Mother*, Nov. 1999, p. 74.

101 *A Catalyst survey of women in senior management*: Ibid.

101 *They also point out that the bigger a company's revenue*: Catalyst "Perspective," Feb. 2000, p. 1.

101 *"couldn't cope any better than the women did"*: Reed Abelson, "A Push from the Top Shatters a Glass Ceiling," *The New York Times*, Aug. 22, 1999, pp. A1, .33.

101 *Its new CFO, Debby Hopkins, left the "phenomenal male dominance"*: Patricia Sellers, "The Fifty Most Powerful Women in Business," *Fortune*, Oct. 16, 2000, p. 144.

105 *"I certainly would have kept going"*: Elizabeth Becker, "Army Mothers Find Obstacles on Route to General's Office," *The New York Times*, Nov. 29, 1999, pp. A1, A16.

106 *"I don't attempt to get balance"*: Fawn Germer, "Star Power," *Working Woman*, March 2000, p. 26.

106 *She also recently filed a sexual harassment complaint*: Steven Lee Myers, "Female General in Army Alleges Sex Harassment," *The New York Times*, Mar. 31, 2000, p. A1.

Understanding the Workplace 2000

108 *Teaching "is the most important profession to us"*: Todd S. Purdum, "Teachers Offered a Tax Exemption: California Governor

Would Waive Levies on Income," *The New York Times,* May 14, 2000, p. A.1.

108 *"every department had to make a choice to take money"*: phone interview with Linda Smith, May 1998.

108 *The Navy recently created a new troop carrier*: The USS. *San Antonio,* scheduled for completion in three years. 40% of the crew may be female. "Shipshape, Gender-wise," *Time,* March 27, 2000, p. 34.

108 *"The inhumane demands placed on physicians (long hours on call, rising patient loads) and lawyers (2,000-plus billable hours a year)"*: Sue Shellenbarger, Work and Family Column: "Readers Offer Views About Productivity and Long Work Weeks," *The Wall Street Journal,* Sept. 16, 1998, B1.

109 *According to* The Wall Street Journal, *executives now rank getting and keeping qualified employees as their top priority*: "Work Week," *The Wall Street Journal,* Jan. 18, 2000, p. A1.

109 *Replacing an employee costs on average*: estimates vary from $10,000 up. This one is quoted in Sue Shellenbarger, "To Win the Loyalty of Your Employees, Try a Softer Touch," *The Wall Street Journal,* Nov. 20, 1999, B.1; others, such as a 1999 AON-America@work study, show "costs of more than $10,000," quoted in David Batstone, Get A Life Column, *Business 2.0,* April 2000, p. 343.

109 *Never mind finding good workers*: "Work Week: Special Report About Life on the Job—And Trends Taking Shape There," *The Wall Street Journal,* June 2, 1998, p. A1.

109 *At the top six accounting firms*: David Molpus, "Ernst and Young Workplace," *All Things Considered,* National Public Radio, July 28, 1998.

110 *This spring, 1.2 million college students*: Carl Quintanilla, "College Recruiting Becomes Lavish," *The Wall Street Journal,* June 4, 1998, p. B1.

110 *Fun is the big ingredient*: Vivienne Walt, "Instant Fame for New MBA's," *The New York Times,* May 17, 1998, p. D11.

110 *Xerox, for example, has taken to setting up*: Sue Shellenbarger, Work and Family Column: "What Job Candidates Really Want to Know: Will I Have a Life," *The Wall Street Journal,* Nov. 17, 1999, p. B1.

111 *One savvy candidate won a completely outfitted home office in Malibu*: Bill Breen, "Money Isn't Everything," *Fast Company,* April –May 1998, p. 233.

112 *"The average American worker"*: David Batstone, Get a Life Column: "The Company Store," *Business 2.0,* April 2000, p. 343.

112 *"Getting a better shopping deal"*: Ibid.

112 *"Unlike the last wave of corporate initiatives":* Leslie Kaufman, "Some Companies Derail the 'Burnout' Track," *The New York Times,* May 4, 1999, pp. A.1, A 18. Discusses the Hewlett-Packard experiment.

116 *"Authority has not exactly vanished from corporate America"*: Michael Lewis, "The Artist in the Gray Flannel Pajamas," *The New York Times Magazine,* March 5, 2000, p. 45.

117 *"The humanistic trend"*: Colleen O'Connor, Get A Life Column: "High Touch for High Tech," *Business 2.0,* Feb. 2000, p. 219.

117 *"sensational improvements in stock performance"*: Michael Moskowitz, Best Companies to Work For, Inc., San Francisco, phone interview, March 30, 2000.

117 *"Pretty clear that as people"* Leslie Kaufman, "Some Companies Derail the 'Burnout Track,'" *The New York Times,* May 4, 1999, p. A1.

118 *"work-life issues are a business priority"*: Reed Abelson, "A Push from the Top Shatters a Glass Ceiling," *The New York Times,* Aug. 22, 1999, p. A1.

118 *It's been called "Sanity, Inc."*: *Fast Company,* (cover story), Jan. 1999.

118 *"Utopia, Ltd."*, Timothy D. Schellhardt, "An Idyllic Workplace Under a Tyrant's Thumb," *The Wall Street Journal,* Nov. 23, 1998, p. B1.

119 *"I could make more money elsewhere"*: Ibid.

119 *One result is 4 percent turnover:* Peter Burrows and Peter Elstrom, "The Boss," *Business Week,* Aug. 2, 1999, p. 79.

119 *"It's an enormously successful business model"*: Ibid.

120 *"The story isn't about money"*: Robert Levering and Milton Moskowitz, "The 100 Best Companies to Work For," *Fortune,* Jan. 10, 2000, p. 82.

If Your're Considering Medicine, Business, or Law

130 *Medicine does offer some sane work choices, but mostly women are taking them*: Jennifer Steinhauer, "For Women in Medicine, a Road to Compromise, Not Perks," *The New York Times,* March 1, 1999, p. A1.

130 *Even in the same specialties, women doctors earn far less*: Natalie Angier, "Among Doctors, Pay for Women Still Lags," *The New York Times,* Jan. 12, 1999, p. D7.

147 *"Few of the people who work there are remembering to enjoy themselves."*: Po Bronson, *Nudist on the Late Shift,* New York: Random House, 1999, p. 211.

147 *"Once I have more money than Larry Ellison"*: quoted in Robert D. Hoff, "No Satisfaction in Silicon Valley," *Business Week,* Nov. 8, 1999, p. 15.

147 *the median income in information technology*: Elisabeth Weise, "Families Learn to Live on Internet Time," *USA Today*, May 27, 1999, p. B1.

147 *"Knowledge work requires so much communication"*: quoted in Susan Moran, Get a Life Column: "Stressed for Success," *Business 2.0,* Nov. 1999, p. 283.

148 *Analyst figures are even lower*: figures from John L. Nesheem, *High Tech Start Up,* New York: Simon and Schuster, 1997, quoted in *Business 2.0,* Mar. 2000, p. 140.

148 *In a survey of 1,400 chief information officers in IT*: Susan Moran, Get a Life Column: "Stressed for Success," *Business 2.0,* Nov. 1999, p. 287.

148 *She explains that a lot of corporations cannot dangle the prospects of overnight riches*: phone interview with Jan English-Lueck, Nov.1999.

152 *"to make sure that employees are having fun"*: Amy Wilson, "Job Titles of the Future," *American Way*, Dec. 15, 1999, p. 82.

152 *Present glut of lawyers*: Bureau of Labor Statistics.

153 *billable hours have increased*: Hindi Greenberg, *The Lawyers Career Change Handbook,* New York City: Avon Books, 1998, p. 14.

155 *Wages for first-year lawyers*: "Work Week," *The Wall Street Journal,* Oct. 15, 1999, p. A1. Other figures come from the Bureau of Labor Statistics.

155 *"nearly two-thirds of the associates"*: Renee M. Landers, James B. Rebitzer, and Lowell J. Taylor, "Work Norms and Professional Labor Markets," *Gender and Family Issues in the Workplace,* ed. Francine Blau and Ronald G. Ehrenberg, Ithaca: Russell Sage Foundation, 1997, p. 176.

155 *a poll taken by California Lawyer*: quoted in Hindi Greenberg, *The Lawyer's Career Change Handbook,* p. 10.

155 *"if his revenues or hours drop"*: Robert Kurson, "Who's Killing the Great Lawyers of Harvard?" *Esquire,* Aug. 2000, pp. 83–89, 140. This quote, p. 86. Figures for the directory, p. 84.

155 *"about 80% of incoming Harvard Law School students"*: Ibid., p. 87.

158 *Unfortunately, many of the largest law firms have cut back on their pro bono work*: Greg Winter, "Law Firms Limit Aid to Poor," *The New York Times,* Sept. 10, 2000, p. 2.

159 *As a perk Shearman and Stirling:* Richard B. Schmitt, "From Cash to Travel, New Lures for Burned-Out Lawyers," *The Wall Street Journal,* Feb. 2, 1999, pp. B1.4.

159 *Some, according to the* National Law Journal *are even offering the unheard of luxury of paternity leave*: Adam Bryant, "Looking for a Purpose in a Paycheck," *The New York Times,* June 21, 1998, p. D1.

160*Take advantage of the myriad books: The Lawyer's Career Change Handbook* (see note to p. 187) has an extensive bibliography of these books and sites. Its author, Hindi Greenberg, suggests that before taking a job, investigate the firm through the *Martindale-Hubbell Law Directory,* finding out how many associates have left in recent years, and calling some to find out why. For those who would like change from within, there's *Life, Law and the Pursuit of Balance: A Lawyer's Guide to Quality of Life,* edited by Jeffrey R. Simmons (published in partnership with the Maricopa County and Arizona Bar Associations); for defectors: Deborah Arron's *What Can You Do with a Law Degree? A Lawyer's Guide to Career Alternatives Inside, Outside and Around the Law,* Niche Press.

Striking Out on Your Own

162 *In 1972, only 5 percent of businesses were owned by women*: statistics from "Key Facts," The National Foundation for Women Business Owners, 2000. www.nfwbo.org.

163 *Our Wildest Dreams*: *Women Entrepreneurs Making Money, Having Fun, Doing Good,* New York: Harper Business, 1992.

165 *America's 9 million female entrepreneurs*: statistics from Glenn Yago, Rebecca Ford, and Judith Gordon, *Economic Prosperity, Women and Access to Credit,* Santa Monica, Calif.: Milken Institute, Oct. 2000, pp. 2–3.

165 *Women tend to apply for smaller loans*: Ibid., p. 13.

165 *two-thirds of female-owned businesses*: Thomas J. Stanley, William D. Danko, *The Millionaire Next Door: The Surprising Secrets of America's Wealthy,* New York: Pocket Books, 1996 p. 182.

165 *As of 1998, just over half of the women and men who owned businesses*: "Key Facts," National Foundation for Women Business Owners, 2000. www.nfwbo.org.

166 *"although women generally give great customer service"*: Jennifer Kushell, phone interview, June 2000.

168 *women entrepreneurs have a success rate*: Dorothy P. Moore, E. Holly Buttner, *Women Entrepreneurs: Moving Beyond the Glass Ceiling,* Thousand Oaks, Calif.: Sage Publications, 1997, p. 4

168 *"in order to advance"*: Ibid., p. 23.

169 *While these women all earned more as business owners than they had before, they claimed:* Ibid., p. 166.

170 *45 percent of women working full time earn less than $25,000*: Bureau of the Census, "Money Income in the U.S., 1999."

176 *"In general these couples are rarely willing"*: Kathy Marshack, *Entrepreneurial Couples: Making It Work at Work and at Home,* Palo Alto: Calif.: Davies Black Publishing, 1998, p. 51.

176 *"As long as those tendencies prevail"*: Ibid., p. 51.

Work and Family: If You're Thinking of Kids

184 *More young adults are the product of divorced parents*: : Kendall Hamilton and Pat Wingert, "Down the Aisle," *Newsweek*, July 20, 1998, P. 56.

184 "It's not like I was beaten regularly": Elizabeth Wurtzel, *Prozac Nation: A Memoir*, New York: Riverhead Books, 1995, p. 129.

184 *They don't have a clue*: Ibid.

184 *All of my friends [with kids] had lives that were so hectic*: Lou Ann Walkers, "He Doesn't," *New Woman*, Nov. 1997, p. 145.

185 "*'How,' friends asked*": Ibid., p. 146.

188 *"dinner was now us standing in the middle of the kitchen"*: Karen Karbo, *Motherhood Made a Man out of Me*, New York: Bloomsbury, 2000, quotes from Ann Hodgman, "Please Baby, Please Baby," *The New York Times Book Review*, June 18, 2000, p. 27.

188 *"During that first year of Matthew's life"*: Harriet Lerner, *The Mother Dance: How Children Change Your Life*, New York: Harper Collins, 1998, p. 53.

189 *"I'm a 33-year-old new dad"*: "Straight Talk: Questions on Sex, Relationships, and Marriage Answered by Dr. Alan Barasch," *Dads*, June/July 2000, p. 24.

191 *doesn't come with an owner's manual*: Anne Lamott, *Operating Instructions: A Journal of My Son's First Year*, New York: Fawcett Columbine, 1993.

191 *"When you add the stresses of interrupted sleep"*: Harriet Lerner, *The Mother Dance*, p. 37.

192 *"Oh, the joys of co-parenting"*: Maria Hinojosa, *Raising Raul: Adventures Raising Myself and My Son*, New York: Viking, 1999, p. 155

192 *"By the end of the evening"*: Ibid., p. 230.

194 *According to the Department of Agriculture, it costs $160,000*: Department of Agriculture annual report, 1999.

195 *"I missed meetings"*: Joan Williams, *Unbending Gender: Why Family and Work Conflict and What to Do About It*, New York: Oxford University Press, 2000, quotes from Fallows's book are on pp. 17–18.

196 *yet another huge study of the childcare question*: done by Elizabeth Harvey, Department of Psychology at the University of Massachusetts, published as "Short-Term and Long-Term Effects of Early Parental Employment on children of the National Longitudinal Survey of Youth," *Developmental Psychology*, No. 35, 1999, pp. 445–459.

198 *Psychologist Leah Fisher, director of the Center for Work and Family in Berkeley, California*: phone interview, March, 1999.

200 *81 percent of female high school seniors*: Lloyd D. Johnston, Patrick M. O'Malley, Jerrold G. Bachman, "1998: Monitoring

the Future," Institute for Social Research at University of Michigan, a longitudinal study of high school seniors' goals since 1975.

200 *Radcliffe Public Policy Institute*: quoted in Joe Queenan, "New Magazine Celebrates the Guy Called Dad," *The New York Times,* News of the Week in Review, June 15, 2000, p. 9.

201 *As witness, only 12 percent of men reported a work-life conflict in 1977*: Kyle D. Pruett, Fatherneed: *Why Father Care Is as Essential as Mother Care for Your Child,* New York: The Free Press, 2000, p. 147.

201 *In 1999, to take one of a thousand examples, a Maryland state trooper*: Tamar Lewin, "Father Awarded $375,000 In Parental Leave Case," *The New York Times,* Feb. 3, 1999, p. A11.

201 *Psychologist Francine Deutsch makes this argument in her book*: Francine M. Deutsch, *Halving It All: How Equally Shared Parenting Works,* Boston: Harvard University Press, 1999, p. 47.

202 *"Passive resistance":* Ibid., p. 74.

202 *Deutsch concluded*: Ibid., p. 135.

202 *"I couldn't get away with [not parenting]"*: Ibid., p. 21.

202 *"Don't you understand how ashamed I am"*: Emily Yoffe, "Fugitive in the Family," *The New York Times Magazine,* June 20, 1999, p. 132.

203 *"spectral fathers"*: Susan Faludi, *Stiffed: The Betrayal of the American Man,* New York: William Morrow, 1999, p. 374.

203 *"Eventually I no longer relied on him":* Joan Kofodimus, "Why Executives Lose Their Balance," *Organizational Dynamics,* Summer 1990, p. 61.

203 *Research by Ross Parke, a psychologist of fathering*: Ashley Beitel and Ross Parke's 1998 study, cited in Ross Parke, Armin A. Brott, *Throwaway Dads: The Myths and Barriers That Keep Men from Being the Fathers They Want to Be,* New York: Houghton Mifflin, 1999, p. 119.

204 *"touched, held, looked at their infants":* Ibid., p. 121.

204 *A news article charmingly entitled, "Boot Camp For Dads:"*: James Meadow, *Sarasota Herald Tribune,* Jan 10, 1998, p. A10.

204 *Ross Parke and his colleagues*: *Throwaway Dads,* p. 23.

205 *In Fatherneed, he argues*: *Fatherneed,* p. 22.

205 *"children are born with a drive to find"*: Ibid., p. 2.

205 *They play with kids more*: Ibid., p. 8.

205 *Whatever a fathers parenting style, Pruett emphasizes*: Ibid., p. 25.

205 *Not only are they more exploratory,* Ibid., p. 50.

206 *According to Pruett, studies have actually quantified fatherneed*: Ibid., p. 38.

206 *Involved fathers are less likely*: Ibid., p. 180 (citing the research of Joseph Pleck).

206 *In fact, men who do housework and childcare*: Marcia Byalick and Linda Saslow, *The Three Career Couple: Mastering the Art of Juggling Work, Home, and Family*, Princeton, New Jersey: Peterson's, 1993, p. 91 (cites research of John Gottman).

206 *Another plus: they're more likely to stay happily married: Fathemeed*, p. 175.

206 *"Two parents who are equally involved"*: Robert Frank, *The Involved Father*, New York: St. Martin's Press, 1999, p. 37.

206 *James Levine, author of Working Fathers*: with Todd L. Pittinsky, *Working Fathers: New Strategies for Balancing Work and Family*, Reading, Mass: Addison Wesley, 1997.

206 *Of the over eight hundred fathers I interviewed*: Jerrold Lee Shapiro, *The Measure of a Man: Becoming the Father You Wish Your Father Had Been*, Berkeley, California: Perigee Press, 1995, p. 139.

207 *To this end, Robert Frank advises replacing the traditional baby shower*: *The Involved Father*, p. 133 (see note to p. 251).

207 *A report to the Commission on Family and Medical Leave:* cited in *Fatherneed*, p. 196 (see note to p. 248).

209 *During my three-month paid leave*: Thomas E. Salyers, "Time Off for New Dads," Letters, *The New York Times*, April 30, 2000, p. B24.

209 *"went to court to win an argument against his government":* Warren Hoge, "Cherie Blair vs. Tony Blair, You Might Say, in Court, the Case for Parental Leave," *The New York Times*, May 17, 2000, p. A2.

210 *And, take note, in August following the May birth of his son*: "Showing Off Baby Leo," caption under picture of Blair with infant son, *International Herald Tribune*, "Italy Daily," August 9, 2000, p. 2.

New Rules, New Parents, New Choices

217 *Jamie Rubin, Madeline Albright's assistant secretary of state*: Jeffrey Goldberg, "Diaper Diplomacy," *The New York Times Magazine*, Apr. 30, 2000, p. 32.

217 *Nick Macphee, former VP of Operations at Microsoft*: Wendy Bounds, "Give Me a Break," *The Wall Street Journal*, May 5, 2000 p. W4.

218 *Four of the top five women on Fortune's 2000 "50 Most Powerful"*: Patricia Sellers, "The 50 Most Powerful Women in Business," Fortune, Oct. 16, 2000, p. 156.

219 *As far back as 1993, 1.3 million employed fathers*: cited in Suzanne Braun Levine, Father Courage: *What Happens When Men Put Family First*, New York: Harcourt, Inc. 2000, p. 98.

219 *About 5 percent of fathers are primary caregivers*: Robert Frank, *The Involved Father*, p. 250.

219 *In Europe, a Brussels-based organization called "STUDS":* see www.terracognita.com/wj_male.html.

221 *Stacey Calvert, 36, a soloist ballerina*: Holcomb B. Noble, "Leaping from Childbirth to Ballet Stage," *The New York Times*, May 18, 1999, p. D8.

221 *Renee Fleming, opera diva*: Melanie Rehak, "Lullaby Diva," *The New York Times Magazine*, August 29, 1999, p. 16.

221 *"the only NASA shuttle commander"*: Beth Dickey, "Woman's Work: Space Commander," *The New York Times*, July 24, 1999, p. A8.

221 *"It has made me a stronger parent"*: "Power Moms: Sisters Are Finding Ways to Have It All—Children and Careers," *Ebony*, July 1999, pp. 52–58.

222 *"most apt to experience work/life success"*: Phyllis Moen, Yan Yu, "Having It All: Overall Work/Life Success in Two Earner Families," *Research in the Sociology of Work*, Vol. 7, 1999, pp. 109–110.

224 *"free and easy happiness never emerged":* Francine Deutsch, *Halving It All*, p. 8.

225 *In Deutsch's same study, these working mothers*: Ibid.

225 *"This is not to be confused"*: quoted in Laura B. Randolf, "Sisterspeak: Strong Black Woman Blues," *Ebony*, July 1999, p. 24.

227 *"Rather than lose this talent"* Wendy Bounds, "Give Me A Break," *The Wall Street Journal*, May 5, 2000, p. W1.

227 It may be worth joining a sequencing organization like Mothers and More: see www.mothersandmore.com.

227 *"I track how many times I get home to have dinner":* Lucy McCauly, "Don't Burn Out," *Fast Company*, May 2000, p. 102.

227 *"I have three Golden Rules"*: Ibid., p. 114.

227 *Stacy Snider, the 38-year-old*: Patrick Goldstein, "Empire Builders," *The Los Angeles Times Magazine*, Mar. 26, 2000, pp. 18–20, 41.

227 *Charter Communications CEO*: Sue Shellenbarger, Work and Family Column: "Family Friendly CEO's Are Changing Cultures at More Workplaces," *The Wall Street Journal*, Sept. 15, 1999, p. B1.

228 *"Exhausted from hectic work schedules"*: June Fletcher, "Extreme Nesting," *The Wall Street Journal*, Jan. 7, 2000, p. W1.

229 *"I am a senior manager at a start-up"*: *Fast Company*, Apr. 2000, p. 36.

229 *In Ask the Children*: Ellen Galinsky, *Ask the Children: What America's Children Really Think About Working Parents*, New York: William Morrow and Co., 1999.

No Woman is an Island

246 *"Like any woman who has actually done it":* Shirley P. Burggraf, *The Feminine Economy and Economic Man,* Reading, Mass.: Perseus Press, 1997, p. 189.

247 *The Census Bureau tells us*: Tamar Lewin, "Now a Majority: Families with Two Parents Who Work," *The New York Times,* Oct. 24, 2000, p. A14. The article notes that Amara Bachu of the Census Bureau, who is analyzing current data on women and work, "sees no signs that the trend towards more working mothers has peaked."

247 *In places where men do little parenting, like Italy and Japan*: Michael Specter, "The Baby Bust, a Special Report: Population Implosion Worries a Graying Europe," *The New York Times,* July 10, 1998, p. A1.

250 *"This is not discrimination against mothers"*: "Do Working Parents Merit Help," *The New York Times,* Letters, from Seth Chasin of Oak Park, Calif., May 21, 2000, p. A28.

250 *In The Baby Boon*: Elinor Burkett, *The Baby Boon: How Family Friendly America Cheats the Childless,* New York: The Free Press, 2000.

251 *"Parental dividends"*: Shirley P. Burggraf, *The Feminine Economy and Economic Man,* p. 69.

251 *Professor Lotte Bailyn*: Lotte Bailyn's theory appears in *Breaking the Mold: Women, Men, and Time in the New Corporate World,* New York: The Free Press, 1993.

251 *"modified work patterns"*: Eric Pace, "Mirra Komarovsky, Authority on Women's Studies, Dies," *The New York Times,* Feb. 1, 1999, p. A22.

252 *"To eliminate institutional practices":* Ruth Bader Ginsberg: "Gender and the Constitution," *University of Cincinnati Law Review,* 44, Vol. 1, 1975, pp. 28–30.

252 *In a January 2000, poll done by EDK Associates*: cited in Bob Herbert, In America Column: "Women Vote Too," *The New York Times,* Jan. 27, 2000, p. A.27.

253 *In a more recent poll called "Women's Voices 2000"*: Bob Herbert, In America Column: "Focus on Women," *The New York Times,* Sept. 28, 2000, p. A31.

253 *"I'm not a feminist, but"*: Jennifer Baumgardner and Amy Richards, Manifest: *A Young Women, Feminism, and the Future,* New York: Farrar, Straus, and Giroux, 2000, p. 48.

253 *"The only problem is that"*: Ibid., p. 18.

254 *"As a young women I have more choices"*: Kate Farrar, Connecticut Naral "Letter to Supporters," July 2000.

256 *"It's not that we don't want to support [do-gooders]"*: quoted in Tamara Straus, "Irony with Soul: Dave Eggers Writes the Hippest of Memoirs," hipMama.com, Feb. 18, 2000, see www.alternet.org/story.html?storyID=401.

256 "want to breathe fire": Ibid.

258 *"Work is a major source of satisfaction"*: Kathy Marshak, *Entrepreneurial Couples*, p. 57 (see note to p. 217).

258 *"once time pressure is added"*: Joanne B. Ciulla, *The Working Life*, p. 185.

259 *In his last year as president, Bill Clinton pledged to make working parents a "protected class":* Lee Walzak, "Clinton Sets a Parent Trap for the GOP," *Business Week*, May 3, 1999, p. 55.

259 *Ten New York City labor unions*: Steven Greenhouse, "Unions Unite in a Campaign for Childcare," *The New York Times*, Mar. 2, 1998, p. B1.

259 *the government provided $52 million*: Francine D. Blau, Marianne A. Ferber, Anne E. Winkler, *The Economics of Women, Men, and Work*, 3rd edition, Upper Saddle River. Prentice Hall, 1998, p. 111.

260 *In one example, cited in* The New York Times: Suzanne Daley, "A French Paradox: 35 Hour Work Week May Turn Out to Be Best for Employers," *The New York Times*, Nov. 11, 1999, p. C1.

260 *"The ability to go home"*: Joanne B. Ciulla, *The Working Life*, p. 183.

261 *"Surely there must be some give"*: "Mothers and Markets," *The New Republic*, Mar. 6, 2000, p. 42.

262 *In 1995, "Cost, Quality and Child Outcomes in Child Care Centers"*: "Cost, Quality and Child Outcomes in Child Care Centers," Public Report, April 1995, University of Colorado at Denver, Department of Economics.

262 *Dr. T. Berry Brazelton*: T. Berry Brazelton and Stanley Greenspan, *The Irreducible Needs of Children: What Every Child Must Have to Grow, Learn, and Flourish*, Cambridge, Mass.: Perseus Books, 2000. His two major points are from an interview with him in Katy Kelly, "Child docs to parents: Stay home and save your kids," *U.S. News and World Report*, Oct. 30, 2000, p. 65.

264 *A higher percentage of women in Congress vote for choice*: Bob Herbert, In America Column: "Women Vote Too," *The New York Times*, Jan. 27, 2000, p. A27.

Bibliography

Abelson, Reed. "A Push from the Top Shatters a Glass Ceiling." *The New York Times*, Aug. 22, 1999, p. A1.

———. "Part Time Work for Some Adds Up to a Full Time Job." *The New York Times*, Nov. 2, 1998, pp. A1, A16.

Albom, Mitch. *Tuesdays with Morrie*. New York: Doubleday, 1997.

Allen, Kathleen, and Hansen, Karen. *Entrepreneurship for Dummies*. Indianapolis, Ind.: IDG Books Worldwide, 2000.

Angier, Natalie. "Among Doctors, Pay for Women Still Lags." *The New York Times*, Jan. 12, 1999, p. D7.

———. "For Women in Astronomy, a Glass Ceiling in the Sky." *The New York Times*, Feb. 15, 2000, p. D5.

———. "Nothing Becomes a Man More than a Woman's Face." *The New York Times*, Sept. 1, 1998, p. B9.

Arron, Deborah. *What Can You Do with a Law Degree?: A Lawyer's Guide to Career Alternatives Inside, Outside and Around the Law.* Washington, D.C., Niche Press, 1999.

Auletta, Ken. Annals of Communications: "In the Company of Women." *The New Yorker*, Apr. 20, 1998, p. 75.

Bader Ginsberg, Ruth. "Gender and the Constitution," *University of Cincinnati Law Review*, 44, Vol. 1 (1975), pp. 28–30.

Bagby, Meredith. *Rational Exuberance: The Influence of Generation X on the New American Economy*. New York: Dutton, 1998.

Bailyn, Lotte. *Breaking the Mold: Women, Men, and Time in the New Corporate World*. New York: The Free Press, 1993.

Banks, Melissa. *The Girls Guide to Hunting and Fishing*. New York: Bantam Books, 1999.

Bannon, Lisa. "Why Girls and Boys Get Different Toys." *The Wall Street Journal*, Feb. 14, 2000, p. B1.

Barasch, Alan. "Straight Talk: Questions on Sex, Relationships, and Marriage." *Dads*, June/July 2000.

Batstone, David. Get a Life Column: "The Company Store." *Business 2.0*, April 2000.

Baumgardner, Jennifer, and Richards, Amy. *ManifestA: Young Women, Feminism, and the Future*. New York: Farrar, Straus, and Giroux, 2000.

Becker, Elizabeth. "Army Mothers Find Obstacles on Route to General's Office." *The New York Times,* Nov. 29, 1999, p. A1.

Becker, Penny Edgell, and Moen, Phyllis. "Scaling Back: Dual-Earner Couples' Work-Family Strategies." *Journal of Marriage and the Family,* No. 61 (Nov. 1999), p. 1001.

Bell, Alison. "Making Work Work." *American Baby,* Feb. 1998, p. 53.

Bing, Stanley. Bing! Column: "Sleep Faster." *Fortune,* Nov. 22, 1999, p. 95.

Blau, Francine D., Ferber, Marianne A., and Winkler, Anne E. *The Economics of Women, Men, and Work,* 3rd edition. Upper Saddle River,: Prentice Hall, 1998.

Bounds, Wendy. "Give Me a Break." *The Wall Street Journal,* May 5, 2000, p. W4.

Bouris, Karen. *The First Time: What Parents and Teenage Girls Should Know About Losing Your Virginity.* Emmeryville, Calif.: Canari Press, 1994.

Braun Levine, Suzanne. *Father Courage: What Happens When Men Put Family First.* New York: Harcourt, 2000.

Brazelton, T. Berry, and Greenspan, Stanley. *The Irreducible Needs of Children: What Every Child Must Have to Grow, Learn, and Flourish.* Cambridge, Mass.: Perseus Books, 2000.

Breen, Bill. "Money Isn't Everything." *Fast Company,* April-May 1998, p. 233.

Broad, William J. "Blasting Off on a Mission for Cosmic Science." *The New York Times,* July 13, 1999, p. D3.

———. "Three Women Wait Anxiously for Their Spacecraft to Reach Mars." *The New York Times,* Apr. 18, 1999, p. A10.

Bronson, Po. *Nudist on the Late Shift.* New York: Random House, 1999.

Bryant, Adam. "Looking for a Purpose in a Paycheck." *The New York Times,* June 21, 1998, p. D1.

Bumiller, Elizabeth. "Free Fall in the Financial District." *The New York Times Magazine,* Nov. 15, 1998, p. 74.

Burggraf, Shirley P. *The Feminine Economy and Economic Man.* Reading, Mass.: Perseus Press, 1997.

Burkett, Elinor. *The Baby Boon: How Family Friendly America Cheats the Childless.* New York: The Free Press, 2000.

Burrows, Peter, and Elstrom, Peter. "The Boss." *Business Week,* Aug. 2, 1999, p. 79.

Byalick, Marcia, and Saslow, Linda. *The Three Career Couple: Mastering the Art of Juggling Work, Home, and Family.* Princeton, N.J.: Peterson's, 1993.

Callaghan, Polly, and Hartman, Heidi. *Contingent Work: A Chart Book on Part Time and Temporary Employment.* Washington, D.C.: Economic Policy Institute, 1991.

Calvo, Dana. "Female Anchors on Local TV Paid 28% Less." *The Los Angeles Times*, June 1, 2000, p. A1.

Caroll, Jon. Escape column: "The Stepford Economy." *Business 2.0*, Nov.1999, p. 336.

Catalyst. *Perspective*. New York: Catalyst, Feb. 2000.

Chasin, Seth. "Do Working Parents Merit Help?" *The New York Times*, May 21, 2000, p. A28.

Ciulla, Joanne B. *The Working Life: The Promise and Betrayal of Modern Work*. New York City: Times Books, 2000.

Collins, Gail. "A Social Glacier Roars." *The New York Times Magazine*, May 16, 1999, p. 78.

Daley, Suzanne. "A French Paradox: 35 Hour Work Week May Turn Out to be Best for Employers." *The New York Times*, Nov. 11, 1999, p. C1.

Dallas, Sandra. "From Desk to Disaster Area and Loving It." *Business Week*, Nov. 8, 1999, p. 14E2.

Daum, Meghan. "My Misspent Youth." *The New Yorker*, Oct. 18,25, 1999, p. 162.

Dean, Cornelia. "After a Struggle, Women Win a Place 'on the Ice.'" *The New York Times*, Nov. 10, 1998, p. D1.

Deutsch, Francine M. *Halving It All: How Equally Shared Parenting Works*. Cambridge, Mass: Harvard University Press, 1999.

Dickey, Beth. "Woman's Work: Space Commander." *The New York Times*, July 24, 1999, p. A8.

Douglass, Marcia, and Douglass, Lisa. *Are We Having Fun Yet: The Intelligent Women's Guide to Sex*. New York: Hyperion, 1997.

Edwards, Tamala M. "Flying Solo." *Time*, Aug. 28, 2000, p. 48.

Eggers, Dave. *A Heartbreaking Work of Staggering Genius: Based on a True Story*. New York: Simon and Schuster, 2000.

Faludi, Susan. *Backlash: The Undeclared War Against American Women*. New York: Crown Publishers, 1991.

———. *Stiffed: The Betrayal of the American Man*. New York: William Morrow, 1999.

Fallows, Deborah. *A Mother's Work*. New York: Houghton Mifflin, 1985.

Families and Work Institute. "National Study of the Changing Workforce." New York: Families and Work Institute, 1997.

———. "Business Work-Life Study." New York: Families and Work Institute, 1998.

Farrar, Kate. "Letter to Supporters." Connecticut Naral, July, 2000.

Fiermen, J. "Why Women Still Don't Hit the Top." *Fortune*, July 30, 1990, p. 40.

Fletcher, June. "Extreme Nesting." *The Wall Street Journal*, Jan. 7, 2000, p. W1.

Frank, Robert H. *Luxury Fever: Why Money Fails to Satisfy in an Era of Excess*. New York: The Free Press, 1999.

Frank, Robert. *The Involved Father*. New York: St. Martin's Press, 1999.

Galinsky, Ellen. *Ask the Children: What America's Children Really Think About Working Parents*. New York: William Morrow and Co., 1999.

Germer, Fawn. "Star Power." *Working Woman*, March 2000, p. 26.

Gerson, Kathleen. "Children of the Gender Revolution: Some Theoretical Questions and Findings from the Field." In *Family In Transition*, 11th edition, Arlene and Jerome Skolnick, eds. Needham Heights, Mass.: Allyn and Bacon, 2000.

Godfrey, Joline. *Our Wildest Dreams: Women Entrepreneurs Making Money, Having Fun, Doing Good*. New York: Harper Business, 1992.

Goldberg, Carey. "Ethics Ruling Faults Massachusetts's Official." *The New York Times*, Aug. 24, 2000, p. A14.

———. "M.I.T. Acknowledges Bias Against Female Professors." *The New York Times*, Mar. 23, 1999, p. A1.

Goldberg, Jeffrey. "Diaper Diplomacy." *The New York Times Magazine*, April 30, 2000, p. 32.

Goldin, Claudia. "Career and Family: College Women Look to the Past." In *Gender and Family Issues in the Workplace*, Francine D. Blau and Ronald G. Ehrenberg, eds. New York: Russell Sage Foundation, 1997, pp. 20–58.

Goldstein, Patrick. "Empire Builders." *The Los Angeles Times Magazine*, Mar. 26, 2000, p. 18.

Goodman, Ellen. "It's No Wonder Women Enter Politics a Decade Later than Men." *The Hartford Courant*, Jan. 11, 2000, p. 33.

Greenberg, Hindi. *The Lawyers Career Change Handbook*. New York: Avon Books, 1998.

Greenhouse, Steven. "All College Graduates, Please Apply." *The New York Times*, June 4, 2000, p. A12.

———. "Unions Unite in a Campaign for Childcare." *The New York Times*, Mar. 2, 1998, p. B1.

Hamilton Kendall and Wingert, Pat. "Down the Aisle." *Newsweek*, July 20, 1998, p. 56.

Harvey, Elizabeth. "Short-term and Long-term Effects of Early Parental Employment on Children of the National Longitudinal Survey of Youth." *Developmental Psychology*, No. 35, (1999), pp. 445–459.

Healy, Michelle. Lifeline Column, *USA Today*, July 9, 1999, p. D1.

Herbert, Bob. In America Column: "Focus on Women." *The New York Times*, Sept. 28, 2000, p. A31.

———. In America Column: "Women Vote Too." *The New York Times*, Jan. 27, 2000, p. A27.

Hinojosa, Maria. *Raising Raul: Adventures Raising Myself and My Son.* New York: Viking, 1999.

Hochschild, Arlie. *The Second Shift.* New York: Viking Penguin, 1989.

Hodgman, Ann. "Please Baby, Please Baby." *The New York Times Book Review,* June 18, 2000, p. 27.

Hoff, Robert D. "No Satisfaction in Silicon Valley." *Business Week,* Nov. 8, 1999, p. 15.

Hoge, Warren. "Cherie Blair v Tony Blair, You Might Say, in Court, the Case for Parental Leave." *The New York Times,* May 17, 2000, p. A2.

Horn, Wade F., Feinstein, Alice (editor), and Rosenberg, Jeffrey. *The New Father Book: What Every Man Needs to Know to Be a Good Dad.* Des Moines, Iowa: Meredith Books, 1998.

Howe Verhovek, Sam. "Record for Women in Washington Legislature." *The New York Times,* Feb. 4, 1999, p. A14.

Iovine, Julie V. "Castle First, Prince Later: Marketing to Ms." *The New York Times,* Oct. 21, 1999, p. B1.

Jacobs, Jerry, and Gerson, Kathleen. "Who Are the Overworked Americans?" *Review of Social Economy,* Vol. LVI, No. 4 (Winter 1998), pp. 443–459.

Janofsky, Michael. "Pittsburgh Is Showcase for Women in Policing." *The New York Times,* June 21,1998, p. A14.

Johnston, David Cay. "Vice Chairman of Fidelity to Retire Next Week." *The New York Times,* p. C1.

Johnston, Lloyd D., O'Malley, Patrick M., and Bachman, Jerrold G. "1998: Monitoring the Future." Institute for Social Research at University of Michigan.

Kahn, Joseph. "Morgan Stanley Is Target of Sex Bias Inquiry." *The New York Times,* July 29, 1999, p. C1.

Karbo, Karen. *Motherhood Made a Man Out of Me.* New York: Bloomsbury Publishing, 2000.

Kaufman, Jonathan. "An Aspiring Game Mogul Finds a Boss's Life 'Weird'." *The Wall Street Journal,* June 18, 1998, p. B1.

Kaufman, Leslie. "Some Companies Derail the 'Burnout' Track." *The New York Times,* May 4, 1999, p. A1.

———. "The Dot.Com World Opens New Opportunities for Women to Lead." *The New York Times,* Mar. 9, 2000, pp. C1.

Kelly, Katy. "Child Docs to Parents: Stay Home and Save Your Kids." *U.S. News and World Report,* Oct. 30, 2000, p. 65.

Knight Ridder News Service."High Tech Culture Failing to Draw Girls." *The Honolulu Advertiser,* April 11, 2000, p. A1.

Kofodimus, Joan. "Why Executives Lose Their Balance." *Organizational Dynamics* (Summer 1990), p. 61.

Koretz, Gene. "Economic Trends," "Hazardous to Your Carreer: The Risk of Taking Unpaid Leaves." *Business Week,* Jan. 17, 2000, p. 26.

———. "Economic Trends: Wives with Fat Paychecks." *Business Week,* Sept. 7, 1998, p. 22.

Kurson, Robert. "Who's Killing the Great Lawyers of Harvard?" *Esquire* magazine, August 2000, p. 83.

Kushell, Jennifer. *The Young Entrepreneur's Edge: Using Your Ambition, Independence, and Youth to Launch a Successful Business.* Princeton, N.J.: Princeton Review Series, 1999.

Lake, Sosin, Snell, Perry, and Associates. "Family Matters: A National Survey of Women and Men." New York: The National Partnership for Women and Families, Feb. 1998. See www.nationalpartnership.org.

Lamott, Anne. *Operating Instructions: A Journal of My Son's First Year.* New York: Fawcett Columbine, 1993.

Landers, Renee M., Rebitzer, James B., and Taylor, Lowell J. "Work Norms and Professional Labor Markets." In *Gender and Family Issues in the Workplace,* Francine Blau and Ronald G. Ehrenberg, eds. Ithaca: Russell Sage Foundation, 1997, p. 176.

Lardner, James. "World-Class Workaholics." *U.S. News and World Report,* Dec. 20, 1999, p. 52.

Lasch Quinn, Elizabeth. "Mothers and Markets." *The New Republic,* Mar. 6, 2000, p. 42.

Lemann, Nicholas. "The Battle Over Boys." *The New Yorker,* July 10, 2000, p. 80.

Lennon, M. C., and Rosenfeld, S. "Relative Fairness and the Division of Housework: the Importance of Options." *American Journal of Sociology,* No. 100 (1994), pp. 506–531.

Lerner, Harriet. *The Mother Dance: How Children Change Your Life.* New York: Harper Collins, 1998.

Levering, Robert, and Moscowitz, Milton. "The 100 Best Companies to Work For." *Fortune,* Jan. 10, 2000, p. 82.

Levine, James, and Pittinsky, Todd L. *Working Fathers: New Strategies for Balancing Work and Family.* Reading, Mass: Addison Wesley, 1997.

Lewin, Tamar. "Father Awarded $375,000 in Parental Leave Case." *The New York Times,* Feb. 3, 1999, p. A11.

———. "Now a Majority: Families with Two Parents Who Work." The New York Times, Oct. 24, 2000, p. A14.

———. "Partnership Awarded to Woman in Sex Bias Case." *The New York Times,* May 16, 1990, p. A1.

Lewis, Michael. "The Artist in the Gray Flannel Pajamas." *The New York Times Magazine,* Mar. 5, 2000, p. 45.

———. *The New New Thing.* New York: W.W. Norton and Co., 1999.

Lewis, Steven M. *Zen and the Art of Fatherhood: Lessons from a Master Dad.* New York: Plume, 1997.

Marshack, Kathy. *Entrepreneurial Couples: Making It Work at Work and at Home*. Palo Alto: Calif.: Davies Black Publishing, 1998.

McCauly, Lucy. "Don't Burn Out." *Fast Company*, May, 2000, p. 106.

McGeehan, Patrick. "Morgan Stanley Cited for Discrimination Against Women." I, June 6, 2000, p. C1.

Mihm, Stephen."Traveling: A Box Score." *The New York Times*, July 12, 2000, p. D5.

Miller, Stephen C. "Moved by Love, and Work." *The New York Times*, Money and Business, Jan 23, 2000, p. 2.

Moen, Phyllis. and Yu, Yan. "Having It All: Overall Work/Life Success in Two-Earner Families." *Research in the Sociology of Work*, Vol. 7 (1999), pp. 109–110.

Molpus, David. "Ernst and Young Workplace." *All Things Considered*, National Public Radio, July 28, 1998.

Moore, Dorothy P., and Buttner, E. Holly. *Women Entrepreneurs: Moving Beyond the Glass Ceiling*. Thousand Oaks, Calif.: Sage Publications, 1997.

Moran, Susan. Get a Life Column: "Stressed for Success." *Business 2.0*, Nov., 1999, p. 283.

Morgan, Joan. *When Chickenheads Come Home to Roost: A Hip Hop Feminist Breaks It Down*. Touchstone Books, 2000.

Morris, Betsy. "It's Her Job Too." *Fortune*, Feb. 2, 1988, p. 65.

Myers, Steven Lee. "Female General in Army Alleges Sex Harassment." *The New York Times*, March 31, 2000, p. A1.

Nesheem, John L. *High Tech Start Up*. New York: Simon and Schuster, 1997.

Noble, Holcomb B. "Leaping from Childbirth to Ballet Stage." *The New York Times*, May 18, 1999.

O'Connor, Colleen. Get a Life Column: "High Touch for High Tech." *Business 2.0*, Feb. 2000, p. 219.

Oldman, Mark, and Hamadeh, Samer. *America's Top Internships*. Princeton, N.J.: Princeton Review, 2000.

———. *The Internship Bible 2001*. Princeton, N.J.: Princeton Review, 2000.

Orenstein, Peggy. *Flux: Women on Sex, Work, Love, Kids, and Life in a Half Changed World*. New York: Random House, 2000.

Pace, Eric. "Mirra Komarovsky, Authority on Women's Studies, Dies." *The New York Times*, Feb. 1, 1999, p. A22.

Parke, Ross, and Brott, Armin A. *Throwaway Dads: The Myths and Barriers That Keep Men from Being the Fathers They Want to Be*. New York: Houghton Mifflin, 1999.

Perlow, Leslie A. *Finding Time: How Corporations, Individuals, and Families Can Benefit from New Work Practices*. Ithaca, N.Y.: Cornell University Press, 1997.

Pollack, William S. *Real Boys Voices*. New York: Random House, 2000.

Pruett, Kyle D. *Fatherneed: Why Father Care Is as Essential as Mother Care for Your Child.* New York: The Free Press, 2000.

Purdum, Todd S. "Teachers Offered a Tax Exemption: California Governor Would Waive Levies on Income." *The New York Times,* May 14, 2000, p. A1.

Queenan, Joe. "New Magazine Celebrates the Guy Called Dad." *The New York Times,* News of the Week in Review, June 15, 2000, p. 9.

Quintanilla, Carl. "College Recruiting Becomes Lavish." *The Wall Street Journal,* June 4, 1998, p. B1.

Randolf, Laura B. "Sisterspeak: Strong Black Woman Blues." *Ebony,* July 1999, p. 24.

Ratliff, Pam. "Motherhood: A Proud Profession." *Ventura County Parent,* May 1999, p. 16.

Rehak, Melanie. "Lullaby Diva." *The New York Times Magazine,* Aug. 29,1999, p. 16.

Rhode, Deborah L. "Perspectives on Professional Women." *Stanford Law Review,* No. 40 (1988), pp. 1163–1207.

Ricci, Laura. *Views from Women's Eye's: Managing the New Majority.* Austin, Tex.: R3 Press, 1997.

Riesman, David. *The Lonely Crowd.* New Haven, Conn.: Yale University Press, 1969.

Rosener, Judy B. *America's Competitive Secret: Women Managers.* Oxford: Oxford University Press, (Oxford Paperbacks), 1995.

Sadker, Daniel. "Gender Games." *The Washington Post,* Op. Ed., July 30, 2000, p. A37.

Salyers, Thomas E. "Time Off for New Dads." Letters, *The New York Times,* Apr. 30, 2000, p. B24.

Schaffer, William, A. and Schaffer, Bill. *High Tech Careers for Low Tech People.* Ten Speed Press, 1999.

Schevitz, Tanya. "40% of U.S. Doctoral Degrees Earned by Women in '96–97." *The San Francisco Chronicle,* Nov. 3, 1999, p. 2.

Schleinholtz, Debra F., ed. "Cracking the Glass Ceiling: Strategies for Success," a study done for the Glass Ceiling Commission of the U.S. Department of Labor. New York: Catalyst, 1994.

Schmitt, Richard B. "From Cash to Travel, New Lures for Burned-Out Lawyers." *The Wall Street Journal,* Feb. 2, 1999, p. B1.

Schor, Juliet. *The Overspent American: Upscaling, Downshifting, and the New Consumer.* New York: Basic Books, 1998.

Schwartz, Delmore. "In Dreams Begin Responsibilities," *In Dreams Begin Responsibilities.* 1948. Reprint, New York: New Directions Books, 1978.

Sellers, Patricia. "The 50 Most Powerful Women in Business." *Fortune,* Oct. 16, 2000, p. 154.

———. "These Women Rule." *Fortune,* Oct. 25, 1999, p. 94.

Shapiro, Jerrold Lee. *The Measure of a Man: Becoming the Father You Wish Your Father Had Been.* Berkeley, Calif.: Perigee Press, 1995.

Sharkey, Joe. Business Travel Column: "The World Bank Gauges the Toll Travel Takes on Employees and Looks for Ways to Soften the Effect." *The New York Times,* May 10, 2000, p. C6.

Sheehy, Gail. *Passages: Predictable Crises of Adult Life.* New York: Bantam, 1977.

Shellenbarger Sue. Work and Family Column: "To Win the Loyalty of Your Employees, Try a Softer Touch." *The Wall Street Journal,* Nov. 20, 1999, B1.

———. Work and Family Column: "Students Get Lessons in How to Manage a Well-Balanced Life," *The Wall Street Journal,* Feb. 24, 1999, p. B1.

———. Work and Family Column: "Family Friendly CEO's Are Changing Cultures at More Workplaces." *The Wall Street Journal,* Sept. 15, 1999, p. B1.

———. Work and Family Column: "Readers Offer Views About Productivity and Long Work Weeks." *The Wall Street Journal,* Sept. 16, 1998, B1.

———. Work and Family Column: "What Job Candidates Really Want to Know: Will I Have a Life?" *The Wall Street Journal,* Nov. 17, 1999, p. B1.

———. Work and Family Column: "Would Your Teen Give You High Marks on Career-Handling?" *The Wall Street Journal,* May 20, 1998, p. B1.

Simmons, Jeffrey R., ed. *Life, Law and the Pursuit of Balance: A Lawyer's Guide to Quality of Life.* Published in partnership with the Maricopa County and Arizona Bar Associations, Phoenix, Ariz.: 1996.

Sonnert, G., and Holton, G. *Who Succeeds in Science? The Gender Dimension.* New Brunswick, N.J.: Rutgers University Press, 1996.

Specter, Michael. "The Baby Bust, A Special Report: Population Implosion Worries a Graying Europe." *The New York Times,* July 10, 1998, p. A1.

Stanley, Thomas J., and Danko, William D. *The Millionaire Next Door: The Surprising Secrets of America's Wealthy.* New York: Pocket Books, 1996.

Steinhauer, Jennifer. "For Women in Medicine, a Road to Compromise, Not Perks." *The New York Times,* Mar. 1, 1999, p. A1.

Stone, Judith. "Trust Us." *Mirabella,* Apr. 2000, p. 118.

Straus, Tamara. "Irony with Soul: Dave Eggers Writes the Hippest of Memoirs." hipMama.com, Feb. 18, 2000, see www.alternet.org/story.html?storyID=401.

United States Merit Systems Protection Board. "A Question of Equity." Report to the President and Congress. Oct. 1992.

University of Colorado at Denver, Department of Economics. "Cost, Quality and Child Outcomes in Child Care Centers." Apr. 1995.

Valian, Virginia. *Why So Slow? The Advancement of Women*, Cambridge. Mass.: The M.I.T. Press, 1998.

Waldfogel, Jane. "Understanding the 'Family Gap' in Pay for Women with Children." *Journal of Economic Perspectives*, Vol. 12, No. 1 (Winter 1998), pp. 143–153.

Walkers, Lou Ann. "He Doesn't." *New Woman*, Nov., 1997, p. 145.

Walt, Vivienne. "Instant Fame for New MBA's." *The New York Times*, May 17, 1998, p. D11.

Walzak, Lee. "Clinton Sets a Parent Trap for the GOP." *Business Week*, May 3, 1999, p. 55.

Weise, Elisabeth. "Families Learn to Live on Internet Time." *USA Today*, May 27, 1999, p. B1.

Wells, Susan J. "What Happens if Harriet Makes More than Ozzie." *The New York Times*, Aug. 1, 1999, p. B10.

Wilgoren, Jodi. "With Labor Day Comes More Labor, Less Play." *The Los Angeles Times*, Sept. 7, 1998, p. A1.

Williams, Joan. *Unbending Gender: Why Family and Work Conflict and What to Do About It*. New York: Oxford University Press, 2000.

Wilson, Amy. "Job Titles of the Future." *American Way Magazine*, Dec. 15, 1999, p. 82.

Winter, Greg. "In the Boom, Desperately Seeking Bean Counters." *The New York Times*, June 28, 2000, p. C11.

Winter, Greg. "Law Firms Limit Aid to Poor." *The New York Times*, News of the Week in Review, Sept. 10, 2000, p. 2.

Wolf, Naomi. *The Beauty Myth: How Images of Beauty Are Used Against Women*. New York: William Morrow and Company, 1991.

———. *Fire with Fire: The New Female Power and How to Use It*. New York: Random House, 1993.

Wu, Amy. My Money, My Life Column: "Twentysomethings' Lament." *The New York Times*, Sept. 31, 1999, p. B15.

Wurtzel, Elizabeth. *Prozac Nation: A Memoir*. New York: Riverhead Books, 1994.

———. *Bitch: In Praise of Difficult Women*. New York: Doubleday, 1999.

Yago, Glenn, Ford, Rebecca, and Gordon, Judith. *Economic Prosperity, Women and Access to Credit*. Santa Monica, Calif.: Milken Institute, Oct. 2000.

Yoffe, Emily. "Fugitive in the Family." *The New York Times Magazine*, June 20, 1999, p. 132.

Zemke, Ron, Raines, Claire, and Filipczak, Bob. *Generations at Work: Managing the Clash of Veterans, Boomers, Xers, and Nexters in Your Workplace*. New York: AMACOM Books, 2000.

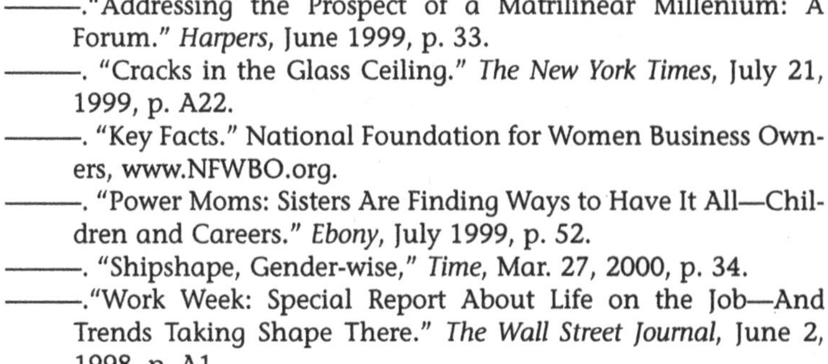

———."Addressing the Prospect of a Matrilinear Millenium: A Forum." *Harpers*, June 1999, p. 33.

———. "Cracks in the Glass Ceiling." *The New York Times*, July 21, 1999, p. A22.

———. "Key Facts." National Foundation for Women Business Owners, www.NFWBO.org.

———. "Power Moms: Sisters Are Finding Ways to Have It All—Children and Careers." *Ebony*, July 1999, p. 52.

———. "Shipshape, Gender-wise," *Time*, Mar. 27, 2000, p. 34.

———."Work Week: Special Report About Life on the Job—And Trends Taking Shape There." *The Wall Street Journal*, June 2, 1998, p. A1.

Index

Abandonment, fear of, 78
Abortion, 252, 253–254
See also Reproductive freedom
Abrams, Joyce, 77–78, 79, 81–82
Absenteeism, 44, 261
Academy of Management Journal, 44
Active Element, 255
Activism, xiii, 255
Adam.com, 151
Aetna, 115, 120
Affirmative action, 249, 252
Aflac, perks at, 120
Afterschool programs, 248, 262, 263
Agilent Technologies, 114, 219
Air Force
career in, 102–104, 106
joint-spouse policy of, 105
Albright, Madeline, 217
Alecci, Lisa: negotiating by, 114
Allen, Kathleen, 165–166
on female entrepreneurs/obstacles, 167
on financial expertise/women, 166
Allen, Paul, 227
AMA, 141
Amanpour, Christine, 217
Ambition, 91, 196, 226
sacrificing, 198, 248
American Association of University Women, 95
American Astronomical Society, 53
American Bar Association, 158
American Cancer Society, 3
American Century, perks at, 119
American Express, 47
America Online (AOL), 44, 261
America's Top Internships, 99
An Income of Her Own, 163
Apprenticeships, 125, 164
"Ask Amy" (Web site), 255
Ask the Children (study), 229
Associates, 153, 155
AT&T, survey by, 42
At-Home Dad's convention, 219
At-home parents, 217, 219, 223, 224, 225
designating, 199
Avon Products, Inc., woman CEO for, 23
Ayyildiz, Kent: documentary by, 219

B.A., power of, 109–111
Baby boomers, xi, xii
Generation XX and, 32
goals of, xiii
impact of, xiv, 23
workplace and, 18
Baby Boon: How Family Friendly America Cheats the Childless, The
(Burkett), 250
Baby-sitters, 236, 237–238
entertainment by, 240
"Babysitter's Club, The" book series, 241
Baby-Sitters of America, 228
Backlash (Faludi), xiii
Bagby, Meredith
on career status, 24
on material girls/boys, 47–48
Bailyn, Lotte: on humane policies, 251
Baird, Zoe: undocumented aliens and, 249
Balance, 37, 96, 99, 105, 150, 246, 247
achieving, 10, 11, 13, 24, 25, 140, 228, 264
concerns about, 12, 100, 221–226
harmony and, 92
importance of, xi, 90, 110
meaning and, 92
men and, 201, 227
values and, 91
Bankers, gender perception of, 165–166
Banks, Melissa, 71–72, 79
Batstone, David: on work-life balance, 112
Battle-of-the-sexes theory, 135
Baumgardner, Jennifer, xiv, 253
Beauty Myth, The (Wolf), xiii
Beckwith, Allison, 164–165

Ben and Jerry's, 25
Benchmark, 173
Benefits, 95, 114
  problems with, 43–44
  See also Perks
Bergson, Pamela, 172–173, 181
Berry, Matt, 219
Billings, Hillary, 69, 80, 81, 264
  career of, 149–152
  family life of, 150–151
  RedEnvelope and, 149
  on work ethic/family, 152
Bing, Stanley: on sleep, 44–45
Birchhead, J. Gary: work week of, 45
Birthrate, drop in, 247
Bitch (Wurtzel), xiii
Blair, Tony, 209, 210
Blancheflower, David: on happy marriage/value, 86
Bohling, Donna, 193, 234
Bonding, 187
  men and, 54, 206, 208, 209
  potential for, 233
Bonuses, 118, 145, 159
  signing, 100, 108, 110
"Boot Camp for Dads: Cuddle That Baby, Maggot," 204
Boston Consulting Group, 121, 123, 124
Boston Globe, The: on shared parenting, 199
Bowman, Joan: on negotiating, 113
Boy code, 79
Boyfriends, choosing, 84
Boykin, June: on rural childcare, 263
Boy Scouts of America, 228
boyzChannel, 62
Bramoco, perks at, 120
Brass ceiling, 105
Brazelton, T. Berry: on childcare, 262
Bright Horizons, 263
Bronson, Po
  on Silicon Valley entrepreneurs, 147
  on uber geeks, 148
Brooks, Garth, 218
Bureau of Labor Statistics
  on flexible schedules, 259
  on median salaries, 94
Burggraf, Shirley P., 246, 251
Burkett, Elinor: on parents/unfair advantages, 250
Burnout, 99, 116, 180
Business
  accommodation by, 249, 251, 261
  boom in, 258
  business of, 141–142
  family, 175–176
  men and, 248
  micro-, 170
  starting, 181
  teenagers and, 161–162
  women and, 161–162, 168, 169, 176, 182
  work madness of, 141
Business 2.0
  on employee happiness, 117
  on work-life balance, 112
Business Enterprise Trust, seed money from, 169
Business school, 126, 141
Business Week, on 100 Best Companies, 117
Bust (zine), 255
Buttner, E. Holly
  family life and, 51
  on women entrepreneurs, 168

California Lawyer, poll by, 155
Calvert, Stacey, 220–221
Calvin Klein, part-time work at, 115
Camp $tart-up, 163, 164
Capital, 170
  lack of access to, 165, 169
  working, 161
  See also Venture capital
Career Choices, 27
Career paths, 30, 100, 211
Careers
  family and, 24, 197
  life and, 25
  motherhood and, 35, 77
  limits of, 226
  planning, 84, 96–98
  sacrificing for, 136
  switching, 222, 245–246
Caregiver-child ratios, 239
Caregivers, 236, 237, 248
  attachment to, 238
  childcare and, 240
  entertainment by, 240
  full-time, 258
  problems with, 238
  turnover of, 239
  See also Primary caregivers
Caretaking, 249, 251, 259
Carlson, Ben: advice from, 90–91
Carroll, Jon: on Stepford economy, 11, 147
Carrol School of Management (Boston College), data base of, 27

Case, Steve: salary for, 261
Catalyst, 26–27
  glass ceiling and, 26
  research by, 51, 101
Catino, Annette, 174–175, 181
CCH, Inc., survey by, 44
Census Bureau, on employed mothers/children, 247
Center for Men (McLean Hospital), 79
Center for Work and Family (Boston College), 117, 198
Centropia, 125
CEOs
  female, 23, 52
  workplace culture and, 117–118, 121
Changes, 245
  cultural, 22, 258–262, 264
  economic, 22
  encouraging, 19
  healthy, 82
  in parenthood, 188, 213, 215
  in politics, 22
  postponing, 260
  second order of, 82
  in values, 144
  workplace, xii, 14, 21, 114, 116–121, 142, 264
Charity work, 3, 119, 121, 172
Charles, Prince: parenthood and, 187
Charles Schwab, Independent Means and, 164
Chavez, Cesar, 74
Cher, 179
"Chickclicks" (Web site), 255
Childcare, 16, 27, 75, 93, 159, 264
  ambivalence about, 236
  caregivers and, 240
  emergency, 119, 120
  extended family/friends and, 240
  finding, 196, 224, 236–237, 249
  as full-time job, 197
  help with, 212
  immigrants and, 249
  maternity leave and, 259
  men and, 202, 206
  mental health and, 196
  military and, 108
  money for, 262–263
  myth/reality of, 236–240
  NOW and, 252
  on-site, 118, 248, 251
  quality, 194, 252, 260, 262, 263
  rural, 263
  salaries in, 258, 262
  subsidized, 94, 250, 262
  See also Daycare
Child development, 239
Childhood
  insight into, 10
  rituals of, 238
Childrearing, 252, 258
  economics and, 220
  men and, 201, 203
  money for, 194
Children
  cost of raising, 194
  elders and, 234
  equal relationships with, 35
  impact of, 14, 36, 183–184, 197
  intimacy with, 205
  marriage and, 35
  neglecting, 30, 206
  neighbors and, 233
  significant others and, 231–232
  social life and, 233–234
  staying home with, 13, 15
  supporting, 36, 39, 135
  thinking about, 81, 186, 187
"Children of the Gender Revolution" (Gerson), 35–36
Children's World, 263
Child Welfare Hotline, 193
Chin, Wendy: Scient and, 146
Chisholm, Shirley, xiii
Choices, xvii, 229, 254, 264
  children's, 234
  for doctors, 139–140
  fear/guilt about, 196
  for lawyers, 157
  lifestyle, 114, 139–141
  losing, 253
  making, 77–78, 97
  parenting and, 64, 222, 232
  sane, 130
  women's, 130, 196
Citigroup's Salomon Smith Barney, discrimination at, 54–55
Citizen Schools in Boston, 125
Ciulla, Joanne B., 87, 258, 260
Clark, Jim: restlessness of, 147
Clinton, Bill, 249, 259
ClubInvest, 164
Club $tart-up, 164
Coca Cola, layoffs at, 47
Cole, Paula, 59
Collective wisdom, group-think and, xiv
College attendance, impact of, xvii
College Boards Advanced Placement, on women/technology, 95
Collins, Eileen Marie, 23, 221

Commission on Family and Medical Leave, on paternity leave, 207
Commission on National Security for the 21st Century, 102
Communication, 33, 52
Community
  creating, 231–232
  parents and, 231–232
  self-centered and, 257
Community services, 143, 230
Commuting, 5, 42, 136
Competition, 72, 169
Compromises, 203, 222
Connections, 86–87, 91, 171
  desire for, 157
  importance of, 87
  social, 70–71
Consulting, 116
  life after, 144–149
  normalization of, 144
  work madness of, 141
Container Store, perks at, 119
Cook County Hospital, residents at, 138
Cooperation, 127, 167
Co-parenting, 224, 225, 226
Cornell University Careers Institute, 31
Corning, experimental unit at, 251
Corporate culture, 100
"Cost, Quality and Child Outcomes in Child Care Centers" (study), 262
Council on Foreign Relations, 102
Count-Me-In, loans from, 170
Country Kids Farm, 93
Crunch, 14, 15
Cultural revolution, 11, 12, 121
Culture, 35, 189, 245
  baby-sitters and, 237
  caring, 19
  changes in, 22, 28, 258–262, 264, 265
  equality and, 32
  family-oriented, 146
  Generation X women and, 11–12
  identity and, 28
  succumbing to, 201
  traditional, 79
  work, 101, 121

"Daddio" (sitcom), 219
"Daddy and me" classes, 213
Daddy deficit, suffering from, 206–207
Dads, 189, 201
Dad's Magazine, 201
Dad-To-Dad, 219
Damia, Alicia: planning by, 186
Dannon, part-time work at, 115
Dating, 29, 37, 50, 69, 72, 171–172
Daum, Meghan, 48, 49
Davis, Gray: teachers/tax breaks and, 108
Daycare, 24, 190, 257, 259
  educational, 239
  family, 237, 238–240
  licensed, 238–39
  socialization and, 239
  See also Childcare
Debt
  accumulation of, 47
  credit card, 48–49, 139
  impact of, 45, 46–49, 58
  school, 89, 130
Deloitte and Touche, 120
  turnover rate at, 109
Dentist-on-wheels, 44, 112
Department of Agriculture, on childraising costs, 194
Depression, impact of, xii, xv
Deutsch, Francine M., 68
  on at-home mothers/husbands, 225
  on balance, 224
  on parenting/men, 201, 202
DeWolf, Betsy: daycare center of, 239
Diana, Princess: parenthood and, 187
Dickie, Jane, 203
Digital girls, 265
Dinks, 184, 185
Discrimination, 49–50
  avoiding, 32, 52
  ethnic, 254
  vs. female entrepreneurs, 51
  gender, 52, 53–57, 100, 117, 163, 168, 250
  handling, 51, 55, 56–57, 58
  legal cases about, 57–58
  patterns of, 54
  sex, 55, 57, 254
  termination and, 57–58
  workplace, 34–35
Divorce, 73
  fatherhood and, 202
  impact of, 184, 187, 211, 220
  relationships and, 184
Doctors
  internships and, 129
  lifestyle choices for, 139–140
  male/female compared, 130, 137
  negligence by, 130
  as victimizers, 132
  workload of, 108–109, 132, 133
  See also Medicine

Doctors Without Borders, 90
Dollar Diva/Dollar Dude, 164
Domestic work, 21, 69, 200, 248–249
Downscaling, 47, 211
Drag coefficient, 142, 222, 258
Dreams, 143, 183, 190, 196
  achieving, 25–26
  exploring, 10, 12–13
  giving up, 247
  material, 46
  responsibilities and, 10
  strategies for, 13
  See also Goals
Drexel Burnham, Malnick at, 142
Driscoll, John, 85
Drury, Gita: Active Element and, 255
Dual-income families, 31
  workplace/public policy and, 21
Dubinsky, Donna, 218, 265
Dunn, Patricia, 23

Earning power, 195
  losing, 32
  parenting and, 194
  parity in, 200, 246
  work potential and, 31
Eason, Yla: entrepreneurship of, 169
Economics, 11, 12, 13, 21, 125, 195
  changes in, 22
  childrearing and, 220
  cultural emphasis on, 85
  politics and, 256
EDK Associates, poll by, 252
Education, xv, 21, 27, 32, 49–50, 91, 247, 250, 254, 257
  early childhood, 92–93
  funding, 264
  gap in, 164
  spiritual enrichment from, 93
  women and, 22
  workaholism and, 129
Edward, Prince, 60
Egalitarianism, 61–62, 64, 82
  See also Equality
Eggers, Dave, 256, 257
Electra, Carmen, 60
Electronic revolution, backlash against, 12
Eli Lily, leave from, 224
Ellison, Larry, 147
Ellwanger, Meghan, 164
E-mail
  answering, 147–148
  marketing, 171
Emergencies
  childcare during, 119, 120
  swapping help for, 212
  work, 116, 237
Emotional survival instincts, 72, 76
Employees
  appreciating/encouraging, 124
  getting/keeping, 109
  replacing, 109
  satisfaction for, 121
English-Lueck, Jan, 147, 148
Ensler, Eve, xiii
Entrepreneurs, 182
  couples as, 175, 176, 177–181
  family life and, 215
  personality type of, 176
  See also Female entrepreneurs
Entrepreneurship for Dummies (Allen), 165
Equal Economic Opportunity Commission, discrimination and, 53–54
Equality, 51, 56, 226, 259, 263
  achieving, 32
  affirmative action and, 252
  believing in, 69
  caretaking and, 249
  culture and, 32
  desire for, 21, 63
  gender, theories of, 34–35
  men/women and, 15, 70, 198
  parenting and, 35, 210
  public acceptance of, 32
  reality of, 55
  relationship, 61, 65–66
  See also Egalitarianism
Equal pay for equal work, 252, 253, 254
Ericson, Eric, 198
Ernst and Young, 109
Esquire, on overworked lawyers, 155
"estronet" (Web site), 255
Executive placement companies, 113
Extavour, Kemba, 156, 157, 264
  life of, 40, 41
  salary for, 47
  work life of, 42, 50, 51, 57, 83, 152

Face-time, importance of, 100
Fallows, Deborah, 195
  on childcare, 196
Fallows, James, 195
Faludi, Susan, xiii, 202–203
Families and Work Institute, 45, 229
Family
  balance and, 259
  career and, 24

devotion to, xiii, 133
extended, 230, 240
identity and, 14
importance of, 4, 5, 7, 24, 41, 110, 151
pressure on, 43, 133
support from, 4, 105, 229, 230, 248
thinking about, 187
women and, 27, 64
work and, 13, 14, 16, 25, 27–30, 32, 117, 152, 207, 224, 240–244
Family and Medical Leave Act (1993), 27, 44
Family and Work Institute, 206
Family, Career, and Community Leaders of America, 24
Family crises, 39, 120, 193
Family friendly policies, described, 119–120
Family life, 31, 51, 230, 248
entrepreneurship and, 215
family business and, 176
free-form, 197, 218, 219, 265
men and, 203, 206
neighbors and, 233
problems with, 17, 211
time for, 134, 242
Family lifesavers, 229–236
Farrar, Kate: on choices, 254
Fast Company, 229
on balance, 227
on SAS, 118
survey by, 25, 111
Fast track, 32, 114
work/life balance and, 226
Fatherhood, 9, 203, 210, 214
books on, 200–201
clumsy stage of, 226
divorce and, 202
magazines on, 201
marriage and, 202
model for, 205
professional, 220
post-feminist-era, 189–190
Fathemeed (Pruett), 205, 206
Fathers
absent, 202–3, 211, 222, 226, 247
at-home, 217, 219
as helpers, 207
help for, 219
involved, 206, 215
men as, 200–210
seminar for, 204
separation anxiety and, 205
work/life balance and, 219
Feiwell, Jean
work day of, 241–242
work/family and, 240–244
FEMALE. *See* Formerly Employed Mothers at the Leading Edge
Female entrepreneurs, 51, 125, 126, 265
advantages for, 167–168
business and, 162, 163
challenges for, 165
control/advancement by, 168
employment by, 165
gender discrimination against, 167
handicaps for, 167, 182
revenues by, 165
success for, 168–170
training for, 163
venture capital and, 175
Feminine Economy and the Economic Man, The (Burggraf), 251
Feminine side, 72, 79
Feminism, 35
personal level, 253
politics and, xv, xvi, 253, 254
Third Wave, xiii
thoughts on, 252–254
"50 Most Powerful Women in Business" (*Fortune*), 218
Filipczak, Bob, 25
Financial security, xv, 73, 91–98, 164, 166
relinquishing, 247
Finova Group, perks at, 119
Fiorina, Carly, 101, 218, 265
glass ceiling and, 52
Fire With Fire (Wolf), xiii
First USA, perks at, 119
Fisher, Leah: on traditional partnerships, 198
Fitzpatrick, Kellyann, 24
Five-year plans, 126
Flare.Com, 165
Fleet Boston Bank, Independent Means and, 164
Fleet Financial Services, experimental unit at, 251
Fleming, Renee, 221
Flexibility, 6–7, 11, 37, 136, 145, 224, 260
creating, 240
employer, 4
importance of, 98, 127
negotiating, 195
schedule, 3, 101, 106, 115, 259
See also Sequencing
Flexible Resources, 114–115, 223

Flex-time, 118, 148, 226, 250, 251, 252
  at law firms, 158, 159
  negotiating, 113–116
  pressing for, 248, 249
Floating holidays, 145
Flux (Orenstein), 14
Focus Media, 213, 214
Ford Foundation, study by, 43
Formerly Employed Mothers at the Leading Edge (FEMALE), 224
Fortune, 30
  on balance, 120
  on 100 Best Companies, 117
  on SAS, 119
  on sleep, 45
  on women in business, 218
Fortune 500 companies, 101, 162, 251
Forum on Children and Families, 263
Fox.com, UBUBU and, 125
Fox Family Channel, girls/boys sections to, 62
Frank, Robert, 219
  on children/communication, 206
  on fathers as helpers, 207
  on luxuries, 49
Free-lancing, 116, 171, 199
Free market, 248, 249
Fried, Mindy: on productivity/stress, 117
Friends, 9, 36, 151
  childcare and, 240
  children's, 234
  making, 89, 126, 231, 232–233
  support from, 264
"Friends" (television show), 39, 40, 48
"Functional Design Catalogue, The," 178
Future 500, The, 255
Future Homemakers of America, 24

Gallup, poll by, 44
Garland, Eric: on men/balance, 201
Gates, Bill, 121
Gelb, Les, 102
Gemmell, Bonnie, 264
  entrepreneurship of, 177–181
  on Rob, 181
Gemmell, Max, 178
Gemmell, Rob
  on Bonnie, 181
  entrepreneurship of, 177–181
Gemmell, Sarah, 178
Gender discrimination, 52–53, 57, 117, 250
  breaking, 163, 168
  issue of, 100
Gender roles, 34
  blending, 26–27, 80
General Electric, 65, 115, 118
Generations at Work (Zemke, Raines, and Filipczak), 25
Generation X, 86
  credit card debt for, 48
  reactiveness of, 18
Generation X women, culture and, 11–12
Generation XX, 12
  Baby Boomers and, 32
  described, 22–23
  discrimination against, 54–55
  parenthood and, 183–184, 191
  popular culture and, 39
  secret weapons of, 32–35
Generation XX women, rise of, 22–23
Generation XY, xi
  coming of age of, 11
  professional savvy of, xii
  renaming, 10–12
  revolution and, xiii
Gerber, Sharon, 204
Gerson, Katherine, 35–36
Gerson, Risa, 159, 224, 264
Ghio, Renato: planning by, 186
Ginsburg, Ruth Bader, 23
  on equality/affirmative action, 252
Girlfriends, protecting, 72
Girl Scouts, 172
Girls Guide to Hunting and Fishing, The (Banks), 71–72
GirlStory, 125
girlzChannel, 62
Glass ceiling, 17, 61, 153, 182
  bypassing, 168, 173
  family responsibilities and, 26
  hitting, 163
  trap doors and, 49–58
Glenn-Davis, Janeith, 221
Go (movie), 39
Goals, xii, xiii, 217
  compromising on, 18
  defining, 85
  pursuing, 196
  See also Dreams
Godfrey, Joline
  digital girls and, 265
  entrepreneurship of, 162–165
  on models, 165
Goldin, Claudia: on earnings/work potential, 31
Goldman Sachs, perks at, 119
Goodman, Ellen: on Swift, 55
Goodnight, James: SAS and, 118

Gore, Al, 23
Gottlieb, Diane, 77, 89
  on economic riches, 85
  on emotional awareness, 72
Gottlieb, Sasha, 90
  balance and, 92
  mentors of, 89
Graham, Bob, 102
Grandparents, 4, 248
  help from, 234–235, 236
  surrogate, 235
  See also Senior citizens
Granite Rock, perks at, 119
Grey, Andrew: perks and, 111
Group-think, collective wisdom and, xiv
Growth, 105, 143–144
Guardian Insurance, Independent Means and, 164
Guilt, 196
  mothers/fathers and, 206–207, 211, 214
Gurgle (magazine), 190

Half-time work. *See* Part-time work
Halving It All (Deutsch), 201
Hancock, Ellen, 218
Hankin, Harriet, 173–174, 181
Happiness, 11, 86
Harris, Bretall, Sullivan and Smith, 142
Hart, Gary, 102
Hartley, Adriana, 146
  maternity policy and, 145
Harvard Law School, unhappy graduates of, 155
Harvey, Elizabeth: on childcare/mental health, 196
Hay Group, 109
Health insurance, 27, 44, 174–175, 250
Heartbreaking Work of Staggering Genius, A (Eggers), 256
Heron, Katrina, 218
Hewlett Packard, 52, 101
  attrition rate at, 112
  perks at, 120
  work/life balance at, 118
High Tech Careers for Low Tech People (Schaffer), 96
Hinojosa, Maria: on co-parenting, 192
Hip hop, impact of, 257
hipMama (Eggers), 256
HMOs, 174, 175
Hochschild, Arlie: on equal relationships/women, 65–66
Holton, Gerald, 52
Home, xii
  men/women at, 135
  workplaces and, 246
HomeAdvisor.com, 80
Home Book, 178
Homedaddy (Ayyildiz), 219
Home Depot, Independent Means and, 164
Homemakers, providers and, 60, 62, 63
Home offices, 261
Hopkins, Ann, 54
Hopkins, Debby, 101, 218
"Hot Company" (game), 164
Househusbands, 104, 217, 218, 219
Housekeeping, 16, 25, 135, 192, 249
  men and, 206
  sharing, 68–69, 198–199
Hughes, Karen, 93–94
Humanitarian groups, 90
Human resources, 52, 118
Husbands, choosing, 7

IBM, 164
  leave from, 224
  perks at, 120
Identities, 87, 196
  assault on, 27–32
  culture and, 28
  family and, 14
  postmodern, 215
  preserving/strengthening, 37, 215
  work, 28, 197
Immigrants, childcare and, 249
Independent Means, 125, 162
  partners for, 164
  web site for, 164
Individuality, xiii, xvi, 245–246
Industry Standard, The: on saving time, 228
Information technology
  median income in, 147
  work madness of, 141, 148
Innovation, 80, 143–144
Intergenerational estrangement, xvi
Internet, 164
  UBUBU and, 123–124
Internet Business Guide (Resnick), 171
Internship Bible, The, 99
Internships, 125, 129
  difficulties with, 130
  finding, 99
Interviews, xii, 29, 33, 73
  information from, 99, 100, 110–111
  negotiating during, 113
  See also Recruiting
Interwoven, perks by, 111

Intimacy, 205
avoiding, 192, 203
creating, 28
maintaining, 245
Investment banking, work madness of, 141, 142
Investors' Circle, 164
Invisible hand, 246, 249, 252
involvedfather@aol.com, 219
Irreducible Needs of Children, The (Brazelton), 262
Isolation, 230
materialism and, 136
"It's No Wonder Women Enter Politics A Decade Later Than Men"
(Goodman), 55
"It takes a village" approach, 230

Jane (zine), 255
Jealousy, maternal, 237–238
Jerks, avoiding, 80–82, 149
Jerry Yang's of America, 85
Job bias, banning, 259
Job mobility, 147
Job placement, 34
Jobs. *See* Careers; Work
Jobs, Steve, 177
Job sharing, 101, 114, 118
Johnson and Johnson, 100, 120
Journal of Developmental Psychology, The, 196
Judiesch, Michael, 43

Kalish, Benjamin, 2, 3, 4, 8
caring for, 10
Greg and, 9
Kalish, Carol Ann, 16, 31, 40, 41, 46, 69, 100, 156, 158, 235, 264
story of, 1–10
strategy by, 17–18
on workplaces, 19
Kalish, Greg, 69, 79, 190, 235
story of, 1–10
work of, 8–9
Kaplan, Samantha, 140, 141
on debt, 130
planning by, 131
Kavaler, Betsy, 133, 141, 222, 256, 264
dismissal of, 134
generation isolation and, 136
girlfriends of, 137
models for, 135
sacrifice for, 134
urological surgery and, 136–137
week of, 131
women's medicine and, 257
Kellogg Company, six-hour day at, 260
Kennedy, Claudia: on work/life balance, 106
Kent, Jerald: family time for, 227
Khosla, Vinod, 227
King, Billy Jean, 23
Klein, Naomi, 256
Kleiner Perkins, Caufield, and Byers, 227
Kofodimus, Joan, 203
Komarovsky, Mirra, 251–252
Koogle, Tim: salary for, 261
Koplowitz, Kay: entrepreneurship of, 169–170
Koppel, Ted: Morrie and, 88
Kornhaber, Arthur, 90, 234
on businessified culture, 87
on spiritual currency, 86, 87
Kurson, Robert: on overworked lawyers, 155
Kushell, Jennifer, 190, 264
entrepreneurship of, 166–167
Young Entrepreneurs Network and, 166

Labor, traditional division of, 16
Labor unions, childcare/maternity leave and, 259
La Leche League, handbooks by, 201
Lamont, Margaret, 14–15
on life factors, 13
Lamott, Anne, 191
Landers, Renee M.: on rat race model, 155
Lane, Jenai, 161–162, 169
Lara, Concepción, 125
Lardner, James, 45
Lasch-Quinn, Elisabeth, 261
Law
changing practice of, 156–160
overwork in, 152–156
rat race model of, 155, 156
unfriendliness in, 129
workaholics in, 129
Law firms, 100
glass ceiling at, 153
interviewing at, 5, 6
working at, 3, 40, 50, 57, 83–84, 152, 155, 156, 158, 159
Law school
attending, 4, 5
professors at, 154
Lawyers
choices for, 157

salary/perks for, 153–154, 157
supply of, 152, 157
workload of, 108–109, 155
"Lawyers for Literacy" project, 3
Leadership, 5, 95, 101
Lear, Norman, 169
Leaves of absence, 97, 118, 133, 224, 227
See also Maternity leave; Parental leave; Paternity leave
Leisure, productivity and, 113
Lemann, Nicholas, 79
Lepore, Dawn, 218
Lerner, Harriet: on parenthood, 188–189, 191
Lerner, Steve, 188, 189
Leven, Meale, Bender, and Rankin (law firm), 40, 50
Levine, James, 218, 234
lecture by, 219
on men/work-family balance, 206
Levy, Jordan: parenting by, 210–215, 233
Levy, Samantha, 211
caring for, 213, 214
Levy, Sherry, 232, 264
on grandparents, 234
on parental leave, 212
parenting by, 210–215, 233
Lewis, Michael, 116, 147
Life
career and, 25
designing, 10, 37, 84
enjoying, 151–152
spiritual side of, 98
workable, 96, 244
work and, 15, 27, 28, 40, 117
Life-and-death decisions, 131
Life designs, xii, xiii, 9, 11, 12–19, 31
brass tacks of, 98–102
rethinking, 139–140
Lifestyles, 2–3, 18, 114, 153, 208
affluent, 182
changing, 224
credit-card, 48–49
healthy, 227
inconsistent, 36
money and, 154–155
multiplicity of, 265
postmodern, 217
supporting, 98
Lillian Vernon, 178
Lipponen, Paavo: paternity leave for, 210
Loans, 170
school, 1, 89, 126, 157
Lonely Crowd, The (Riesman), 87
Los Angeles Times, The, 41
on women television news anchors, 55–56
Lowe, Amy, xvi-xvii
bonding by, 233
negotiations by, 199
on parenthood, 199–200
Lucent Technologies, 101, 120
Luxury Forever (Frank), 49
Lyness, Karen, 43

Macphee, Nick, 217
Macy's, 150, 162
Malnick, Carol, 76, 142–144
Management Recruiters International, 42
Management Resources International, 85, 113
Management style, female, 167
Management-training workshops, 101
Marcus, Barbara
on Feiwell, 242
sabbatical for, 243
work/family and, 240–244
Marcus, Ben, 243
Marcus, Michael, 241, 243
Marketing, 167
opt-in, 171–72
Marriage, 29, 37
children and, 35
commuter, 136
dual-income, 11, 21, 31, 189, 195
equal, 35, 64, 65, 73
fatherhood and, 202
happy, value of, 86
models of, 184
parenthood and, 191
professional decisions and, 198
strengthening, 208
stress on, 136
Marshack, Kathy: entrepreneurship of, 176
Martin, Erin, xvi, 42, 113
analysis by, 30
on men/women, 67, 68
work life of, 28–29
Massachusetts State Ethics Commission, Swift and, 55
Materialism, xii, 46, 47–48
coming to terms with, 29
isolation and, 136
overwork and, 49
slipping into, 123
Maternal control
giving up, 225
paternal instinct and, 204

Maternity leave, 138, 145, 150, 209, 212
childcare and, 259
rescinding, 120
See also Parental leave; Paternity leave
McGovern, Gail, 45
McKenzie, Katy, 104, 105
McKenzie, Kimber L., 264
career of, 102–106
work/life balance and, 104–105
McKenzie, Mark, 104, 105
Medicaid, 133, 139
Medicine
changing, 141
down-to-earth, 139–140
life in, 129–141
models of, 134
personal life and, 137
women in, 130
workaholics in, 129
work madness of, 129, 130
See also Doctors
Menninger, Karl, 87
Mentors, 89, 92, 89, 150, 264
finding, 33, 98
importance of, 101, 166
medical, 140
See also Models
Merck, perks at, 119
Meritocracy, 33, 144
Merlino, Nell, 170
Merrill Lynch, layoffs at, 47
Meyers, Ann, 44
Meyers, Rachel, 43
MGM Home Entertainment, Levy at, 211, 212
Miami Herald, The: Resnick at, 171
Micro lenders, 161
Microprocessors, impact of, 21
Microsoft, 80
Middlebury College, dismissal from, 134, 194
Military
careers in, 102–104, 106
childcare and, 108
Milken, Michael, 142
Millionaire Next Door, The, 181
Milone, John, 127
Minton, Joe, 43
Models
importance of, 165, 166
See also Mentors
Model 2000 woman, 153
Moen, Phyllis: on work/life success, 222
Mommy track, 16, 34, 114, 248
Money, 91, 95
lifestyle and, 154–155
prestige and, 212
seed, 169, 170
work and, 98
Money-is-all model, 41
Moore, Ann S., 14
Moore, Dorothy P., 51
on women entrepreneurs, 168
Morgan, Joan: on superwoman problem, 225
Morgan Stanley, 96, 97
discrimination at, 54
work at, 28–29, 35, 42, 98
Moskowitz, Michael, 117, 118
Mother Dance, The (Lerner), 188
Motherhood
career and, 35, 77
dreams of, 247
hiding, 105
navigating, 14
problems with, 15, 16, 190, 211
professional, 194, 196
reading about, 24
sacredness of, 197
traditional, 17, 64, 248
work and, 13, 16, 245
"Motherhood: A Proud Profession," 24
Motherhood Made A Man Out of Me (Karbo), 188
Mothers
at-home, 215, 225
working, 223
Mother's Work, A (Fallow), 195
Mt. Sinai Hospital, 131, 139
Movies, female image in, 62
Mulcahy, Ann: balance and, 100
"My Misspent Youth" (*New Yorker*), 48

Nannies, 213, 236, 249
entertainment by, 240
using, 212, 237–238
Narcissistic men, falling in love with, 65
National Abortion and Reproductive Rights Action League (NARAL), 254
National Association for Law Placement, on associates, 159
National Foundation for Women Business Owners, The, 169
National Institute for Occupational Safety, 44
National Law Journal, paternity leave and, 159

National Organization of Women,
childcare and, 252
National Women's Business Council, 169
NearCom, 213, 214, 215
Neely, Heather, 31, 256, 257
on caring culture, 19
on Generation X peers, 18
planning by, 30
Neely, Tim, 30
Negotiations, 91, 92, 113–116, 193
trickiness of, 198, 199
Neighbors, 233
Neiman Marcus, 162
Nelson Capital, Malnick at, 142, 143
NetCreations, 170, 171
Netscape, 147
perks by, 44, 112
Networking, 101, 232
self-centered and, 257
tech work and, 148
women's, 169
New Economy, 168, 177
New Father Book: What Every Man Needs To Know To Be a Good Dad, The
200–201
New New Thing, The (Lewis), 116, 147
New Republic, The, 261
Newsday, 159
Newsweek, 224
New Yorker magazine, 79
New York Times, The, 32, 105, 226
on discrimination vs. mothers, 250
on Fiorina appointment, 52
on paternity leave, 209
on Prince Edward, 60
on Rippys, 80
on service industries, 260
on women's salaries, 95
on work-life balance, 112
New York Times Magazine, on RedEnvelope, 149
Non-profits, 163
Nordstrom, 162
Nudist on the Late Shift (Bronson), 147
Numbers' crunchers, 124
Nurturing, 70, 197, 237, 258
fathers and, 206
importance of, 208, 259
subtlety of, 73
Nurturing men, 183, 205, 264
finding, 65, 68–73
support from, 69
OAD. *See* Office of the Appellate Defender
O.A.S. *See* Organization of American States
Obligations, check-list of, 26
O'Connor, Colleen: on employee happiness, 117
O'Connor, Sandra Day, 23
Office of the Appellate Defender (OAD), 158
Off Road Capital, 223
100 Best Companies to Work for in America (*Fortune*), 227
On-the-job training, 40
Opportunities, 17–18, 91
Orenstein, Peggy: on "Crunch," 14
Organization of American States (O.A.S.), 89
Oswald, Andrew: on happy marriage/value, 86
Our Wildest Dreams: Women Making Money, Having Fun, Doing Good
(Godfrey), 163
Overspent American, The (Schor), 48
Over The Rainbow, 93, 94
Overworked American, The (Schor), 45

Paralegals, 154
Parental dividends, 251
Parental leave, 97, 120, 133, 212, 224, 251
paid, 250, 260, 261
pressing for, 248
regulations for, 259
taking, 208
unemployment benefits and, 261
See also Maternal leave; Paternity leave
Parenthood, 64, 183, 232
books on, 229
changes in, 188, 213, 215, 222
difficulties in, 187–188, 203, 232, 243
earning power and, 194
equality and, 35, 135, 210
family support and, 229, 230
impact of, 185, 191
improving, 213, 229–230, 236, 240
macro view of, 193–200
marriage and, 191
men and, 14, 69, 204, 208, 209
micro view of, 187–193
part-time work and, 195, 208
post-modern, 210–215
preparation for, 213

primary, 135
reversed roles in, 136, 220
sacredness of, 197
shared, 198–199, 246
sleep and, 188
styles of, 205
time for, 214, 223
work and, 223
Parents
challenges for, 226
community and, 231–232
dealing with, 39
drive-by, 228–229
dual-career, 195
help for, 226, 234–235, 240
independence/control for, 140
single, 194
unmarried, 185
working, 186, 259
Parity, 22, 63, 195
earning power, 200, 246
partnership, 195
Parke, Ross, 203, 204
Partnership, 137, 152, 168, 190, 246
achieving, 54
negotiating, 198
Part-time work, 43, 145, 154, 224
demanding, 249
at law firms, 158
negotiating, 113–116
options for, 260
parenthood and, 193, 195, 208
Passages (Sheehey), 33
Paternal instinct, 205
maternal control and, 204
Paternity leave, 159, 217
avoiding, 201, 207–208
taking, 209–10
See also Maternal leave; Parental leave
Pearson, Sarah, 36, 37, 72, 264
Bob and, 70–71, 78–79
Perks, 157
companies offering, 119–120
enticing with, 111–113
financial, 118
at law firms, 159
taking advantage of, 120–121
See also Benefits
Perksatwork.com, 111
Person, Ethel: on singles/couples, 65
Personal life, 40, 91, 109, 120, 143, 242
caring for, 126
conflicts in, 176
finding, 38, 87, 88, 156
loss of, 12
medicine and, 137
professional life and, 105, 137
time for, 12, 117, 151
workaholism and, 17
work identities and, 197
Pfau, Bruce, 109
Pfeffer, Jeffrey: on SAS, 119
Phillpotts, Beth Davis, 36, 37, 67, 97, 140, 235, 264
Garfield and, 138, 141
on improving society, 257
life for, 137
reflection by, 138
salary of, 138–139
Physicians. *See* Doctors; Medicine
Physician's assistants, 131
Pilgrim, Trip, 229
Planning, 36, 104–105, 131, 154
business, 213
financial, 223
importance of, 98, 161
strategic, 171, 208
Platt, Lewis, 101
work/life balance and, 118
Politics, xi-xii, 37, 57
changes in, 22
economics and, 256
feminist, xv, xvi, 253
men and, 248
sexual, 34
women and, 27, 255–257
Pollack, William S.: on boy code, 79
"Pop and Politics" (Web site), 255
Popular culture, Generation XX and, 39
Pottery Barn, 150
Preferred Provider Organizations (PPOs), 174, 175
Prejudice, 55, 57
Preschool, money for, 262
Pressures. *See* Stress
Price Waterhouse, 54
PricewaterhouseCoopers, 25, 109
Primary caregivers, 218
men as, 201, 205, 206, 219
women as, 209
See also Caregivers
Priorities, xvii, 118, 229
Proctor and Gamble, 25
Productivity
increase in, 251, 260
leisure and, 113
obsession with, 11
part-time work and, 115
stress and, 117

Professionals, 16, 41
life among, 40
personal life and, 105, 137
respecting, 117
traditional wives and, 66
women, 22–23
Professions
gentler-sex, 22
helping, 8–9
life-friendly, 129, 196
people-loving, 94, 107
Promise Keepers, 203
Promotions, 113, 114, 118, 243
prospects for, 109
turning down, 105
Providers, homemakers and, 60, 62, 63
Prozac Nation (Wurtzel), xiii, 184
Prudential Securities
Independent Means and, 164
survey by, 63
Pruett, Kyle
on clumsy fathering stage, 226
on developmental research, 205
on fatherneed, 206
on paternal instinct, 204
on primary caregivers/men, 205
Psychological moorings, 84–91
Publishing jobs, parenting and, 199

QualCare, Inc., 174, 175
Qualcom, perks at, 119
Quality of life, 107, 264
Quantity time, 17
Quinn, Trini, 73–76, 264
Quinn, Willie, 73–76, 79
Quixi, help from, 228

Radcliffe Public Policy Institute, 200
Raines, Claire, 25
Raskins, Pat: on identity/voice, 87
Rational Exuberance (Bagby), 24
Rat race model, 155, 156
Raz, Shlomo, 131, 132–133
Rebitzer, James B.: on rat race model, 155
Recruiting, 108, 144, 145
novel, 110
questions for, 100
See also Interviews
RedEnvelope, 149
Relationships, 37, 86–87
bad, 71
divorce and, 184
equal, 58, 61, 73, 76–80, 82, 245
long-distance, 235
nurturing, 71, 77, 80
traditional, 76
work and, 80, 176, 197
Renahan, Kevin, 100
Reproductive freedom, 149, 256
See also Abortion
Residency, impact of, 130, 131, 132, 138
Resnick, Rosalind, 170–172, 178, 181
Responsibilities, 116, 200, 225, 229
family, 26, 27
dreams and, 10
glass ceiling and, 26
rank and, 106
sharing, 80–81, 237
Revolution
cultural, 11, 12, 121
electronic, 12
Generation XY and, xiii
RHI Consulting, flex-time at, 148
Rhode, Deborah L.: on sex discrimination, 55
Richards, Amy, xiv, 253
Ridgeview, perks at, 120
Riesman, David, 87
Rietano Davey, Susan
on achievements/opportunities, 91
on schedule flexibility, 115
on sequencing, 223–224
on thinking about money, 91
Riot Grrrls, xiii
Ripken, Cal, Jr., 201
Rippy, Dan and Laura, 80
Roe v. Wade (1973), 254
Roland, Gabriel, 36
Romance, 65, 83, 87
egalitarian, 59
hidden agenda for, 60
Rosenman and Colin (law firm), 157, 158
Rubin, Jamie, 31, 111, 217
career of, 96–97, 98
trailblazing by, 26
Rudman, Warren, 102
Rules, The (novel), 71–72
Russo, David: on SAS, 119

Sabbaticals, 101, 119, 145, 240, 261
encouraging, 227, 243, 248
paid, 250
structuring, 242
Sachs, Tamara, 139–141, 181, 264
Sacrifice, 133, 134, 136, 198, 228, 248

self-, 61
success and, xvii
Salaries, 47, 110, 138–139, 153–154, 157, 258, 261
differences in, 95
equal, 57
men's, 10
media, 94
quality of life and, 107
self-worth and, 88, 92, 136
starting, 46, 95
for teachers, 107, 108, 262
women's, 95
Same-sex couples, parenthood and, 185
Same-stage parents, 232, 233
Sandler, Adam, 86
San Francisco Chronicle, on Stepford economy, 11
Sanity, benefits of, 107, 180
San Jose National Bank, perks at, 120
SAS Institute, 118–119
Savoca, Nancy: on motherhood, 191
Schaffer, William, 96
Schedules, flexibility in, 3, 101, 106, 115, 259
Schieffelin, Allison K.: discrimination against, 54
Scholarships, 95, 130
Scholastic Books, 240, 241
School for Social Research (University of Michigan), 200
Schor, Juliet, 45, 48
Schwartz, Delmore, 10
Scient, Inc.
life at, 144–149
perks at, 145
Security
financial, xv, 73, 91–98, 164, 166, 247
looking for, 24
Self-employment, 181–182
Self-esteem, 7, 75, 85
low, 63, 64, 65, 137
male, 203
Self-financing, 170–172
Self-worth, 29, 236
salary and, 88, 92, 136
Senior citizens
help from, 234–236
See also Grandparents
Separation anxiety, 205
Sequencing, 223–224
Service industries, help from, 228, 260
Seventeen, Godfrey in, 163
Shah, Julie: activism of, 255
Shapiro, Ellen Sklars: on parenting, 193
Shapiro, Jerrold Lee: on fathers/guilt, 206–207
Shearman and Sterling (law firm), perks at, 159
Sheehey, Gail, 33
Shellenbarger, Sue
on doctor/lawyer workload, 108
on recruiting, 100
Shroeders Bank, The, 96, 97
Sidewalk.com, 80
Significant others, children and, 231–232
Silicon Valley
life in, 142, 147
social responsibility in, 143
workplace revolution in, 142
Singles, parenthood for, 185
Sisters in Action, 255
Sisters of the Sorrowful Mother, 174
Skowcroft, Brent, 102
Sleep, 44–45, 188, 232
"Sleep Faster" (*Fortune*), 45
Sloan, Margaret: sex discrimination and, 57
Sloan Center for the Study of Working Families, 222
Smith, Adam: revisiting, 246–252
Smith, Eve: revisiting, 246–252
Smith, Linda: on military/childcare, 108
Snider, Stacey, 227
Snowball.com, ad for, 48
Social arrangements, changing, 247
Social life, 72, 232, 242, 265
children and, 233–234
cultivating, 88
keeping, 245
Social Security System, 251
Societal impediments, internalizing, 58
Sowell, Shaunna, 101
Special treatment, defining, 250
Spencer, Casey, 223, 224
fatherhood of, 219, 220
homemaking and, 220
Spencer, Kelani, 220
Spiritual currency, 87, 264
thinking about, 86, 90
trading in, 92
Spiritual values, 90, 94
Spouses Training Under Duress Successfully (STUDS), 219
Springboard 2000, 169
Star Media, 42
Start-ups, 148–49, 164, 165, 179, 180
Starwood, Barry, 150
Status (American Astronomical Society), 53

Steele, Liz, 90
Steinem, Gloria: sex discrimination and, 57
Stepford economy, 11, 147
Stereotypes
gender, 51, 66
increase in, 62
Stewart, Patrick: UBUBU and, 125
Stiffed (Faludi), 202–3
Strategies, 4, 6, 35–38, 103, 104, 124, 157, 171, 173–74, 208
developing, 17–18, 33, 37, 232
dreams and, 13
investment, 180–181
importance of, 18
Stress, 31, 43, 50, 85, 136
dealing with, 2, 4, 106, 112, 258
financial, xii
gender, 202
productivity and, 117
social, 4, 37
STUDS. *See* Spouses Training Under Duress Successfully
Success, 57, 81, 92, 94, 129
falling short of, 32
sacrifice and, xvii
societal impediments to, 58
Sun Microsystems, 96, 227
Superwoman problem, 225, 245
Support systems, 228, 230
Sweat-equity, 173–174
Swedish Medical Research Council, women applicants to, 56
Swetschinski, Galia, 158, 160, 193, 264
on money, 153–155
values of, 154
work of, 152–153
Swift, Jane: prejudice against, 55

Tag teaming, 10
Talents, assessing, 88, 102
Task Force on Relations with Columbia, 102
Taylor, Lowell J.: on rat race model, 155
TD Industries, perks at, 119
Teachers, 33
salaries for, 107, 108, 262
tax breaks for, 108
Technology, 172
impact of, 116–117
networking and, 148
sequencing and, 223–224
women and, 95, 104, 147, 167
See also Information technology
Teenagers, business and, 161–162
Teen Business Plan, 163, 165
Telecommuting, 101, 116, 118, 251
"Ten Things Every Working Parent Needs To Know" (Levine), 219
Termination, discrimination and, 57–58
Third Wave Foundation, 255
Thomas, Denise, 77–78, 81, 223, 224
Time
buying/finding/making, 226–229
controlling, 139
negotiating, 113–116
parenting and, 223
Toys R Us, girls/boys sections to, 62
Tracey, Margaret, 221
Tradition, 31
going against/with, 197–198
Trap doors, glass ceilings and, 49–58
Trudell, Cynthia, 218
Tuesdays with Morrie, 88
Turnover, 47, 112, 119, 121
caregiver, 239
costs of, 109–110
employee happiness and, 117
part-time work and, 116
rate of, 110, 145, 147
reducing, 261
21st Century Youth Leadership Movement, 255
24-Hour Woman, The (movie), 40
"24 Hour Woman, The" (Savoca), 191
Type-A personalities, work of, 109, 242

Uber geeks, 148
UBUBU, 121–127, 149
UCLA Medical Center, Kavaler at, 131
Unbending Gender (Williams), 195
Undocumented aliens, hiring, 249
Unemployment, 259, 261, 262
U.S. Chamber of Commerce, unemployment insurance and, 261
U.S. Labor Department, parental leave and, 259
United States Merit Systems Protection Board, 52
U.S. News and World Report, 45, 195
Universal Pictures, 227
Universal Studios, 219
Urological surgery, 132, 134, 136–137
Urry, C. Megan, 53
USA networks, UBUBU and, 125

Vacations, 27, 138, 145, 188, 227, 231, 236, 243, 260, 261

budgeting for, 197
taking, 210, 211, 213
Vagina Monologues (Ensler), xiii
Valian, Virginia
on gender discrimination, 56
on self-image, 57
Values, 18, 29, 83, 90, 121, 217
assessing, 86, 102
balance and, 91
changes in, 144
expressing, 135–136
knowing, 85, 88
prestige/income, 29
Vanderbilt Law Review, on overworked lawyers, 155
Van Tol, Peter, 157
Vault.com, 116
Venture capital, 165, 166, 167, 227
female entrepreneurs and, 175
seeking, 173, 175
Vickers Willis, Sarah, 149, 264
UBUBU and, 121–127
on work/authenticity, 125
Voice, importance of, 87
Volunteer activities, work and, 91
Vulnerabilities, 72, 83

Wallerstein, Judith: on divorce/relationships, 184
Wall Street Journal, The
on college grads/job market, 110
on doctor/lawyer workload, 108
on getting/keeping employees, 109
Minton in, 43
on recruiting, 100
on sabbaticals, 226–227
on SAS, 118
on service industry, 228
Warren, Lissa, 13, 14, 17
Warshawsky, Daniel, 158, 159
Wendt, Lorna: suit by, 65
Wethington, Elaine: on work/family, 16
When Chickenheads Home to Roost (Morgan), 225
"Where Have All The Cowboys Gone?" (Cole), 59
Whitman, Meg, 30
"Who Succeeds in Science: The Gender Dimension" (Holton), 52
"Why Executives Lose Their Balance" (Kofodimus), 203
Why So Slow? (Valian), 56
Wilderotter, Maggie: golden rules of, 227
Williams, Joan: on Fallows, 195
Williams, Parker, Harrison, Dietz & Getzen (law firm)
interviewing at, 5
working at, 6–7
Wired Magazine, 218
"With Labor Day Comes More Labor, Less Pay" (*Los Angeles Times*), 41
Wolf, Naomi, xiii
Women In Medicine, 141
Women's Business Development Center, 169
Women's Commission, study by, 164
Women's Economic Network, 169
Women's March on Washington (1970), 252
Women's rights, xvi, 27, 62
Women's Voices 2000, 253
Women's work, 64, 67, 68
doing, 61, 63
Woods, Kimba: undocumented aliens and, 249
Woods, Tiger, 201
Work
analyzing, 18–19, 37
changing, 14, 90, 103, 114, 209
content-driven, 241, 242
enjoying, 37–38
family and, 13, 14, 16, 25, 27–30, 32, 117, 152, 207, 224, 240–44
finding, 8, 85, 99
full-time, 21, 113–116
giving everything to, 17, 222
grunt, 13, 41, 42
importance of, 24, 85, 98
knowledge, 147
life and, 15, 27, 28, 40, 117
men/women at, 23, 135
money and, 98
motherhood and, 13, 16, 245
parenting and, 223
relationships and, 80, 176, 197
spiritual side of, 98
See also Professions
Work/family balance, 28, 184, 221–226, 259
men and, 206
Work-less-live-more ethic, 25
Work/life balance, 3, 7, 27, 36, 81, 100, 106, 112, 142–144, 168, 176, 222
business and, 261
fast track and, 226
fathers and, 201, 219
importance of, 101, 118, 259
planning, 104–105, 145, 219
relationships and, 80

Workaholism, xi, 18, 27, 30, 41, 81, 88, 172, 178, 195
defense against, 12, 17
graduate degrees and, 129
growth of, 45, 156
investment banking and, 142
men and, 248
slipping into, 123
work life and, 44, 154
Work and Play, 239
Work environment, 85, 149
Work ethic, 19, 79, 154
backlash against, 152
creating, 19
family and, 152
revenue driven, 153
Working Fathers (Levine), 234
Working Life: The Promise and Betrayal of Modern Work, The
(Ciulla), 87
Working Mother, on 100 Best Companies, 117
Work life, xii, 99, 248
designing, 89, 107, 112, 245
independent, 36
workaholics and, 44
Workplaces, xi, 18, 52
changes at, xii, 14, 21, 34, 114, 116–121, 142, 264
family time and, 207
gender relations and, 34, 58
home and, 246
humane, 17, 117–118, 121–127
problems in, 1, 25, 47, 109
public policy and, 21
values at, 258
Work proposals, writing, 115–116
Work weeks, 45, 46, 109, 250
World Bank, health insurance claims at, 44
"World Class Workaholics" (*U.S. News and World Report*), 45
World Trade Organization meeting, protest at, 256
WRQ, perks at, 119
Wu, Amy, 85–86
Wurtzel, Elizabeth, xiii, 184
www.activelement.org, 255
www.bid4vacations.com, 172
www.fatherslove.com, 219
www.feministmajorityfoundation, 99
www.grandparenting.org, 234
www.internshipsininformation, 99
www.newdads.com, 219
www.slowlane.com, 219
www.thirdwavefoundation.org, 255

Xerox, 110, 251
perks at, 119

Yahoo!, 86, 261
Y Generation girls, Godfrey and, 162
Young Entrepreneurs Association, 190
Young Entrepreneurs Edge, The (Kushell), 166
Young Entrepreneurs Network, The, 166, 167
Young Mothers League, 16
Youssef, Niven, 41, 47
debt for, 46
work life of, 42, 50, 51, 57, 152, 157
Yu, Yan: on work/life success, 222
YWCA, 125

Zemke, Ron, 25
Zen and the Art of Fatherhood, 200
Zines, pro-women, 255
Zion, Sidney, 130
Zulman, Carol, 81
on self-esteem, 64
on traditional motherhood, 64
on women's beliefs, 63
Zulman, Tanya, 63, 64